One Word From God Can Change Your Life

KENNETH
COPELAND
PUBLICATIONS

One Word From God Can Change Your Life

ISBN-13 978-1-60463-059-6   30-0730

14 13 12 11 10 09   12 11 10 9 8 7

© 2002 Eagle Mountain International Church Inc aka Kenneth Copeland Ministries

Kenneth Copeland Publications
Fort Worth, TX 76192-0001

For more information about Kenneth Copeland Ministries, call 800-600-7395 or visit www.kcm.org.

Contents

Introduction

Introduction

One Word From God Can Change Your Life FOREVER!

When the revelation of this statement exploded on the inside of me, it changed the way I think...about everything! I had been praying for several days about a situation that seemed at the time to be overwhelming. I had been confessing the Word of God over it, but that Word had begun to come out of my head and not my heart. I was pushing in my flesh for the circumstance to change. As I made my confession one more time, the Spirit of God seemed to say to me, *Why don't you be quiet?!*

I said, "But, Lord, I'm confessing the Word!"

He answered inside me, *I know it. I heard you. Now just be still and be quiet a little while, and let the Word of God settle down in your spirit. Quit trying to make this thing happen. You're not God. You're not going to be the one to make it happen anyway!*

So I stopped. I stopped that situation in my mind and began to get quiet before the Lord...and this phrase came up in my spirit...*One word from God can change anything.*

So I started saying that. I said it off and on all day. It came easily because it came from God—not from my own thinking.

Every time I was tempted to worry or think of ideas concerning my circumstances, I'd think, *Yes, just one word from God...*

I noticed when I'd say that, the peace of God would come on me. It was so calming. As a result, a habit developed in me. People would bring me issues. They'd say, "Well, what about..." And I'd either say aloud or think to myself, "Yeah, that may be so, but one word from God will change anything."

It began to be the answer for everything. If I was watching television and the newscaster was telling about a disaster, and the people being interviewed were saying things to the effect of "Oh, what are we going to do? It's all been blown away, burned up or shook up...," I'd say, "Yeah, but one word from God can change anything."

It really developed into a strength for me, and it can for you, too. That's why we've put together the *One Word From God* book series...there could be just one word in these inspiring articles that can change your prayer life forever.

You've been searching, seeking help...and God has the answer. He has the one word that can turn your circumstance around and put you on dry ground. He has the one word that gives you all the peace that's in Him. He is your Intercessor. He wants to give you the desires of your heart as you delight yourself in Him. He wants you perfect and entire, wanting nothing (James 1:4).

God loves you. And He has a word for you. One word that can change your life *forever!*

Kenneth Copeland

One Word From God
Can Change
Your Prayer Life

The Time to Pray

Chapter I

"Pray without ceasing."
— I THESSALONIANS 5:17

Gloria Copeland

If you have your ear turned toward God these days, I suspect you've heard Him say something to you about prayer. He's been calling you to spend more time in it, to make it a higher priority in your life.

How do I know? Because He's been telling me the same thing. In fact, the more people I talk to about it, the more convinced I am that God is calling all His people to prayer.

The reason is simple. These are the last of the last days. God is ready to move through us in magnificent and supernatural ways. But He can't do that if we're not walking in the spirit. He can't work through people who are so busy with the affairs of the flesh that they can't hear His voice.

He needs people who will pray—not just when they happen to think about it, but every day. He needs people who will build their whole lives around prayer and make it their No. 1 priority.

Have you ever noticed how Jesus operated when He was on the earth? He placed great importance on prayer. His prayer life was absolutely amazing. The night before He chose the 12 disciples, He was in prayer all night long!

Well, Jesus didn't do things one way and tell us to do something else. He expects us to follow His example.

First Thessalonians 5:17 tells us to "pray without ceasing." Ephesians 6:18 tells us to pray "always with all prayer and supplication in the Spirit." All through the New Testament we're told to pray! And now it's time for us to do our job. I don't mean just one or two of us—I mean the whole army of God.

Your natural human reaction to that call for prayer may be to say, "Hey, I hardly have time enough to handle all the crises in my life as it is now. I can't afford to spend any more time in prayer!" But, the truth is, you can't afford not to. You need to tap in to what time spent with the Father can do for you.

That's what I did. Some time ago, God spoke to me that if I'd give Him a tithe of my time—just an hour or two a day in the Word and prayer—all would be well with me. And not only with me, but that I'd be a blessing to the people around me.

He's made that same promise to you. It's right there for you to read in Romans 8:28. There the Holy Spirit says: "And we know that all things work together for good to them that love God, to them who are the called according to his purpose."

Most people take that verse out of context and say the Bible promises that all things (including demonic things like sickness, death and poverty) work together for good, period. But that's not true. If you'll back up and read the surrounding scriptures, you'll find that promise follows a discussion about praying aided by the Holy Spirit—where the Holy Spirit makes intercession for us according to the will of God. Remember Romans 8:26 says He helps us to pray. This is not something the Holy Spirit does apart from us. *The Amplified Bible* says He comes to our aid and bears us up in our weakness when we don't know how to pray as we ought. By His help, we pray in the spirit the perfect will of God!

It's when we begin to make prayer our priority—to lay aside the natural things and take up the things of God and walk in the power of the Spirit—that the glory of God will be reflected in us.

If we want to have the power of God in our lives, we have to get rid of this tunnel vision we've had. We have to quit spending all our time thinking about our little surroundings, our little life, and what we're doing day to day. We have to start giving ourselves to things that will make an eternal difference. We have to start giving ourselves to prayer.

You know God hasn't put us here on the earth just so we could make it through life in relative comfort and then go on to heaven. He's put us here so we can dominate the world of the natural while we're here and do His works just as His Son,

Jesus, did. Jesus said we would do even greater works than He did (John 14:12).

But we're not going to be empowered to do those things by sitting around watching television. We're going to be empowered to do them when we start making Jesus' priorities our priorities; when we start wanting what He wants more than anything else.

God has glorious plans for us in the spirit realm. But if we don't spend time in that realm, praying and listening to God, we're not going to get in on those plans.

I heard a story some time ago about some Eastern European believers that illustrates what I'm talking about. It took place a few years ago when the underground church in Eastern Europe had to meet out in the woods and in secret places to keep from being raided by the KGB.

During that time, there was this one group of believers who had a spy among them. As a result, no matter where they met, the police always showed up. So, do you know what they did? They stopped announcing the location of the next meeting. They simply said, "We'll meet wherever the Holy Spirit tells us to. So whoever wants to be there will have to listen to the Spirit to find out where to go." The next time they met, every person showed up except one.

All of us have the ability to listen to our spirit like that. In America, we've not operated in that realm very much. But we're going to. How are we going to? By praying in the spirit and listening to God! The more we do that, the more accurately we'll hear.

Think of your spirit like a kind of inner radio. If you don't tune it to exactly the right frequency, all you get is static and meaningless noise. But if you tune in to the station exactly, everything comes in loud and clear.

God is wanting us to fine-tune ourselves in the realm of the spirit. He's wanting us to tune our spirits so we can pick Him up clearly and definitely. He wants us to be able to hear His voice so we can obey it.

Most, however, haven't been willing to take the time to do that. We've come to the point where if we knew God wanted us to do something, we'd do it. But we won't get quiet before Him long enough to hear Him say what He wants us to do.

That's why He's telling us to put prayer first, to make communication with Him top priority, to shut out the world and spend time in prayer and in the Word. When we do that, He can begin to fine-tune our spirits to hear His voice. His voice is indistinct to us because we spend so much of our time caught up in natural things.

As we begin to come into this place of hearing, we'll be in one accord because we'll all know what the mind of the Spirit is. We'll have our minds and hearts in tune with what God's doing—and then when we come together, there will be an explosion of God's power that will turn the world upside down!

This calling to live in the spirit and in power is drawing us forward. In my spirit, I can see it like a carrot dangling in front of a horse. It is so close to us. All we have to do to reach it is to take a few more steps, to learn to listen to the Spirit of God, and make the adjustments He tells us to make.

I tell you, it's exciting. I've seen enough of the kind of life that's available in God to know that there's not anything in the world more valuable. But if you're going to lay hold of it, you're going to have to get quiet and pray. You're going to have to get unbusy with the affairs of life. You're going to have to set aside all the clamor of the world and get with God.

"Oh, Gloria," you say, "you just don't know how hectic my life is. I just can't do that!"

Yes, you can. It's just a matter of rearranging your priorities.

Think of it this way. If you walked through your kitchen tomorrow morning on your way to work and Jesus was sitting at your kitchen table, what would you do? Would you say, "Jesus! I'm so glad to see You! I wish I had time to visit. If I'd gotten up earlier, I could spend some time with You. But I watched television so late last night and I've been so busy lately—so much work at the office and everything. How about I try to catch You later?"

Ridiculous, isn't it? What would you really do if Jesus were physically sitting at your kitchen table in the morning?

You'd fall on your face before Him. You'd hang on to every moment and say, "I'm not going to work today, Jesus. There are so many things we need to talk about. I can't pass up an opportunity like this."

It wouldn't matter that you were tired. It wouldn't matter how busy things were at the office. You'd get before Him and begin to worship and enjoy times of refreshing from the presence of the Lord until your body wasn't tired any longer.

Do you understand that Jesus actually is closer than your breakfast table? His Spirit is in you—waiting to fellowship with you. When you're tempted to sleep late tomorrow, think about that.

Think about the sweet Spirit of God saying, *I want to help you this morning. I'm here to strengthen you. You know that problem you've been having? I want to apply spiritual power to it so it will disappear from your life.*

Think about the fact that God is waiting on you. That He has some things He wants to show you. Things you've been beating your head against the wall trying to figure out. He's just waiting to counsel you, to show you the answer.

I'll tell you this: God is not going to make you pray. Jesus is not going to make you pray. The Holy Spirit is not going to make you pray. But they are all three calling you to it. They're preparing to go into action the moment you begin.

The eternal, all-powerful Creator of heaven and earth, the Almighty God, is ready right now to meet with you in prayer. He's made your prayers His priority. The question is, have you?

Principles of Effective Prayer

"Be careful for nothing; but in every thing by prayer and supplication with thanksgiving let your requests be made known unto God."
— PHILIPPIANS 4:6

*Kenneth
Copeland*

Have you ever had so many needs that you felt like a prophet would have to pray all night to get them taken care of?

I have!

Shortly after becoming a Christian, I requested prayer for my financial needs. I expected the preacher to make such inspired intercession that everyone would fall on their knees. I imagined him weeping over my problems as Jesus wept over Lazarus' death. But to my amazement, he merely laid his hand on my chest, bowed his head and said, "Lord, bless him. Meet his every need, in the Name of Jesus." Then he turned and walked away!

What a disappointment! My problems were *big!* I figured it would take a *big* prayer to cover them. But you see, I was operating in unbelief, and this man of God was operating in faith. He was concentrating on the answer—Jesus—and not on my problems.

Since then, I've learned a lot about prayer. I've stepped beyond shooting scattershot prayers, just hoping for something to happen, and I've learned to follow the guidelines to prayer that are given in the Word of God. You see, God never meant for us to stumble around in the dark when we pray. Philippians 4:6 says, "Be careful for nothing; but in every thing by prayer and supplication with thanksgiving let your requests be made known unto God." God intends to answer our requests. He wants us to get results when we pray. But first, we have to put away our childish ideas about prayer and replace them with God's power-packed principles.

For example, one thing we need to learn is that it is not the length of our prayers that gets results.

According to 1 John 3:22-23: "Whatsoever we ask, we receive of him, because we keep his commandments, and do those things that are pleasing in his sight. And this is his commandment, That we should believe on the name of his Son Jesus Christ, and love one another, as he gave us commandment."

Praying all night is not what gets the ear of God; it is believing on and praying in the Name of Jesus. Praying all night is quite an accomplishment, but praying in the Name of Jesus is basing your prayer on His accomplishments, not on yours.

Of course, if you haven't been living a life that is pleasing to God, your prayers will be hindered. Disobedience robs you of your confidence in Him, but even then Jesus is still the answer. He is your Advocate with the Father. Don't run from God when you sin; run to Him! Act on 1 John 1:9. Confess your sin and receive your forgiveness. Don't let sin and condemnation keep God from moving in your life, your heart and your circumstances. Jesus is faithful and just to forgive you when you repent. He wants to answer your prayers.

Another key to answered prayer is praying according to the will of God. The problem is that many believers are in the dark about God's will. Religion has told us, "You never know what God's going to do." But that's not true! He's told us in His Word exactly what He will do.

The written Word brings the will of God out of the realm of obscurity. When we pray in line with the Word, we pray according to the will of God. When we let the Word of God engineer our prayer, "this is the confidence that we have in him, that, if we ask any thing according to his will, he heareth us: And if we know that he hear us, whatsoever we ask, we know that we have the petitions that we desired of him" (1 John 5:14-15).

Prayer based on the Word begins with the answer and doesn't concentrate on the problem. Let's take healing as an example. First Peter 2:24 says that by the stripes that Jesus bore, we were healed. Just as in the forgiveness of your sins, your healing was provided for through the Cross. If the Word says you were healed, then God's will is for you to be well. Let the Word of God settle the issue once and for all. Throw out all the arguments, and believe the Word.

Mark 11:24 says, "What things soever ye desire, when ye pray, believe that ye receive them, and ye shall have them." Notice that it says for you to believe when you pray. Make the decision that God's Word is absolutely true. If God said that you were healed, then believe that you were healed when you prayed, not when you began to feel better.

When you base your prayer on the fact that the answer is already yours, then the only thing left is to begin the application of your faith. Faith is your response to what God has already provided.

Faith is released in two ways: by saying it and by acting on it. If 1 Peter 2:24 says you were healed, then don't say, "I'm sick." Say, "I believe that by the stripes Jesus bore for me, I am healed." And then act like it. Real Bible believing demands action.

If someone came running in your front door and said, "The house is on fire!" and you believed it, you would immediately get out. You wouldn't wait until you saw smoke!

Faith in God's Word works the same way. Don't wait until you feel healed to believe it. Believe it before anything you can see ever happens, or it will never happen. Faith makes prayer work; prayer doesn't make faith work.

If your needs have been piling up, don't panic. Pray! Your spiritual, mental, physical, financial and social needs can be met by the power of Almighty God. Just follow God's principles of prayer and make your requests known unto Him; then start to praise, knowing the results are on the way!

Trade in Your Old Prayers

"Delight thyself also in the Lord; and he shall give thee the desires of thine heart."
— PSALM 37:4

John Avanzini

If your prayers are going unanswered lately, it may be time to trade in your old prayers for some more accurate ones. God answers only those prayers that are in agreement with His will (1 John 5:14). So check your prayers to be sure what you're praying lines up with His will.

There are three steps to finding out what God wants you to pray.

First, study the Word. God's Word is His will, and you'll never know what His will is without knowing His Word intimately (2 Timothy 2:15).

Second, renew your mind. The study of God's Word will transform you so you can know what is the good, acceptable and perfect will of God (Romans 12:2).

Third, be soft and pliable to God's will for your life. Be ready to replace your desires with God's desires. That may sound difficult, but it's actually easy if you follow God's directions.

Psalm 37:4 says, "Delight thyself also in the Lord; and he shall give thee the desires of thine heart." The Hebrew word translated *delight* means "be soft and pliable." So we could say, "Be soft and pliable in the hands of God, and He will give you the desires of your heart."

But if that were all God meant, we would soon be in big trouble. Most of our own desires are not God's desires for us. God isn't saying He'll give us whatever we desire if we are merely soft and pliable. He's saying He will cause our desires to be taken out of our hearts and replaced with His own desires. As we become soft and pliable in His hands, we will exchange our desires for the things He desires.

When what we desire is what God desires for us, we can pray accurately. Let God tell you what to pray, and your prayers will always be answered!

Into His Courts With Praise

"I will praise thee, O Lord, with my whole heart; I will show forth all thy marvellous works. I will be glad and rejoice in thee."
— PSALM 9:1-2

Kenneth Copeland

For verily I say unto you, That whosoever shall say unto this mountain, Be thou removed, and be thou cast into the sea; and shall not doubt in his heart, but shall believe that those things which he saith shall come to pass; he shall have whatsoever he saith. Therefore I say unto you, What things soever ye desire, when ye pray, believe that ye receive them, and ye shall have them (Mark 11:23-24).

This very familiar scripture has to do with praying in faith, or praying to get results. The most important thing for you to remember about praying accurately is to go to the Word of God, find out what the Word says about the problem and then pray according to that Word.

First John 5:14-15 says when we ask anything according to His will, we know He hears us and we know we have the petitions we desired of Him. When you pray according to God's Word, which is His will, then you know that your prayer is answered.

Jesus said, "Whatsoever ye shall ask the Father in my name, he will give it you" (John 16:23). When you use the Name of Jesus in prayer, you get the ear of God.

Peter wrote that the eyes of God are over the righteous and His ears are open to their prayers. You don't have to pray until you get God's attention. He is listening for your prayer. You have His attention all the time.

When you pray according to Mark 11:23-24, you believe you receive when you pray. This opens the door for thanksgiving and praise. Philippians 4:6 says, "Be careful for nothing; but in every thing by prayer and supplication with thanksgiving let your requests be made known unto God." Thanksgiving and praise are an integral part of prayer. When you believe you receive, then you begin to praise God for the answer. You thank God that it is done for you.

Thanksgiving and praise involve more than just speaking lovely words to God. There is power in the praise of God. Praise was ordained by God for a definite reason. It serves a purpose.

Psalms 8 and 9 point out some things about praise that every believer should know. Psalm 8:1-2 says, "O Lord our Lord, how excellent is thy name in all the earth! who hast set thy glory above the heavens. Out of the mouth of babes and sucklings hast thou ordained strength because of thine enemies, that thou mightest still the enemy and the avenger." Jesus quoted that passage in Matthew 21:16: "Out of the mouth of babes and sucklings thou hast perfected praise." He equates praise with strength.

From these scriptures, we see that God brought praise into existence. He ordained it. Why? "Because of thine enemies, that thou mightest still the enemy and the avenger." Praise stops Satan right in his tracks. It is a weapon we are to use in calling a halt to Satan's maneuvers. Psalm 9 says: "I will praise thee, O Lord, with my whole heart; I will show forth all thy marvellous works. I will be glad and rejoice in thee: I will sing praise to thy name, O thou most High. When mine enemies are turned back, they shall fall and perish at thy presence. For thou hast maintained my right and my cause; thou satest in the throne judging right" (verses 1-4).

When your enemies are turned back...not *if*. There is no question about it. Remember: We wrestle not against flesh and blood, but against Satan's forces. When you praise God, your enemies have to turn back. They will fall and perish at your presence. You can see why praise is so important in the life of a believer. It is a vital weapon in your warfare against Satan and his forces.

Usher In His Presence

One thing you must realize is that praise is not governed by emotions. God is worthy of your praise whether you feel like praising Him or not. Hebrews 13:15 says, "Let us offer the sacrifice of praise to God continually, that is, the fruit of our lips giving thanks to his name." Under the old covenant, when the people had problems, they went to the priest and he would offer a sacrifice to God. That would bring God on the scene.

Today, under the new covenant, we are to do the same. We are priests under God (Revelation 5:10). As we offer up the sacrifices of praise before our Most High Priest, Jesus, our communication with God is great. Psalm 22:3 says God inhabits the praises of His people. Praise brings God on the scene personally. At times of high praise, the shekinah glory of God will fill the whole place with His sweet presence.

When Solomon finished building the house of the Lord, the trumpeters and singers lifted their voices as one and, with trumpets, cymbals and instruments of music, they praised the Lord saying, "For he is good; for his mercy endureth for ever." The glory of God filled the house so that the priests could not even minister because of the cloud (2 Chronicles 5:13-14). God Himself inhabited the praises of His people.

Jehoshaphat appointed singers unto the Lord to go before the army and say, "Praise the Lord; for his mercy endureth for ever."

When the Israelites began to sing and praise, the Lord set ambushments against their enemies, and their enemies destroyed themselves (2 Chronicles 20:21-23).

The weapon of praise! Singers going before an army? It happened just that way. Israel didn't have to unsheathe a weapon of war. They only had to sing "Praise the Lord; for his mercy endureth for ever."

David was a man after God's own heart. He knew how to praise his God. Until you have the Word dwelling in you richly so that you can speak psalms and praises out of your own spirit, use the praises of David to magnify God. Speak them or sing them out loud to the Father.

> In God I will praise his word, in God I have put my trust; I will not fear what flesh can do unto me. Every day they wrest my words: all their thoughts are against me for evil. They gather themselves together, they hide themselves, they mark my steps, when they wait for my soul.... When I cry unto thee, then shall mine enemies turn back: this I know; for God is for me. In God will I praise his word: in the Lord will I praise his word. In God have I put my trust: I will not be afraid what man can do unto me (Psalm 56:4-6, 9-11).

The Bible says God inhabits the praises of His people (Psalm 22:3). The enemy is turned back, falls and perishes at the presence of our God.

Praise not only honors God and empowers our faith, but it is also a powerful weapon in the realm of the spirit. Remember: Praise will cause Satan and his forces to turn back, fall and perish at your presence.

Keep the Door Open

Abraham "grew strong and was empowered by faith as he gave praise and glory to God" (Romans 4:20, *The Amplified Bible)*. As you praise God and speak of His marvelous works, your faith rises on the inside of you to receive the blessings of God.

Honor God with the words of your mouth. Allow your words to agree with God's words where He is concerned. Look in His Word for good things to proclaim about Him. Publish the Lord's mercy and compassion to those around you. Tell others of the great things He has done in your life.

Notice that David said, "I *will* praise...I *will* show forth all thy marvellous works...I *will* be glad and rejoice...I *will* sing praise" (Psalm 9:1-2). It is a matter of your will. You do not just praise God because you feel like it. You praise God because you *will* to praise Him. Say with David, "I will praise thee, O Lord, with my whole heart." Then watch the Word go to work on your behalf!

One incident during Jesus' earthly ministry clearly shows the importance that praise can have. Luke 17:12-19 describes the cleansing of 10 lepers. All 10 of them were cleansed, but only one turned back to Jesus and glorified God. To that one man, Jesus said, "Arise, go thy way: thy faith hath made thee whole." The others were cleansed. He was *made whole.*

As I was meditating on these scriptures, the Lord showed me a vision. I saw the man come running up to Jesus. He was cleansed—all the disease was gone from his body—but the bottom of his ear was missing. The disease had eaten it away. As he shouted and praised God, the ear was restored. He was *made whole.* Praise made the difference.

If you do not know very much about praising God, then I encourage you to spend time meditating in the Word concerning praise. It will revolutionize your life! I guarantee it! David said, "I will show forth all [Your] marvellous works." If you don't know how to praise God, just find some of the things God has already done throughout the Bible and begin to praise Him for doing them. When I first began doing these things, I would open my Bible and praise God by reading the Psalms out loud. From there I let the Holy Spirit lead me into praising God for things He had done in my life and to saying things that would bless God.

One important thing I have learned is to praise God in the spirit. The real strength comes when we praise the Lord in the spirit, in other tongues. First Corinthians 14:4 says we are edified, or charged up, when we speak in tongues. First Corinthians 14:17 says giving thanks in tongues is giving thanks well. Praising God in this way enables us to praise Him beyond our own intellects. We allow the Holy Spirit to lead us into unlimited praise and thanksgiving. This is surely perfected praise (Matthew 21:16).

Let's say you are faced with a problem. You know what the Word says about it, so you go directly to prayer. You put your faith into action against the mountain—whatever it may be. You pray and believe God for the answer. By believing God in that situation and acting on the Word, you are applying faith power to the mountain. It begins to move. Then Satan gets involved. The only way he can stop you is by injecting unbelief so that you will stop applying pressure to the mountain. He can't stop the mountain from being moved, but he can try to stop you from applying the pressure of your faith to it. The mountain will never move until you apply the faith force necessary to move it. This is where praise comes in.

While you are standing in faith—while you are applying the Word of God to the situation—it is important to keep the praise of God on your lips. Continue to praise God for the answer. Praise Him that the mountain is moved. Don't be moved by the circumstances. Just keep your eyes on God's Word. The Word of God and prayer open the doors for God's power to work. Praise keeps them open. Praise will bring manifestations of the Holy Spirit and His great power.

Activate the power of God in every area of your life by speaking the Word in faith and praising God that His marvelous works have been performed on your behalf.

The Power of Praying in Tongues

"But you, beloved, build yourselves up [founded] on your most holy faith—make progress, rise like an edifice higher and higher—praying in the Holy Spirit."
— JUDE 20, *The Amplified Bible*

Gloria Copeland

You have a weakness. It doesn't matter who you are...or how often you work out at the local gym. If you're a born-again child of God living on planet Earth, you have a weakness. It's a weakness that can knock your legs out from under you just when you think you're standing strong. It can cause you to act like a sinner on the outside when on the inside you're a saint.

What is that weakness? Your flesh.

That's right. That flesh-and-blood body you live in hasn't been reborn as your spirit has. If it controls your life, it will take you from one failure to another. And believe me, if you don't do something to stop it, it will take control.

What you have to do is build up your spirit—strengthen it to the point where it can actually dominate, or rule over, your flesh. If that sounds hard, don't worry. It's not. In fact, God has made it so easy that anyone can do it. Jude 20 will show you how. It says: "But you, beloved, build yourselves up [founded] on your most holy faith—make progress, rise like an edifice higher and higher—praying in the Holy Spirit" *(The Amplified Bible)*.

Most believers don't realize it, but praying in the spirit, or praying in other tongues, is a spiritual exercise that strengthens your inner man. Just as barbells build up your arms, praying in tongues will build up your spirit. If you'll do it faithfully, it will help bring you to the point where your spirit will be able to keep that fleshly body of yours in line.

"Well, Gloria," you may ask, "why can't I just do that by praying in English?"

Because the Bible says your "weakness" gets in the way. Many times your natural mind doesn't have the first idea how to pray as it needs to. It may not know how to pray prayers that will strengthen you against temptations that are about to come your way. Your mind is not informed as your spirit is. Your spirit is in contact with God. That's why, as Romans 8:26-28 says:

> The (Holy) Spirit comes to our aid and bears us up in our weakness; for we do not know what prayer to offer nor how to offer it worthily as we ought, but the Spirit Himself goes to meet our supplication and pleads in our behalf with unspeakable yearnings and groanings too deep for utterance. And He who searches the hearts of men knows what is in the mind of the (Holy) Spirit... because the Spirit intercedes and pleads [before God] in behalf of the saints according to and in harmony with God's will *(The Amplified Bible)*.

Praying in the spirit enables you to pray the perfect will of God for your life. It allows you to step out of the realm of the flesh and into the realm of the spirit so that no matter how weak or ignorant you may be in the natural, you can pray exactly as you need to.

Is it any wonder that speaking in tongues has undergone such persecution—to the point where people were even killed for it in our own country? The devil hates it! He knows it's the only way believers can pray beyond what they know.

He understands (even if we don't) that even baby Christians, newly reborn, can pray in tongues, get the mind of the Spirit, and start growing fast. That's the way the church at Jerusalem grew in the early days, you know. That's all they had. They couldn't turn to the book of Ephesians or the book of Colossians. They just had to use the ability and understanding the Holy Spirit had given them. And when they did, they turned the whole world upside down.

Let me tell you something. This will turn your world upside down too. Or, it might be more accurate to say, it will turn it right side up. It will pump you up and enable you to walk in the power of the Spirit instead of the weakness of the flesh.

But be warned, it won't work for you unless you put it to work. The Holy Spirit is a gentleman. He's not going to come storming in and make you pray in the spirit. He's going to wait on you to decide to do it. He's going to wait for you to put your will in gear.

What happens if you don't? You won't be prepared when trouble comes.

In Luke 21:36, Jesus says, "Watch ye therefore, and pray always, that ye may be accounted worthy [or, as *The Amplified Bible* says, 'that you may have the full strength and ability'] to escape all these things that shall come to pass."

If you want to have the strength and ability to come through troubled times in triumph, you'd better spend some time in prayer.

That's what Jesus urged Peter and the other disciples to do in the Garden of Gethsemane. He knew they were about to face one of the toughest times of their lives. He said, "Watch ye and pray, lest ye enter into temptation. The spirit truly is ready, but the flesh is weak" (Mark 14:38).

But the Scripture tells us they didn't obey Him. They slept instead. And, in Peter's life in particular, we can see the result. When temptation came, he entered in to it and denied the Lord.

You might as well face it. Temptation is going to come to you as long as you live in a flesh body. So you'd better be prepared. You'd better have spent some time praying in the spirit when it comes.

If you've spent much time with the Lord at all, these instructions probably don't come as much of a surprise to you. In fact, I strongly suspect that God has already been speaking to you about spending more time praying in the spirit.

I remember when He first began to speak to me about the importance of it. I'd been asking Him to show me how to quit living my life so much on the natural, circumstantial level and start walking in the spirit. *Pray an hour or two a day in the spirit* was the first instruction He gave me.

I'd been committed to the Word for years at that time. I regularly spent much time reading and meditating on it—and that alone had already revolutionized my life. But I knew there was still something lacking.

What God showed me was that it was time to add to the Word by praying more in the spirit. It's really so simple, I'm surprised I didn't see it before. First Corinthians 14:14 says, "If I pray in an unknown tongue, my spirit prayeth." So when I began to pray more in tongues, I began to give my spirit more outflow. I gave vent to it.

Giving vent to your spirit is the way you walk in the spirit, just as giving vent to your flesh is the way you walk in the flesh. The more I released my spirit through tongues, the more it began to take charge. And I found it worked just as the Bible says: "Walk in the spirit, and ye shall not fulfil the lust of the flesh" (Galatians 5:16). I found it easier to hear and obey my spirit indwelt by the Holy Spirit.

Simple, isn't it? But the devil has tried to hide the simplicity of it from us because he knows if we ever start doing it he'll have no place left. You see, he's limited. He can't touch your reborn spirit. The only thing he has to work on is your flesh. Once you learn what brings the flesh under dominion—once you learn that praying in the spirit applies spirit to flesh and causes the flesh to obey God the way it ought to—the devil won't be able to get a foothold in your life at all!

But listen, the benefits of praying in tongues don't stop there. In fact, that's just the beginning! Listen to what the Apostle Paul wrote about it: "For he that speaketh in an unknown tongue speaketh not unto men, but unto God: for no man understandeth him; howbeit in the spirit he speaketh mysteries" (1 Corinthians 14:2).

What are mysteries? Mysteries are things we don't know. We don't just automatically know, for example, what the perfect will of God is for our lives. We don't know exactly what part we've been called to play in the Body of Christ. We don't know exactly what steps to take and what moves to make each day to fulfill the plan God has laid out for our lives.

And nobody in the world can tell us! As 1 Corinthians 2:9-10 says, "Eye hath not seen, nor ear heard, neither have entered into the heart of man, the things which God hath prepared for them that love him. But God hath revealed them unto us by his Spirit!"

"But how can all those things be revealed to me if I'm praying in a language I don't understand?"

They can't. That's why the Bible tells us to pray that we might interpret. As you begin to pray in the spirit, ask God to give you an understanding of what He's saying. You might not get the interpretation immediately, but eventually it will begin to bubble up inside you. You'll get an impression. A word. A sentence. Say to the Lord, "The things I know not, teach me, and the things I see not, show me." You'll begin to get revelation on things you've never understood before.

That's what you need: Revelation from God! That's what we all need. You know, we're not nearly as smart as we think we are. God has things that are so far better for us than what we've seen that we can't even figure them out. But if we'll pray in the spirit, we'll get into that area out beyond our knowledge and expectation, "above all that we ask or think," as the Bible puts it (Ephesians 3:20).

I'll tell you this: If we all start praying the will of God by the power of the Spirit, this age is going to come to an end quickly! God will be able to get mysteries into the earth. He'll be able to use our mouths and our authority to call forth His plan in the earth.

And, praise God, every one of us—from the least to the greatest—can participate because it's so simple! Every one of us can pray in tongues every day if we choose. You don't even have to be smart to do it. But without a doubt, if you'll do it, it will one day prove to be the smartest thing you ever did.

What Do You Want?

"Let patience have her perfect work, that ye may be perfect and entire, wanting nothing."
— JAMES 1:4

Jeanne Caldwell

My child, what do you want of Me?

With this simple question, God revealed to me a powerful principle of prayer: To be effective, your prayers must be specific. In order to answer your prayers, God has to know exactly what you want.

Here are some guidelines which will help you pray correctly, specifically and effectively:

First, go to the Father in the Name of Jesus and make your requests known. Then, believe that you receive when you pray, and if you have anything against any person, forgive him (Mark 11:24-25).

Second, stand on the promises in God's Word that cover your need. Be specific. Make a prayer list and stick to it. Pray for what you specifically need and what you are specifically believing for, one item at a time.

Third, be patient! "Rest in the Lord, and wait patiently for him" (Psalm 37:7). As long as your prayer lines up with God's Word, He will answer at the right time—His time. So relax, and "let patience have her perfect work, that ye may be perfect and entire, wanting nothing" (James 1:4).

Finally, but most important of all, develop a loving relationship with your heavenly Father. Get to know Him intimately, and you will have unshakable confidence in Him and in His Word.

Specific prayers receive specific answers. Always remember, "If we ask any thing according to [God's] will, he heareth us: And if we know that he hear us, whatsoever we ask, we know that we have the petitions that we desired of him" (1 John 5:14-15).

Chapter 7

The Place of Prayer

"And it shall come to pass in the last days, saith God, I will pour out of my Spirit upon all flesh."
— ACTS 2:17

Kenneth Copeland

There is a particular phrase I've heard spoken countless times over the years, and I like it less every time I hear it. No doubt, you've heard it too.

It comes most frequently on the heels of some tragedy. It's said—usually in drawn-out, religious-sounding tones—when circumstances seem to fall short of what God has promised us in His Word.

The phrase is "Well, Brother, you have to remember...God is sovereign."

As spiritual as that phrase might sound, it really bothers me. It's not that I don't believe God is sovereign. Certainly He is. According to Webster's dictionary, *sovereign* means "above or superior to all others; supreme in power, rank or authority." Without question, God is all those things.

But all too often, when people refer to the sovereignty of God, what they're actually saying is, "You never know what God will do. After all, He's all powerful and totally independent, so He does whatever He wants, whenever He wants."

The problem with that view of sovereignty is it releases us of all responsibility. After all, if God is sovereign, He will do what He wants anyway, so we might as well go watch *Gunsmoke* and forget about it, right?

Wrong. After more than 30 years of studying the Word and preaching the gospel, I've come to realize that God does very few things—if any—in this earth without man's cooperation. Even though it belongs to God—it is His creation and He owns it. Psalm 8:6 tells us God has made man "to have dominion over the works of [God's] hands."

God Himself put mankind in charge. He doesn't intervene in the affairs of earth whenever He wants. He respects the dominion and authority He has given us. So until man's lease on this planet expires, God restricts His power on the earth, taking action only when He is asked to do so.

Since the people who do the asking (the intercessors) are often very quiet people who do their praying in secret, it may appear at times that God simply acts on His own. But regardless of appearances, the Bible teaches from cover to cover that God's connection with man is a prayer and faith connection. When you see Him act in a mighty way, you can be sure there was someone somewhere praying and interceding to bring Him on the scene.

More Than Spectators

Now more than ever before, it is vital for every Christian to understand that. We are in the last of the last days. We are on the edge of the greatest outpouring of God's glory this earth has ever seen. Amazing, supernatural things are beginning to happen just as the Bible said they would.

Yet many believers are just sitting back, watching these events like spiritual spectators. They seem to think God will sovereignly turn over some great heavenly glory bucket and spill signs and wonders over the earth. But it won't happen that way.

How will it happen? Acts 2:17-19 shows us:

And it shall come to pass in the last days, saith God, I will pour out of my Spirit upon all flesh: and your sons and your daughters shall prophesy, and your young men shall see visions, and your old men shall dream dreams: And on my servants and on my handmaidens I will pour out in those days of my Spirit; and they shall prophesy: And I will show wonders in heaven above, and signs in the earth beneath.

If you'll read the last part of that passage again, taking out the punctuation that was put in by the translators, you'll see a divine connection most people miss. You'll see that God is saying when His servants and handmaidens prophesy, when they speak out His divine will and purpose in intercession and faith, then, in response to their speaking, He will work signs and wonders.

That means if this last outpouring of glory is to come in its fullness, all of God's servants and handmaidens must be in their place. What place?

The place of prayer!

Some people would say, "Well, Brother Copeland, we're talking about end-time events here, and I believe God will simply bring them about on His own. He doesn't need any help from us. After all, those things are too important to entrust to mere men."

That's what I used to think too. But God set me straight some years ago. At the time, I had been studying the authority of man and had seen over and over in His Word how the prayers of God's people precede God's actions on the earth. Yet I still hung on to the idea that God still did His most important works independently of man.

One day as I was praying about it, I said, "Lord, You brought Jesus into the earth sovereignly, didn't You?"

No, I didn't, He answered.

"You mean there were people who interceded for the birth of Jesus?" I asked.

Yes.

Then He told me the names of two of them—Simeon and Anna.

50 Years of Prayer

You can find the scriptural account of these two intercessors in Luke 2. There, the Bible tells us that when Jesus was 8 days old, His parents took Him to the temple to be dedicated to the Lord and circumcised into the Abrahamic covenant.

This ceremony was very sacred to the Jewish people, yet right in the middle of it, a man named Simeon walked in and took the baby Jesus in his arms. Nobody said anything to him. Nobody tried to stop him. So it's obvious he was well-known in the temple as a very spiritual man.

How did Simeon know to go to the temple at that particular time? Was it because somebody came and told him that Jesus was being dedicated? No, the Bible tells us "he came by the Spirit" (verse 27). He was led there by God.

What's more, even though Mary herself didn't yet understand who this child of hers truly was, Simeon did, and he prophesied, saying: "Lord, now lettest thou thy servant depart in peace, according to thy word: For mine eyes have seen thy salvation, Which thou hast prepared before the face of all people; A light to lighten the Gentiles, and the glory of thy people Israel" (verses 29-32).

Simeon knew who Jesus was because he had interceded, asking God to send the Redeemer. He had prayed so fervently and so long that God had promised him "that he should not see death, before he had seen the Lord's Christ" (verse 26).

It is amazing enough that Simeon recognized Jesus as the Savior of Israel, but his words reveal he knew even more than that. Read again what Simeon said and you'll see that he knew Jesus was bringing salvation to the Gentiles—a fact the rest of the Church didn't find out until Peter went to Cornelius' house, 10 years after the Day of Pentecost!

Why was Simeon so wise? He was an intercessor. Intercessors know things other people don't know. God tells them divine secrets and mysteries. He gives them inside information.

When Simeon finished prophesying over Jesus that day, in walked a little, 84-year-old widow named Anna. Unlike Simeon, this woman didn't have to be led to the temple by the Holy Spirit—she was already there. In fact, the Bible tells us that she "departed not from the temple, but served God with fastings and prayers night and day" (verse 37).

She hadn't just been there for a week or two, either. She had been residing there ever since her husband died. Since she had only been married seven years and we know from historical records that Jewish women married at about age 16, we can figure she had been praying in the temple for well over 50 years.

That's what I call staying with the program!

Luke 2:38 says that Anna "coming in that instant gave thanks likewise unto the Lord, and spake of him to all them that looked for redemption in Jerusalem." No one had to tell her who Jesus was. She knew the moment she saw Him because, like Simeon, she had been praying for God to send Him for many years.

Just think—even though God is the Almighty, Supreme Creator of this universe, He did not send Jesus into the earth independently. He did it in cooperation with men. He did it in response to the faith-filled words and prayers of His people.

Matthew 18:19 says, "If two of you shall agree on earth as touching any thing that they shall ask, it shall be done for them of my Father which is in heaven." Whether Simeon and Anna knew it or not, they were praying in agreement. They had both interceded, asking God to send His Redeemer, and God answered.

Get With the Program!

What does that mean to us today? It means if we want to see the fullness of this final outpouring of glory, we must get with the program as Anna did. We must get on our knees and start praying for it. We must start speaking out God's Word and His will for this last hour in prophecy and intercession so He can do signs and wonders.

You see, there are certain things that will never happen on the earth unless somebody speaks them. If you'll read through the Bible, you'll discover there are certain events that had to be foretold by the prophets before God would bring them to pass.

Now, I'm not saying Jesus won't come back if you don't pray. Jesus is coming for His people—and He is coming soon. This world has had all the sin it will stand and it's about to come apart. The whole creation is groaning under the stress of it. God will close out this age just as He said He would in His Word—no matter what you and I do. He'll find a Simeon and an Anna somewhere to get the job done.

But if the whole bunch of us believers will pray, instead of just a few, He'll increase the outpouring of glory that will accompany His return. If we'll cry out to God in one accord as the early Church did in Acts 4, this earth will be shaken by the power of God.

God cannot sit still when He hears the cries of His people!

The problem is, most of God's people are too busy with other things to take the time to intercede and cry out to Him. They don't make prayer a priority. Many are so occupied "working" for God, they think they don't need to pray.

But in the end, we'll find out it was the intercessors who were behind every success in ministry. Someday in heaven when the rewards are being handed out, Brother Big will be sitting on the front row expecting a gold trophy because he started the first church in his county. He'll lean over to the fellow next to him and say, "Yes, amen. I pastored that church for 47 years. I led 2,000 people to the Lord and had 1,000 baptized in the Holy Ghost in 1919. I'll tell you boys all about it as soon as I get my trophy."

But when the Lord starts to give the trophy, instead of calling Brother Big's name, He'll say, "Where's Mother Smith?" Then He'll send an angel down to row 7 million to fly Mother Smith up to the front.

When she gets there, He'll put that trophy in her hands and say, "Mother Smith, I want to give you this in honor of those 25 years you prayed and interceded and lay on your face before Me. Because of your prayers, I called Brother Big to come start the first church in your county. Because of your prayers, thousands of people were saved and filled with the Holy Spirit in that church."

Then He'll turn to the front row and say, "Brother Big, I'm rewarding you by allowing you to carry Mother Smith's trophy for her."

Right Place/Right Time

I can tell you whose trophies I will get to carry when that day comes. One of them will belong to my mother and another will belong to a little woman who used to pray with her all the time. That woman would go into my bedroom and get my pillow off my bed. Then she would carry it with her as she walked the floor and interceded for me, leaving her tears on my pillow. I know full well that's why God wouldn't leave me alone in my bed at night.

I'm saved and preaching the gospel today because of those two women. I don't get any credit for it.

I do have some credit coming for the times I interceded and cried out to God on behalf of someone else. But rewards aren't the reason you pray those kinds of prayers. You pray them because you're a bondservant of the One who laid His blood on the line for you. You pray them because of love.

That's the only motivation strong enough, because the job of the intercessor is the toughest job in the kingdom of God. The intercessor carries the spiritual load of everything that happens in the Body of Christ, and it's the most thankless ministry that exists.

When we preachers hold meetings where people get born again, most folks think it was our efforts that brought those people to the Lord. But all we did was preach the message God gave us. The anointing necessary to get lost people saved came because of the prayers of the intercessors.

Revival doesn't come from good preaching. Revival comes from prayer. The great sermon Peter preached on the Day of Pentecost didn't come because Peter was such an outstanding fellow. It came because people had been praying in one accord in one place for many days. About 120 of them prayed until the Spirit of God burst on the scene.

Those people "prayed in" that first great outpouring of the Holy Spirit. And when He came, where do you think He manifested Himself first? In the place where they were praying!

God hasn't changed. He is doing the same thing in our day that He did in Acts 2. But this time, He is moving even more powerfully and gloriously than He did then.

Does your heart hunger to experience that end-time outpouring? Do you want to see firsthand the supernatural signs and wonders He will perform in these last days? Then get in the place of prayer! Become an intercessor, yielding to the Spirit of God in prayer and speaking out His will.

If you'll do that, you won't have to be satisfied with secondhand reports of God's glory. You won't have to say, "I wish I had been there."

Like Simeon and Anna, you'll be in the right place at the right time. You'll have inside information because you won't be just a bystander; you'll be helping to bring forth the glorious return of the Lord!

Want a Change? Make a Change

"Solid food is for full-grown men, for those whose senses and mental faculties are trained by practice to discriminate and distinguish between...good and...evil."
— HEBREWS 5:14, *The Amplified Bible*

Gloria Copeland

If you're new to the things of God, a beginner just learning about the word of faith, no doubt you're eager to launch into a lifestyle of living contact with God by spending time each day in prayer and the Word. That's how I was too when I first learned what the Word of God could do.

No one had to urge me to put the Word first place. No one had to tell me to turn off the television and put down the newspaper. I totally lost interest in those things because Ken and I had our lives in such bad shape that we were desperate for God. We were in trouble. We weren't on the bottom of the barrel. We were under the barrel, and it was on top of us.

We knew that the Word of God was the only answer to our desperate situation. So it was easy for us to sell out to it and spend time in the Word and in living contact with God day and night.

You know, desperation sometimes helps. It encourages you to simplify your life. It inspires you to eliminate the unnecessary things and just go for God. But after you've walked with God for a while and things begin to be comfortable, it's easy to lose the desire you once had for the Word.

That's what happened to me. Once Ken and I paid our debts and began enjoying the blessings of God, I began to let too much of my time be taken up by other things. They weren't sinful things; they were just things I enjoyed doing. Almost without realizing it, my appetite for the things of God began to wane. Instead of hungering more for time with Him than for anything else, I enjoyed other activities and interests more. Those activities would have been fine if I had kept them in the right place, but they occupied too much of my time and attention.

I hardly even noticed it had happened until, one day in 1977, I was attending one of Kenneth E. Hagin's meetings and he began to prophesy. (I still keep the final words of that prophecy in my notebook today.) Part of that prophecy said to purpose in your heart that you will not be lazy, that you will not draw back, hold back or sit down, that you will rise up, march forward and become on fire.

When I heard that, it dawned on me that I had let myself slip spiritually. I realized I'd become lazy about the things of God. I was still spending time in the Word, but not as much as before, and I wasn't as full of zeal either. (That will always be the case. You can't be spiritually on fire without spending a sufficient amount of time with God.)

The Lord began to deal with me about it. I prayed and determined in my heart that I would change things. In order to simplify my life, I asked the Lord to show me what activities I should eliminate and what I should take on.

He led me to drop certain things out of my life that were stealing my time with Him. He also told me to do certain things that would help me get back in the habit of spending time with Him as I should. One specific thing He told me to do was to read one of John G. Lake's sermons each day. Brother Lake had such a spirit and revelation of dominion that each time I read one of those sermons, it opened up my heart to the power of God in a fresh way.

He also led me to get up an hour earlier in the morning so I could spend time with Him before I began my day. When I started, it was wintertime. My alarm clock would go off and my flesh would say, *You don't want to get up. It's too dark! It's too cold!* My bed would feel so wonderful and warm that there were a few mornings during the first few weeks that I'd agree with my body and go back to sleep.

I didn't let that stop me though. If I became lazy and went back to sleep, I'd repent. Then I just asked God to help me, and the next morning I'd go at it again! Eventually, my body became trained.

Your body can be trained to follow God just as it can be trained to follow the devil. Hebrews 5:14 says that mature believers have their "senses and mental faculties...trained by practice to discriminate and distinguish between...good and... evil" *(The Amplified Bible)*. If you practice the things of God, your body will eventually begin to cooperate with you.

For me, getting up earlier was a challenge for a while. But eventually my body learned it wouldn't receive that extra hour of sleep anymore, and it stopped complaining. It became accustomed to getting up at that hour. I also believe for supernatural rest when I have a short night. It works!

The decision to make time for God every morning has been one of the most important decisions of my life. It made such a difference in my spiritual growth. I'm not the same person I was then. People are always talking about how timid and restrained I used to be. I really was, too, but I got over it!

Become Addicted to Jesus

By implementing the changes God instructed me to make, I created a lifestyle of living contact with God. I became addicted to spending time with Him. Do you know what the word *addicted* means? It means "to devote, to deliver over, to apply habitually."

You can create good habits in God the same way you can create poor habits. If you'll habitually apply yourself to making contact with Him daily through prayer and the Word, it will become a way of life to you. You won't even have to think about doing it. It will just come naturally to you.

That's what happened to me. I have developed such a habit of making time with God my first priority that I don't have to get up every day and think, *Well, should I read the Word and pray this morning?* I just do it automatically. It's a way of life for me to spend the first part of my day in prayer now. Even when Ken and I are traveling, even when I have to get up at 4 o'clock in the morning to do it—I do it.

You might think that's extreme. You might think I'm the only one around who is that committed to spending time with the Lord every day, but I'm not. I'm one of many.

I have one friend in particular who is very diligent about it. No matter how early she has to get up in the morning, no matter what else her schedule may hold, she puts her time in the Word and in prayer first place in her day. That's because many years ago she found herself dying of liver cancer. The doctors had diagnosed it and told her she only had a few months to live.

Medical science couldn't help her, so she turned to God's medicine. She began to spend time reading and meditating on scriptures about healing each and every day. As a result, she is alive and well today with no trace of cancer in her body.

My friend knows she owes her very life to God's Word, so she is still faithful and diligent to partake of those scriptures and fellowship with God first thing every morning. She and her husband are ministers of the gospel and, like Ken and I, they often begin their day very early. But she says, "Even if I have to get up at 3 a.m., I'll do it."

Certainly such faithfulness requires time and effort. It's not easy. But if believers fully understood the blessings it brings, they too would be willing to do whatever was necessary in order to make their time with God their first priority every day.

There are great rewards for that kind of faithfulness! The Bible says, "The eyes of the Lord run to and fro throughout the whole earth, to show himself strong in the behalf of them whose heart is perfect toward him" (2 Chronicles 16:9). The word translated *perfect* there doesn't mean without a flaw. It simply means "faithful, loyal, dedicated and devoted."

God will pass over a million people to find that one who is loyal to Him. He scans the earth looking for people who will put Him first and let Him be God in their lives.

God wants to help us. He wants to move in our behalf. He wants to meet our every need and work miracles for us. If you were God, wouldn't you do that? Wouldn't you move in the lives of your children? The Bible says if you know how to give good gifts to your children, how much more the Father gives to His children (Luke 11:13).

Well, we're God's children. We've been born of His Spirit. We look just like God on the inside because He's our Father.

He has us in His heart. He cares about us. He loves each and every one of us as if each were the only child He had. God has a great and wonderful ability to have a family of many millions while treating every member as if they were the only one.

But God can't bless us as He wants to if we won't let Him be God in our lives. He can't pour out His provision upon us if we keep clogging up our heavenly supply line by putting other things before Him. If He is to show Himself strong on our behalf, our hearts will have to be turned wholly toward Him.

Your Desire Follows Your Attention

Maybe today your heart isn't turned wholly toward God. Maybe you're facing the same situation I was facing back in 1977. You've grown busy and lost your appetite for the things of God. You know you ought to be praying more and spending more time in the Word, but you've lost your desire. You just don't want to do it.

If so, you can turn yourself around. You can rekindle your fire for the Lord by making the same kinds of changes I made. Before long, you'll find yourself addicted to God instead of the earthly pursuits that have been so consuming you.

How can I be so sure?

Because God showed me that your desire always follows your attention. Most people think it's the other way around.

They think their attention follows their desire, but that's not the case.

One of the greatest practical examples of the fact that desire follows attention is the average golfer. In the springtime when the weather is nice and there is plenty of opportunity to play golf, most avid golfers become very absorbed in their sport. The more they play, the more they want to play. They think about it, read about it, talk about it. They are constantly wanting to play golf!

But when winter comes, they put away their golf clubs. They stop talking about it and thinking about it. They don't mope around all winter because they can't be on the golf course. Why? Because they've turned their attention to other things, and their desire for golf has weakened.

I've seen that same principle at work in our conventions. People will come to a Believers' Convention, and when they arrive they will often be completely caught up in natural affairs. They'll be preoccupied, worrying and fussing about some business deal at the office or some problem they left at home.

But after just a day or two of attending the meetings and spending hours on end in the Word of God, they'll completely forget about that business deal and that problem. They'll be so absorbed in the Word that those things won't interest them at all.

It doesn't matter how disinterested you may have grown about the things of God. If you will turn your attention toward Him, your heart will follow.

I know that from experience. I turned my attention to the Word of God, spent time listening to tapes, spent time in prayer until I became so addicted to the things of God that I lost interest in many of the other things that had so engaged me before. For example, I enjoy decorating homes and offices, and I used to spend a great deal of time at it. But as I became more involved in the things of God, I just didn't want to spend much time decorating. Now, it's a chore to do that.

What's more, every time I thought about taking up some new project, starting a new hobby or buying something that would require me to spend my time maintaining it, I'd say to myself, *Can I afford this? Can I afford the time it will cost me?* Usually I decided I couldn't. I had come to value the things of God so much and have such great desire for them, I just didn't want to give my time to anything else unless it was absolutely necessary.

A Tithe of Your Time

My resolve to put my time in prayer and the Word first place every day was even further strengthened in 1982 by another prophecy by Kenneth E. Hagin. In that particular prophecy, the Spirit spoke of wading further out into the realm of the spirit, until it's so deep, you can't possibly touch the bottom. But, the Spirit warned, our flesh will hold us back from that. It's only by renewing our minds that we can move into the realm of the spirit. Brother Hagin went on to say by the Spirit of God that if we'd just give an hour or two out of every 24, our lives would be changed and empowered, all would be well, and we would be a mighty force for God.

That prophecy has influenced me and encouraged me tremendously throughout the years, and since I heard it, I have spent at least an hour or two alone with the Lord every day. When I began to do that, there were things in my life and family that I wanted to see changed. There were things in the lives of my children that needed to be improved.

When I heard the prophet say that if I'd spend an hour or two a day with the Lord, things would be well with me, I took God at His word. Today I can give testimony that word was true. It worked. At the writing of this article, everything in my life and the life of my family is good. Things are well with us. My children are healthy, blessed and serving the Lord.

There is no question about it. The time I've spent with God has changed my life. And I can say with certainty that if you'll spend an hour or two a day with Him, it will change your life, too.

How could it possibly be otherwise? How could you spend an hour or two daily with the highest authority and the most kind and loving Being in the universe without having it affect your life?

You may be facing problems today that seem to have no solutions. You may be caught in impossible circumstances. But I want you to know, God can change those things. If you'll give Him a way into your life by making living contact with Him every day, He'll give you a way out of those impossible circumstances. He'll help you solve those problems. He'll move on your behalf until you can say, "All is well with me!"

If you want a change, make a change. Commit yourself to do whatever it takes to maintain living contact with God and spend time with Him every day. Determine right now that by the strength and grace of God, if you have to get up earlier in the morning, you will do it. If you have to go to bed later at night, you will do it. If you have to change jobs, you will do it.

Decide that no matter what it takes, you will maintain your communion with God, and you will guard your heart above all, for out of it flow the issues of life.

Praying With Power

"The earnest (heartfelt, continued) prayer of a righteous man makes tremendous power available—dynamic in its working."
— JAMES 5:16, *The Amplified Bible*

Terri Pearsons

The power of God. That, more than any other thing, is what we desperately need today. We need the power of God released in mighty ways to bring salvation, deliverance, healing and restoration into our lives, our families, our government and our world.

How do we tap into that power? It's no mystery, really. The Bible tells us very plainly in James 5:16: "The earnest (heartfelt, continued) prayer of a righteous man makes tremendous power available—dynamic in its working" *(The Amplified Bible)*.

But let's be honest. Every one of us has prayed prayers we felt weren't answered. We've known people who prayed...and prayed...and prayed, but nothing happened. Those prayers didn't make tremendous, dynamic power available. Somehow they missed the mark.

We can't afford to miss the mark in prayer today. We must have dynamic power. It is essential in this hour. We must learn to stand up in the power of prayer and take dominion, bringing the will of God to pass on earth as it is in heaven.

In God's Image

"Dominion?" you ask. "I'm supposed to take dominion?"

Yes, you were destined and designed by God to be a ruler on this earth, not a victim of circumstance. You must clearly understand that you are to operate powerfully in prayer, because prayer is actually an act of dominion. Your job in prayer is to find the will of God concerning a particular situation, take hold of it in faith, and refuse to let go until this natural world submits to spiritual truth and God's will is carried out in that situation.

You might say that through prayer, you are to be the executor of God's will on the earth.

Does that surprise you? It shouldn't. It was God's plan from the very beginning. Genesis 1:26-28 says, "And God said, Let us make man in our image, after our likeness: and let them have dominion...over all the earth.... So God created man in his own image, in the image of God created he him; male and female created he them. And God blessed them, and God said unto them, Be fruitful, and multiply, and replenish the earth, and subdue it: and have dominion...."

Of course, God didn't intend to simply give man rulership of the earth and then just walk off and leave him with it. No, during those days in the Garden of Eden, He fellowshiped with man. He communed with him, walking with him in the cool of the day (Genesis 3:8). God designed mankind to be so in union with Him that together they would subdue this earth.

But something happened. Adam committed high treason. He disobeyed God and submitted himself to Satan and, therefore, to sin. The day he did that, the life and light of God was extinguished. Adam died spiritually and, as a result, he eventually died physically—and not just Adam but the whole race of man. As Romans 5:12 says, "By one man sin entered into the world, and death by sin; and so death passed upon all men."

A Reborn Race

It was a terrible tragedy, but even so, God would not go back on His Word. He had given mankind dominion, and it could never be reversed.

But God had a plan. He sent His own Son, Jesus, to the earth as a man. Born of the virgin Mary and of the incorruptible Word of God, this Son was born without the nature of sin in His spirit. He was born to be the last Adam (1 Corinthians 15:45), the first of a new race of men, a race who would be born of the Spirit in His image, a race that would once again reign in life as kings with the power and dominion of God.

Jesus lived His life on this earth as a perfect example of how this new race of man was to function. He didn't live as God, although He was divine. The Bible tells us that He let go of every divine privilege and power, "made himself of no reputation, and took upon him the form of a servant, and was made in the likeness of men" (Philippians 2:7).

Jesus was not sent to be an alien-type creature that we could look at and say, "Oh my, isn't He wonderful?" He came to be an example to us of how we could and should be. He came to demonstrate what God wanted to do through us.

If you'll read through the New Testament, one of the most striking things you'll see about Him is the fact that He walked in dominion wherever He went. Acts 10:38 says He "went about doing good, and healing all that were oppressed of the devil." There was nothing the devil could do to challenge Jesus successfully. Jesus was always in control. He cast out demons. He calmed the sea. He stopped the wind. He ended the fig tree's life. He healed the sick. He raised the dead. He multiplied food.

Those who witnessed His life and ministry "were completely astonished at His teaching, for He was teaching as one who possessed authority, and not as the scribes...And they were all so amazed and almost terrified that they kept questioning and demanding one of another, saying, What is this? What new (fresh) teaching! With authority He gives orders even to the unclean spirits and they obey Him!" (Mark 1:22, 27, *The Amplified Bible*).

Even those who resisted Jesus and refused to acknowledge Him as sent from God recognized His dominion. "And they kept saying to Him, By what (sort of) authority are You doing these things, or who gave You this authority to do them?" (Mark 11:28, *The Amplified Bible*).

Position + Relationship = Power

Because of His sinless life, Jesus walked in perfect dominion. God did whatever He asked, not because He was God's Son, but because He held the position of a righteous man. His prayers made much power available, dynamic in its working!

"But that was Jesus!" you say. "What does His prayer life have to do with mine?"

Everything—because the Bible says that through our believing on Him, we've been given the same position of righteousness with God that Jesus has. Ephesians 2:4-6 says it this way: "But God, who is rich in mercy, for his great love wherewith he loved us, even when we were dead in sins, hath quickened us together with Christ, (by grace ye are saved;) and hath raised us up together, and made us sit together in heavenly places in Christ Jesus."

Just think, you're sitting in the seat of dominion with Jesus! You have the right to come boldly before God's throne of grace and obtain help and mercy in your time of need (Hebrews 4:16). You have a right to stand holy and blameless before God, not because of anything you did, but because you received the cleansing blood of Jesus.

So when the Bible talks about the righteous man, it's talking about you!

If you've been around the word of faith very long, you may be thinking, *Yes, I know I'm the righteousness of God in Christ Jesus. I know I have a position of right-standing with God, but my prayers are still lacking power!*

That's because position is not enough. You must also have the relationship. Jesus didn't rely purely on His position as a sinless man; He had communion with God. He fellowshiped with Him. You can see how vital that communion was in Mark 9.

There we see the disciples unable to cast the devil out of a demon-possessed boy. They knew they had the authority to do it because Jesus had given it to them, but for some reason they were unable to successfully exercise that authority. So after Jesus Himself had delivered the boy, "His disciples asked Him privately, Why could not we drive it out? And He replied to them, This kind cannot be driven out by anything but prayer and fasting" (verses 28-29, *The Amplified Bible).*

Notice that Jesus didn't say, "You couldn't cast it out because you're not the sinless Son of God." He told them it was because of their lack of communion with God.

An Intimate Communion

The Bible doesn't reveal a great deal about Jesus' private communion with God through prayer. It does tell us that He spent 40 days in the wilderness before He began His ministry (Luke 4). It tells us that at times He got up a great while before day to pray (Mark 1:35). It tells us that He went into the hills to pray alone and that sometimes He prayed through the night (Luke 6:12).

How are we to know what went on during those prayer times? How can we be sure He was having communion with the Father? By studying the things He said, things such as:

> I assure you, most solemnly I tell you, the Son is able to do nothing from Himself—of His own accord; but He is able to do only what He sees the Father doing. For whatever the Father does is what the Son does in the same way.... My teaching is not My own, but His Who sent Me.... He Who sent Me is true, and I tell the world [only] the things that I have heard from Him.... I do nothing from Myself—of My own accord, or on My own authority—but I say [exactly] what My Father has taught Me (John 5:19, 7:16, 8:26, 28, *The Amplified Bible).*

Jesus fellowshiped with the Father until He knew Him so well that He knew in every instance what the Father would say and do. He could answer and act on God's behalf because He knew God's heart and His ways.

We see that kind of thing happen in natural families all the time. A son might work with his father in business for so long that when the father retires, the son can run the business just as he did.

I know what that's like. I worked with my dad for so many years and listened to him preach so much that I knew what he'd say in almost any situation. If I had to edit one of his two-hour sermons to fit into a 45-minute television broadcast, I could do it without any problem. I knew exactly what points he'd want to leave in and what he'd want edited out.

Can you imagine knowing your heavenly Father that well? It hardly seems possible, but it is!

That's what Jesus wanted us to see. That's why He left behind all the privileges of heaven. He wanted to show us the kind of communion man can have in relationship with God.

He wanted us to realize that through prayer we can develop our relationship with the Father. We can learn to walk with Him and commune with Him. We can tune in to Him and become one with Him just as Jesus was.

If we'll do that, Jesus said, "Whatsoever ye shall ask the Father in my name, he will give it you" (John 16:23). If that's not astonishing enough, He also said, "He that believeth on me, the works that I do shall he do also; and greater works than these shall he do; because I go unto my Father" (John 14:12).

Think for a moment. What works did Jesus do? Those that He saw the Father do. What words did He say? Those He heard the Father say. So if we're going to do what Jesus did, we too must see and hear from the Father!

The Revealer Within You

"Well, I certainly don't know how I could ever do that!"

You couldn't on your own. But, thank God, Jesus didn't leave us on our own. He sent us the Holy Spirit. In John 14 He spoke of that Spirit, saying:

I will ask the Father, and He will give you another Comforter (Counselor, Helper, Intercessor, Advocate,

Strengthener and Standby) that He may remain with you forever, The Spirit of Truth, Whom the world cannot receive (welcome, take to its heart), because it does not see Him, nor know and recognize Him. But you know and recognize Him, for He lives with you [constantly] and will be in you (verses 16-17, *The Amplified Bible*).

Jesus considered the Holy Spirit so valuable that He said it was more profitable for us that He go away so the Spirit could come (John 16:7). That's because Jesus was limited to being with only a few people at a time, but the Holy Spirit is able to dwell with each and every one of us every second of every day.

Exactly what does the Holy Spirit do for us? Jesus tells us in John 16:

When He, the Spirit of Truth...comes, He will guide you into all the truth—the whole, full truth. For He will not speak His own message—on His own authority—but He will tell whatever He hears [from the Father, He will give the message that has been given to Him] and He will announce and declare to you the things that are to come.... He will honor and glorify Me, because He will take of (receive, draw upon) what is Mine and will reveal (declare, disclose, transmit) it to you. Everything that the Father has is Mine. That is what I meant when I said that He [the Spirit] will take the things that are Mine and will reveal (declare, disclose, transmit) them to you (verses 13-15, *The Amplified Bible*).

How can you hear what the Father is saying? The Holy Spirit will tell you! How will you see what the Father is doing? The Holy Spirit will reveal Him to you! He'll enable you to commune with God, talk to Him and flow with Him just as Jesus did.

The Apostle John said it this way: "But as for you, (the sacred appointment, the unction) the anointing which you received from [God], abides (permanently) in you; [so] then you have no need that any one should instruct you. But...His anointing teaches you concerning everything" (1 John 2:27, *The Amplified Bible*).

That verse doesn't mean we don't need teachers in the Body of Christ. It simply means you as an individual believer don't need anyone to tell you right from wrong. You don't need anyone to reveal God's will to you. You have this unction, this Holy One inside you, to lead you, talk to you and guide you. You have a knowing on the inside of you that comes from the Spirit of God.

This knowing enables you to first of all receive revelation from the written Word of God. Then as you look in that Word, the voice of the Spirit will begin to speak to you on the inside. The more time you spend in the Word and in prayer, the more familiar you'll become with that voice.

As the intimacy of that communion grows, you'll find yourself getting the kind of results in prayer you've always longed for. You'll not only step into the position of dominion, but also into an abiding relationship with God that opens the way for Him to give you all that you ask.

You'll discover firsthand the awesome truth recorded in James 5:16. "The earnest...prayer of a righteous man makes tremendous power available—dynamic in its working"! *(The Amplified Bible)*

Chapter 10

Pray Like Harvest Depends on It

"This is the confidence that we have in him, that, if we ask any thing according to his will, he heareth us: And if we know that he hear us, whatsoever we ask, we know that we have the petitions that we desired of him."
— 1 JOHN 5:14-15

Kenneth Copeland

If there were ever a time we needed to pray, it is now.

It's a time for prayer because of the darkness the world is going through. Satan is killing people with diseases, drugs, depression and every other weapon he can get in his hands.

It's time to pray because this generation of believers is in a very, very special time in history. We are at the end of an age. The 6,000 years of man's lease (and Satan's lordship) on the earth are coming to a close. The 1,000 years of Jesus' millennial reign are immediately ahead.

But before Jesus comes, God will fulfill every promise He has made during the 6,000 years of man's history on earth. The Body of the Anointed One is about to have its hands full of harvest.

The key to seeing the kind of results God wants His last-days generation to walk in is not just shooting some scattershot type of prayer and hoping something might happen. James wrote, "Ye have not, because ye ask not. Ye ask, and receive not, because ye ask amiss, that ye may consume it upon your lusts" (James 4:2-3). Success comes when we pray accurately according to the will of God.

Praying the Will of God

So many believers wring their hands and worry about whether or not they're praying according to God's will. Many of them have been taught a wrong view of God's sovereignty. They think that His ways are beyond finding out and that it is more spiritual to pray, "God, whatever Your will is in this situation, You just go ahead and do it."

Just think what kind of confusion that causes. Whatever results from that kind of praying is credited to God—good or bad! To really honor God's sovereignty, we must pray what He has already declared to be His will.

Praying the will of God is the only kind of praying that can consistently, confidently be expected to bring results. We weren't created to waste time standing around looking puzzled, especially in these days. We just need to grab our Bibles and find out what the will of God is. God's Word IS His will. He has made some very specific promises in it. And it's His will to fulfill every one of them.

Think about what you did when you prayed for salvation. You didn't pray, "God, I'm sick and tired of this life under Satan's control, and I want You to be my Lord and Savior. But I don't want to tell You what to do. Whatever Your will is—to set me free or to keep me in this miserable condition, to send me to heaven or to send me to hell—You just do it."

No. You prayed for God to save you just as His Word said He would. You prayed accurately according to His Word that He is "not willing that any should perish" (2 Peter 3:9). You prayed expecting results according to the promise that "If thou shalt confess with thy mouth the Lord Jesus, and shalt believe in thine heart that God hath raised him from the dead, thou shalt be saved" (Romans 10:9).

Maybe you wondered at first, *Did God hear me?* then later discovered that 1 John 5:14-15 says, "If we ask any thing according to his will, he heareth us: And if we know that he hear us; whatsoever we ask, we know that we have the petitions that we desired of him."

Find Out What the Word Says

These same principles work in any area of prayer. Do you need healing in your body? Don't pray what the doctor says or what your religious tradition has told you. Pray, "By His stripes I am healed" (1 Peter 2:24). Do you have financial needs? Don't pray your problem. Pray what God has said He will do: "My God shall supply all my need according to His riches in glory by Christ Jesus" (Philippians 4:19).

God wants His will to be done on earth as it is done in heaven. Find the promise that applies to your situation, and pray the answer instead of the problem. Don't just pray what you remember the Word of God says. Read it! Even if you've read that promise a hundred times, read it again. Feed on what it says again and again. One day, you'll read a familiar verse and suddenly God will give you the greatest revelation you've ever had in your life. And it will be exactly what you needed to know to pray effectively about your current situation.

First John 5:14-15 says, "This is the confidence that we have in him, that, if we ask any thing according to his will, he heareth us: And if we know that he hear us, whatsoever we ask, we know that we have the petitions that we desired of him."

When you pray God's Word knowing His will in advance, you are no longer praying just hoping to get results. You're not rattling off a bunch of religious sounding words. You're praying expecting to get results. You're praying accurately because you are praying the very words God has given as His will to be done on earth.

So, before you pray, make the decision to get results. Then pray the Word, expecting God to move. That's the way we bring demonstrations of God's glory on earth while people are being increasingly tempted and terrorized by Satan's deception. That's the way we position ourselves to receive harvest that will come so quickly that the sower overtakes the reaper.

Jesus is the Alpha and Omega—the Beginning and the End—the First and Last. So let's start with His Word and finish with His Word. Give Jesus the first word in everything you do, and watch Him bring in a harvest like no previous generation has ever seen.

Chapter 11

Fellowship: The Foundation of Powerful Prayer

Lynne Hammond

"I know whom I have believed, and am persuaded that he is able to keep that which I have committed unto him against that day."
— 2 Timothy 1:12

Judging strictly by appearances, it might seem that the Church of the Lord Jesus Christ is doing quite well in the area of prayer these days. Pick up almost any church bulletin in any city and you'll find listed midweek prayer meetings, prayer luncheons, prayer requests, perhaps even a printed prayer for the week.

Walk into any church service and you'll hear at least one prayer—probably two or three—before it's done. Listen in on the conversations of Christians and you'll hear them say, "I need you to pray for me, Brother." And, no doubt, you'll hear the same response every time, "Oh, yes. I will, I will."

One would think, with all this talk about prayer, the windows of heaven would be opened wide, spilling the blessings of God upon us. Jesus plainly promised that "whatsoever ye shall ask in my name, that will I do, that the Father may be glorified in the Son" (John 14:13). So we should be swimming in waves of revival, prosperity, healing and miracles of every sort. Our every conversation should be overflowing with joyful reports of answered prayer. The Church should be bursting forth with such earthshaking evidence of God's mighty delivering power, and sinners should be banging on our doors by the thousands, begging us to show them the way of salvation.

But clearly, that is not the case.

I do not mean to say we have seen no results from our praying. There have always been glimmers and even lightning strikes of the power and presence of God throughout the earth. There have been praying people and even praying congregations here and there who have moved mountains as they lifted their hearts to God—and every day their numbers are increasing. Yet even so, we must admit that in our day, the Church as a whole has not experienced what the Bible has promised would come to us through prayer.

Corporately, we have not seen buildings shake under the power of God as we unite in prayer as the Church did in Acts 4. Individually, we have not been able to speak with absolute certainty the words of the Apostle John: "And this is the confidence that we have in him, that, if we ask any thing according to his will...we know that we have the petitions that we desired of him" (1 John 5:14-15).

As a result, many Christians have allowed prayer to slip from their list of priorities. (One survey reported the average Christian invests less than two minutes a day at it.) Many others have struggled through the disappointments of unanswered prayer, trying to explain away their lack of results with theological arguments. "Well," they say, "perhaps it simply wasn't God's will this time."

But I believe every true Christian knows deep in his heart that despite what the theologians may say, our problem is not that God is saying a loving no to many of our requests. It's that our prayers too often lack the depth that heaven requires. They seem to come from the head, not the heart. Instead of being propelled from our spirit toward God with an earnestness and faith that cannot be denied, they often wobble from our uncertain lips and fall helplessly to the floor.

They have a form of godliness, but they deny the power thereof.

In time past, we were fooled by that form. We were like the shopper standing in the department store who sees the mannequin out of the corner of his eye and, thinking for a split second the mannequin is real, the shopper turns to speak to it.

But, praise God, we're not being fooled any more. We've looked that prayer mannequin square in the face and said, "You're not the real thing!"

We've turned our faces toward God and begun crying out as the disciples did two thousand years ago, "Lord, teach us to pray!"

And He is answering us. He is restoring to us not just the principles nor the mechanics, but the very spirit of prayer.

I Know Whom I Have Believed

It is that spirit we most desperately need. For although principles and formulas are valuable teaching tools, many times we have focused on them to the exclusion of God Himself. We have unwittingly grieved His tender Spirit by approaching Him almost as if He were a machine instead of a Person. We've followed step-by-step formulas as though by systematically pushing scriptural buttons and pulling spiritual levers, we could get Him to produce the results we desire.

Many of us have even recognized the truth—that it takes faith to receive from God. So we've studied the Bible, confessed particular verses over and over and memorized every key to spiritual success. Yet too often, instead of causing us to flourish in faith and prayer, our endeavors have left us dry and spiritless. Why is that? It is because we can't have real faith just by knowing principles. Real faith comes from knowing the Person behind the principles.

That's why the Apostle Paul in his great statement of faith wrote, "I know whom I have believed, and am persuaded that he is able to keep that which I have committed unto him against that day" (2 Timothy 1:12). Paul didn't say, "I know what I have believed." He didn't say, "I know the principles and steps I have believed." He said, "I know the Person of the Lord Jesus Christ."

You see, real praying comes from the heart hungry to know God. It comes when we cry out, as David did in Psalm 42: "As the hart pants and longs for the water brooks, so I pant and long for You, O God. My inner self thirsts for God, for the living God.... [Roaring] deep calls to [roaring] deep at the thunder of Your waterspouts; all Your breakers and Your rolling waves have gone over me" (verses 1-2, 7, *The Amplified Bible*).

When a person is hungry, the deepest part of his spirit begins to call out to God for something to fill that hunger. He might not even know what it is he is calling for, but God knows, and this cry touches the depths of His heart and causes Him to respond.

If we want true power in prayer, we must cultivate that kind of hunger. We must let the deep within us begin to call out to the deep in God. We must desire to know Jesus with such an intensity that every other desire pales beside it.

The fact is, however, that kind of desperate desire doesn't grow in the hearts of those whose relationships with God consist of simply going to church a couple times a week. It doesn't come to those who fellowship with God only at public gatherings of believers.

No, if we are to have true spiritual passion, we must develop a love affair with the Lord—and love affairs are never in public! We must seek out times of private, daily communion with Him, times of waiting before Him and worshiping Him. Instead of being content just to check in with Him now and then, we must learn to lift our hearts to Him continually, moment by moment.

You Can Pray Like Elijah!

Such constant and intimate fellowship is the key to vibrant and powerful prayer. For Jesus said, "If you live in Me—abide vitally united to Me—and My words remain in you and continue to live in your hearts, ask whatever you will and it shall be done for you" (John 15:7, *The Amplified Bible*).

The word "ask" in that last verse has a far deeper meaning than most people realize. It implies you and God are so intertwined, your life and His life so closely joined together, that when you ask Him something, it's not really just you asking—it's Him asking, too.

That's the kind of asking that the Old Testament prophet Elijah did.

"Oh, Sister Hammond," you say, "I couldn't possibly pray with the power of Elijah."

Why not? The Bible says he was a human being just like we are (see James 5:16-18). He had all the same struggles and natural weaknesses we have. He is not set forth as an unusual fellow who lived off in the spiritual stratosphere somewhere. He is given to us as an inspiration and an example of earnest praying. Yet his prayers changed the course of nature. They changed people and nations. They projected God in full force to the world.

How was he able to do that?

Read 1 Kings 17 and you'll find out. There we see Elijah coming boldly before Ahab, the wicked king of Israel, announcing, "As the Lord, the God of Israel lives, before Whom I stand, there shall not be dew or rain these years, but according to My word" (verse 1, *The Amplified Bible*).

Notice Elijah didn't just meander around. He didn't say, "Well, you know, I feel kind of impressed that it might be the Lord's will for rain not to fall around here for a while." No, he was firm and clear. He said, "Here's how it will be. Absolutely. Period. End of conversation." He reveals the reason for his confidence and power in the phrase "the Lord, the God of Israel... before Whom I stand."

That was the secret of Elijah's praying. He had stood in the power and presence of God. He didn't just make up those words he spoke to Ahab on his own. He received them from God Himself. In the times of fellowship, such as those he'd spent beside the brook Cherith alone with God, Elijah had come again and again before Him in prayer, and because he had stood in that place, he could speak and pray with world-shaking authority.

Make a Change

You and I have a far greater covenant than Elijah did. Through the precious blood of Jesus, God has opened for us a new and living way so that we can come boldly before the throne of grace to obtain mercy and find grace to help in time of need (Hebrews 4:16). He has given us a freedom of access to Him the Old Testament saints never knew. He's made available to us all the resources and power of heaven.

But what have we done with those privileges? For the most part, we've done very little. We've been too busy making a living or watching television or perhaps even participating in church activities to take advantage of them. As a Church, we have pacified our spiritual hunger with the junk food the world has offered us, while we've let the dust collect on our Bibles and the cobwebs grow in our prayer closets.

Right now you may be thinking, *Yes, it's true. I have done that in the past, but I want to change it now. What can I do?*

Simply repent before God. Honestly acknowledge that you have desired other things more than Him. You cannot pretend to be hungry when you are not. But you can begin to call out to Him and say, "Lord, please forgive me and make me hungry for You."

You can, from this day on, say as David did, "Your face, Lord, I will seek" (Psalm 27:8, *New International Version).* Set aside time to fellowship with God in prayer and in the Word every day, not out of a sense of religious duty, but because you want to whet your spiritual appetite and you know the fragrance of His presence as you meet Him daily in some quiet place will stir the hunger in your heart. It will awaken the craving that sleeps within every true child of God. It will remind you of how empty you are without Him and cause you to cry out from the depths of your soul, "Lord, I want to know You!"

In the natural course of this earth, wherever there's a vacuum, that vacuum causes the air to rush in and fill its emptiness. Thus, the wind blows there. The same is true in the spirit. If we'll empty ourselves of the distractions and desires of this world and crave Jesus alone, He will rush into our lives with the wind of the Holy Spirit. He will meet us with an intensity and an outpouring we have, until now, only read about in the pages of books.

We will know not just the form of prayer...but its power.

Chapter 12

The Power of Agreement

"If two of you agree on earth about anything that they may ask, it shall be done for them by My Father who is in heaven."
— MATTHEW 18:19, *New American Standard*

The prayer of agreement is one of the most powerful tools God has given us. It is a prayer that Jesus Himself guaranteed would bring results every time. "If two of you agree on earth about anything that they may ask," He said, "it shall be done for them by My Father who is in heaven" (Matthew 18:19, *New American Standard).*

When you don't see the results He promised, I've found the problem usually lies in one of four areas.

1. Run a harmony check.

The word *agree* that Jesus uses in Matthew 18:19 can also be translated "to harmonize" or "to make a symphony." A symphony is composed of many instruments, which, when played together, seem to be a single voice.

If you've ever heard a symphony, you know that when the individual instruments are tuning up, each one playing separately from the other, it's not much to hear. But when the conductor raises his baton and all those instruments begin to harmonize, the sound they make is tremendously powerful.

The same thing is true in prayer. Believers agreeing together in the Holy Spirit are a powerful, unstoppable force. That's why Satan fights Christian families. That's why he doesn't want men and women unified in marriage. He wants us fighting and fussing all the time because he knows it will hinder our prayers (see 1 Peter 3:7).

Any time you fail to get results from the prayer of agreement, run a harmony check. Ask the Holy Spirit to show you if you're in strife with your wife (or anyone else). Then follow the instructions in Mark 11:25, where Jesus tells us, "When ye stand praying, forgive, if ye have aught against any: that your Father also which is in heaven may forgive you."

It is not sufficient for you and your wife simply to agree on the particular issue you are praying about. You must also be in harmony in other areas as well. So make a harmony check!

2. Establish your heart on God's Word.

The prayer of agreement will only work if it is based on the Word of God. You and your wife might jump up one day and agree that you'll own a hundred oil wells by midnight, but you'll never see that prayer of agreement come to pass, because it's not founded on the Word of God.

So go to the Word first. Find the promise that covers the particular situation you're praying about. Then write it down and meditate on it until, as Psalm 112:7 says, your "heart is fixed, trusting in the Lord."

3. Fix your mind on the Word.

Second Corinthians 10:5 tells us to bring "into captivity every thought to the obedience of Christ." You must do that if you're to see results from your prayers of agreement. Do what the Bible says and "think on these things" (Philippians 4:8). What things? Things from the Word of God!

Say to yourself, "I'll not think on anything contrary to this agreement." Then, when Satan tries to slip in negative thoughts and break down your faith, you'll have to tell him, "No, no, no, devil! I don't believe what you say. I believe what the Word says."

Then get out your Bible. Go back to the Word and soak your mind in it. Obey Proverbs 4 and "keep it before your eyes."

4. Act as if it's done.

This is where so many believers miss it. They pray the prayer of agreement, taking a faith stand together. Then as soon as they walk out of the prayer closet, they start wringing their hands and saying, "Oh my, I just don't know what we're going to do if this problem doesn't get solved!"

Don't make that mistake. Once you've settled the issue through the prayer of agreement, refuse to act as though that issue is a problem anymore. Instead, just start praising God. In every way you can, act as though all is well.

When people ask you about the matter, just answer them with faith. Say, "Glory to God, that issue is handled. My wife and I have agreed in prayer. God is honoring our agreement. And as far as we're concerned, that problem is behind us."

The prayer of agreement is a powerful tool. So don't be discouraged by your past experience. Just make the necessary adjustments, and keep on in agreement. Run a harmony check. Establish your heart on the Word. Fix your mind on the Word. Act as if it's done. And anything you ask shall be done for you by your Father in heaven.

Chapter 13

A Blaze of Praise: The Secret of Supernatural Combustion

Gloria Copeland

"Let the saints be joyful in glory...Let the high praises of God be in their mouth, and a twoedged sword in their hand."
— PSALM 149:5-6

Something peculiar is happening to believers these days. They're beginning to rejoice.

If you've been in many meetings where the Holy Spirit has moved, you know what I mean. God is pouring out a spirit of joy so strong it causes people to laugh for hours. Some of them literally end up on the floor doubled over laughing with the joy of the Lord.

Recently, during the Southwest Believers' Convention, that joy swept through the convention center, affecting literally thousands of people. It so filled Ken that he could hardly minister. The next morning, however, he could not only stand and preach, he felt stronger than he'd felt in 10 years.

That's supernatural...but it's not surprising, because the Bible says, "The joy of the Lord is your strength" (Nehemiah 8:10).

I have to tell you, though, when God's people start to praise Him and rejoice with that kind of abandon—it makes some Christians nervous. As a result, many of them are folding their arms, sitting back, saying, "I'm not going to be caught acting like that"...and as a result, they're missing out on a powerful move of God.

I don't want that to happen to you. I don't want you to hold back when the Spirit of God is moving. I want you to be able to step by faith into His flow and receive the rich blessings He's pouring out in these last days.

I'm confident that's what you want, too. So let me share with you a few things I've learned about rejoicing from the Word of God.

Tell "Dignity" Goodbye

Some years ago, when I first began to catch sight of the supernatural power of joy, I did a study on it. During that study, I discovered that one of the biblical words for *joy* is translated "to shine." Another word means "to leap." Another means "to delight." But in every case, joy is more than an attitude; it is an action.

As I studied, I also found out that joyful praise gives God pleasure. Psalm 149 says: "Praise ye the Lord. Sing unto the Lord a new song, and his praise in the congregation of saints. Let Israel rejoice in him that made him: let the children of Zion be joyful in their King. Let them praise his name in the dance: let them sing praises unto him with the timbrel and harp. For the Lord taketh pleasure in his people" (verses 1-4).

It doesn't offend God when we boisterously praise Him. He likes it. It gives Him pleasure to see us shine and leap and express our delight in Him.

"Let the saints be joyful in glory.... Let the high praises of God be in their mouth, and a twoedged sword in their hand" (verses 5-6).

I know that by natural standards, that kind of exuberant praise doesn't look very dignified. But as believers, we need to get past the point where we care about that. We need to focus instead on pleasing God. We should have such a desire to please Him that we don't care how we look to other people.

"But, Gloria, that's easy for you to say. You're comfortable with expressing yourself to God in praise."

I haven't always been. I was so conservative when I first began to walk with God that it took me a long time to even begin to lift my hands in praise. But I broke through that "dignity," and so can you.

Of course, there are always some believers who try to please God and look good at the same time by "praising God quietly in their hearts." Although there's a time for quiet worship, the Bible says joy isn't always quiet. In fact, joy shouts.

"But let all those that put their trust in thee rejoice: let them ever shout for joy, because thou defendest them" (Psalm 5:11).

You may not know this, but when you get to heaven, it's not going to be quiet. The throne room of God is a noisy place.

Isaiah 6 tells us: "In the year that king Uzziah died I saw also the Lord sitting upon a throne, high and lifted up, and his train filled the temple. Above it stood the seraphims.... And one cried unto another, and said, Holy, holy, holy, is the Lord of hosts: the whole earth is full of his glory. And the posts of the door moved at the voice of him that cried, and the house was filled with smoke" (verses 1-4).

The throne room is a loud place that's filled with the glory of God. Living ones are crying "Holy, holy, holy" until the very door posts shake!

I'm telling you, God is not all laid back as some people think. He is not getting old. He isn't even slowing down. His very presence causes people to get so excited they shout.

Do you ever go to a football game and cheer and shout? Is that normal? Certainly! You'd look pretty strange sitting silently on the bench trying to look dignified.

Well, I think it's normal when we get excited worshiping God. In the throne room they think it's normal to cry, "Holy, holy, holy is the Lord God Almighty. The whole earth is full of His glory!"

That's what's normal up there. So if we're going to pray, "Thy kingdom come, Thy will be done on earth as it is in heaven," then we need to learn to act down here as they act up there. We need to learn a holy shout!

Is Jesus Nervous?

Now let's see what Jesus says about praising God. After all, He's the Head of the Church. If He gets nervous when people start praising loudly, then we'd better slow down. (But I've already looked this up, and I know He doesn't.) I'll tell you who did get nervous, though—the Pharisees.

The Gospel of Luke tells us about a time when "the whole multitude of the disciples began to rejoice and praise God with a loud voice for all the mighty works that they had seen.... And some of the Pharisees from among the multitude said unto him, Master, rebuke thy disciples" (Luke 19:37-39).

The Pharisees didn't like that kind of praise. But that's not surprising. The religious folks didn't like anything Jesus did, because nothing He did fit their traditions. And, since they'd lost the power of God in their lives, tradition was all they had!

Make a note of this: When you lose contact with the power of God, you lose your excitement about worship. You start adopting traditions and rituals—and if anyone violates those, it offends you.

That's what happened to the Pharisees. How do you think Jesus responded? Do you think He restrained His disciples so they wouldn't offend anyone? No. He said, "I tell you that, if these should hold their peace, the stones would immediately cry out" (Luke 19:40).

Jesus never tried to please the Pharisees. He only pleased God. He just told them, "If my disciples don't praise Me, the rocks will do it!" That's what Jesus thinks about praise. He's in favor of it—no matter how badly it bothers some folks.

Your Greatest Desire

When we become like Jesus and desire God so intensely that we're willing to cast aside our desire to please men and praise Him without reserve, we'll truly see the glory of God.

Why? Because God manifests Himself where He's wanted. He shows up where hearts are hungry. He's not going to reveal Himself to a great degree among people whose hearts are partially turned to Him and partially turned toward something else.

God told Moses, "As truly as I live, all the earth shall be filled with the glory of the Lord" (Numbers 14:21). That's what He wants. He's wanted it for a very long time. But He has to have a people who will allow Him to be their God—with nothing else before Him. They have to want Him and His presence more than they want to be respected in their neighborhood. They have to want Him more than anything else life has to offer.

Today He is finding people who are willing to do that. People who literally praise God with all their heart.

If you are one of those people, you've probably already found out that some people don't like it. The glory of God offends them, and they don't want to be around you.

Not surprisingly, very often it is the religious people who will criticize you most harshly. After Jesus healed the blind man, the religious leaders told him, "Don't give that Jesus any credit—He's a sinner" (John 9:24, my paraphrase).

The sick, hungry people of the world won't say things like that. They're not like the people who have been "religionized." They want help and they don't care where they get it.

They have the same attitude as the man who was born blind. He said to the Pharisees, "Whether he (Jesus) be a sinner or no, I know not: one thing I know, that whereas I was blind, now I see" (verse 25).

Now That's Power!

If you're not sure you have the strength to face the criticism of the religious people, I have good news for you. You can get that strength by rejoicing, because the Bible says, "The joy of the Lord is your strength" (Nehemiah 8:10).

Joy and praise together release strength on the inside of you and power on the outside. Psalm 9:1-3 says it this way: "I will praise thee, O Lord, with my whole heart; I will show forth all thy marvellous works. I will be glad and rejoice in thee: I will sing praise to thy name, O thou most High. When mine enemies are turned back, they shall fall and perish at thy presence."

God inhabits our praises (Psalm 22:3). And when His presence begins to come into our midst, our enemies fall back. They can't stand the presence of God. "Let God arise, let his enemies be scattered: let them also that hate him flee before him. As smoke is driven away, so drive them away: as wax melteth before the fire, so let the wicked perish at the presence of God. But let the righteous be glad; let them rejoice before God: yea, let them exceedingly rejoice" (Psalm 68:1-3).

Now that's power! When God's people rise up in praise and worship and celebrate the victories of God, His enemies are scattered.

No wonder Satan has tried so hard to get God's people to sit still. No wonder he has bound us up with traditions that taught us to sit back in dignified silence. (The word *dignity* means "to be self-possessed.") For most of us, our traditions have taught us not to do the very things the Bible says we are to do when we worship and praise.

Burn, Brother, Burn!

But tradition's day is over. I'm telling you, when the Spirit begins to move, inhibition has to flee. The Bible says, "And they...shall be like a mighty man, and their heart shall rejoice as through wine" (Zechariah 10:7).

You know what happens when people drink wine—they lose their inhibitions! That's what happened to the disciples on the Day of Pentecost. They had been hiding out only days before, but when the Holy Ghost came upon them, suddenly they were out on the streets acting so wild everyone thought they'd been drinking.

Listen, what God considers "dignified" and what you consider dignified are two different things. God wants you free. He doesn't want you bound up with traditions or fear of what other people might think.

He wants you free to laugh. He wants you free to leap and praise and sing. He wants you free to rejoice. He wants you so free that other people won't understand it—they'll just want it!

Never underestimate the drawing power of joy. It's like a blazing fire that captures the attention of people in darkness. In fact, in a dream I had many years ago, God called it "spontaneous combustion."

I didn't even know what the term meant until the next day. When I looked it up in a dictionary, here's what I found: *Spontaneous combustion*—"the process of catching fire and burning as a result of heat generated by an internal chemical reaction."

That's it! Joy—the process of catching fire and burning as a result of heat which comes from the Holy Ghost.

It's time to rejoice, to rise up out of our exhaustion and implement the power of praise. When you do, you'll enter a domain of power, freedom and the joy of the Lord. A domain that's alive and shining with the presence of God.

So throw off those old inhibitions. Take God at His Word. Leap. Shout. Sing. Let yourself catch fire in the Spirit and never stop burning.

One Word From God
Can Change
Your Finances

Breaking the Power of Debt

Chapter 1

"If the Son therefore shall make you free, ye shall be free indeed."
— JOHN 8:36

John Avanzini

A strong sense of hopelessness.... That is the way many Christians describe their inner feelings about their finances. They feel as if they are aimlessly adrift in an endless stream of borrowing. Unpaid bills occupy more and more of their thoughts. They honestly believe there is no way out of their debt dilemma.

Please note that I am not speaking of dishonest people, but hardworking, honest folks who are doing all they know to do. However, try as they may, they keep sliding further and further into debt.

The Joy Is Gone

In most homes, both husband and wife are forced to work. Yet, even with two wage earners, money always seems to be in scarce supply.

For most families, the joy is gone from payday. All that remains is the Friday night ritual of rushing the paycheck to the bank so the checks they wrote Thursday will not bounce. After the paycheck is deposited, they draw out a few dollars from the automatic teller machine for their once-a-week, Friday night splurge. This consists of a modest meal at a fast food restaurant and a short walk through the mall. Long gone are the days of shopping, for they must now pay for their past credit sprees.

For a pitiful few hours, the wage earner feels good, enjoying a small portion of the fruit of his labor. All too soon Saturday morning arrives, and with it comes the full reality of the fruit of debt. The wage earner must now face his mountain of bills— bills that were only partially paid last payday.

God Is Left Holding the Bag

Check after check is written until, finally, the last pressing obligation is paid. With this task accomplished, the stark reality comes to light. There is only enough left to barely scrape by until next payday.

In the crushing pressure of having only enough to make ends meet, the tithe, which is so vital to receiving God's blessings in life, is usually ignored. At best only a portion of it is paid. This is usually justified with a promise that soon things will be better and then God will get what is His.

For the next six days, the average wage earner has to put off having any fun or doing anything special. To the Christian, the most painful part of this existence is having to say no to God concerning giving into His kingdom. This is an empty cycle that is routinely made from Friday to Friday by those who have come under the control of the spirit of debt.

Wake Up to a Better Way!

Wake up! That's no way for the children of God to live! Surely, this is not God's best for your life! He must have a better plan. Deep down in your spirit, you know He wants something more for your life than barely existing from payday to payday!

Hear the good news! The same God who wants you to walk in His saving grace, the same God who wants you to experience His miracle healing power, the same God who wants your family to be entirely whole also wants you to operate in total financial abundance.

His principles of biblical economics are clearly stated in His Word! If you follow them, they will free you of your payday-to-payday blues. From them you will learn how to boldly get started on your road to a debt-free lifestyle.

A Progressive Walk

God is as concerned about your financial success as He is about every other part of your life.

When you first started to walk with Him, you had to learn to recognize the lies of the devil. They were holding you captive. The world had taught you that drinking and parties were the fun way to live. But as you progressed in your Christian walk, you realized that that kind of thinking is flawed. You began to understand that drinking almost always leads to alcoholism and wild parties open the door to sexual sins. You found that if you were to experience God's best, you would have to say no to sin and yes to God's way of doing things.

The further you walked in God's ways, the less complicated your world became. Inner peace began to grow. Much to your own surprise, you started having more fun instead of less fun. Since the troubles and torments that accompany the world's wicked ways have begun to melt away, your life has become much more worthwhile.

Well, Child of God, I've got good news for you. This same freedom that you are experiencing in this area of your life is also available to you in your finances!

Please do not misunderstand. I'm not talking about something that will force you into the lifestyle of a miser. I'm talking about something that will enable you to experience a miracle in your finances—a miracle that will transform your finances from barely making it to abundance, from not enough to more than enough, from little to much.

Does such a miracle exist? Can we actually go forward in some financial healing line, have someone lay hands on us, and walk away with all of our bills marked paid in full?

Before I answer that question, let us get one thing straight. No man has the ability to miraculously release people from their debts. Miracles are not from men. Miracles are given by God and received, through faith, by men.

I have laid hands on many people and seen them healed; however, I have never healed anyone. Each time someone has been miraculously healed, that person had to receive the miracle from God.

The same biblical principle applies to the miraculous release from debt. Each time the miracle of debt cancellation takes place, it comes directly from God to those who receive it through faith.

A Widow Received This Miracle

Make no mistake about it. The miracle of canceled debt is taught in God's Word. One very powerful illustration involves a widow woman and her two sons.

This widow was left with a great debt at her husband's death. She was hopelessly bound until the miracle of debt cancellation set her free. Her debt was so large that her two sons were sentenced to become bond servants to the creditor. It took everything she had. She was left with nothing more than a small pot of oil. She was brought to the very door of destitution. In her advanced years, she was cruelly sentenced to the life of a beggar.

Thank God for her faith. Her decision not to seek help from the creditor proved to be the wisest move of her life. In the midst of her desperate problem, she turned to her man of God. All the creditor could offer her was more debt, but God presented her with the opportunity to receive the miracle of canceled debt. All she had to do was exercise the faith to do exactly what her man of God told her to do.

The following verses tell us about her powerful miracle of debt cancellation:

Now there cried a certain woman...unto Elisha, saying, Thy servant my husband is dead...and the creditor is come to take unto him my two sons to be bondmen. And Elisha said unto her...what hast thou in the house? And she said...a pot of oil. Then he said, Go, borrow thee vessels.... And when thou art come in, thou shalt... pour out into all those vessels, and thou shalt set aside that which is full.... And it came to pass, when the vessels were full...the oil stayed. Then she came and told the man of God. And he said, Go, sell the oil, and pay thy debt... (2 Kings 4:1-7).

There it is, right from the pages of your own Bible! A miraculous cancellation of debt! The scriptural account of this particular event opened with an impossible mountain of debt. It demanded payment. Even if it meant the ruination of the woman and her two sons, it had to be paid. Then, in just a few hours, this woman was completely debt free!

With this miracle from God's Word, we see proof positive that He has a miraculous solution for the debt problems of people just like you and me. What we need to do is dig into the Bible and find it, then mix it with faith and put it to work in our lives.

Build Your Financial Foundation

"Beloved, I wish above all things that thou mayest prosper and be in health, even as thy soul prospereth."

— 3 JOHN 2

Gloria Copeland

Never try to build a house without first laying a foundation.

I don't care how eager you are to get it finished, how excited you are about filling it with furniture and decorating it all just right—take the time to put down a solid foundation first. If you don't, that house will be so unstable it will soon come tumbling down.

That's simple advice, isn't it? Everyone with any sense at all knows it. Yet in the spiritual realm, people make that mistake all the time. They see a blessing God has promised them in His Word, and they are so eager to have it, they ignore the foundational basics of godly living and pursue just that one thing.

That's especially true in the area of prosperity. Often, people are so desperate for a quick financial fix, they just pull a few prosperity promises out of the Bible and try to believe them—without allowing God to change anything else in their lives. Of course, it doesn't work and those people end up disappointed. Sometimes they even come to the conclusion that it wasn't God's will for them to prosper after all.

But I can tell you today, from the Word of God and from personal experience: It is definitely God's will for all of His children to prosper!

That's why He inspired the Apostle John to write, "Beloved, I wish above all things that thou mayest prosper and be in health, even as thy soul prospereth" (3 John 2).

Notice there, however, that John didn't just say, "I want you to prosper." He said, "I want you to prosper as your soul prospers." He tied financial prosperity to the prosperity of our mind, will and emotions.

God's plan is for us to grow financially as we grow spiritually. He knows it is dangerous to put great wealth into the hands of someone who is too spiritually immature to handle it. You can see dramatic evidence of that fact in the lives of people who have acquired financial riches through this world's system, apart from God. In most cases, such riches just help people to die younger and in more misery than they would have if they'd been poorer.

That's because they use their wealth to sin in greater measure. They use it to buy all the cocaine they want and drink all the alcohol they want. They use it to pay for an immoral lifestyle that eventually destroys them.

The wages of sin is death. That is an inescapable fact. So, when people get money and use it to sin, it does them more harm than good. As Proverbs 1:32 says, "The prosperity of fools shall destroy them."

Seek First Things First

In light of that truth, it's easy to see why God wants us to increase financially at the same rate we increase spiritually. He wants us to outgrow our fleshly foolishness so our prosperity will bring us blessing and not harm.

"But Gloria," you say, "I need financial help fast!"

Then get busy growing. Get busy building your foundation for prosperity.

How? By finding out what God says in His Word and doing it.

You see, the foundation of prosperity is a continual lifestyle built on the Word of God. It is doing whatever God tells you to do, thinking whatever He tells you to think, and saying whatever He tells you to say.

Godly prosperity is the result of putting God's Word—all of it, not just the parts about financial prosperity—first place in your life. It comes when you apply His principles on a continual basis—not just because you want money, but because Jesus is your Lord and you want to follow Him. It comes when you start obeying the instructions Jesus gave us in Matthew 6:25-33:

> I tell you, stop being perpetually uneasy (anxious and worried) about your life, what you shall eat or what you shall drink, and about your body, what you shall put on. Is not life greater [in quality] than food, and the body [far above and more excellent] than clothing? Look at the birds of the air; they neither sow nor reap nor gather into barns, and yet your heavenly Father keeps feeding them. Are you not worth more than they? And which of you by worrying and being anxious can add one unit of measure [cubit] to his stature or to the span of his life? And why should you be anxious about clothes? Consider the lilies of the field and learn thoroughly how they grow; they neither toil nor spin; Yet I tell you, even Solomon in all his magnificence (excellence, dignity and grace) was not arrayed like one of these. But if God so clothes the grass of the field, which today is alive and green and tomorrow is tossed into the furnace, will He not much more surely clothe you, O you men with little faith? Therefore do not worry and be anxious, saying, What are we going to have to eat? or, What are we going to have to drink? or What are we going to have to wear? For the Gentiles (heathen) wish for and crave and diligently seek after all these things; and your heavenly Father well knows that you need them all. But seek for (aim at and strive after) first of all His kingdom, and His righteousness [His way of doing and being right], and then all these things taken together will be given you besides *(The Amplified Bible)*.

I remember back before Ken and I knew we could trust God to take care of us financially, I thought it was my job to worry about how we were going to pay our bills. I spent a great deal of my time thinking things like, *What am I going to do about this light bill? How am I going to keep the electricity from being shut off?* To me it would have been irresponsible not to worry about such things!

Then I found out it wasn't God's will for me to worry. It was His will for us to believe Him to care for us. I also learned that as believers, we're not to seek after material riches. We're not to pursue money like people do who are without God. They have to pursue it. They don't have a covenant with God, so if they don't seek material goods, they won't get them!

But we're not like those people. We're not in the world without God and without a covenant (Ephesians 4:12-13). We have God's promise of provision. He has assured us in His Word that He will not only meet our needs, but give us an abundance.

It's important for us to remember, however, that a covenant is always between two parties. It has two sides to it. A covenant says, If you do this, then I'll do that.

God's part of the covenant is to prosper us—spirit, soul and body as well as financially. What is our part of the covenant? It's not to seek after that prosperity. If we do that, we'll get side-tracked. Our part of the covenant is to seek first His kingdom, His way of doing and being right!

Our part is to say, "Lord, I'll do whatever You tell me to do. I'll obey Your Word and do what is right in Your sight—even if it looks like it will cost me."

Of course, obeying God's Word never costs in the long run. It pays! You always put yourself in a position for increase when you seek after God and do things His way.

I'll be honest with you though, there will be times when you can't see how that increase is going to come. Ken and I know about those times. We've been through them.

When we saw in the Word of God that we were to "Keep out of debt and owe no man anything, except to love one another" (Romans 13:8, *The Amplified Bible*), we weren't too excited about it. At that time in our lives, it looked to us like we'd never be able to do anything financially without borrowing money.

We thought, *How will we ever get a car? How will we get a home? How will we finance our ministry? We're doomed!*

But we had already decided to obey God no matter what the cost, so we committed to Him to get out of debt even though we thought it would be to our disadvantage. Of course, that decision has since turned out to be one of the wisest financial decisions we've ever made.

That's the way it always is. Obeying God always works to your advantage in the end!

Become a Candidate for Increase

It's easy to see how following God's instructions to get out of debt affected our prosperity. But the fact is, our decision to obey other, seemingly unrelated commands we saw in the Word also had an impact on our finances.

That's because you can't separate God's financial principles from the rest of His principles. They all work together. So you have to take the whole Bible to have a good foundation for godly prosperity.

The primary commandment Jesus gave us, for example, is to "love one another" (John 15:12). To the casual observer that commandment may seem to have nothing to do with money, yet to have true prosperity love must be the guiding force of your life. You must be quick to apply scriptural principles for living like these found in 1 Peter 3:8-11:

> Finally, all [of you] should be of one and the same mind (united in spirit), sympathizing [with one another], loving [each the others] as brethren (of one household), compassionate and courteous—tenderhearted and humble-minded. Never return evil for evil or insult for insult—scolding, tonguelashing, berating; but on the contrary blessing— praying for their welfare, happiness and protection, and

truly pitying and loving them. For know that to this you have been called, that you may yourselves inherit a blessing.... For let him who wants to enjoy life and see good days...keep his tongue free from evil, and his lips from guile (treachery, deceit). Let him turn away from wickedness and shun it; and let him do right *(The Amplified Bible)*.

Think of it this way. Every right action you take, every godly decision you make, every time you go love's way instead of the selfish way, you're putting another block on your foundation of prosperity.

When you pray for your enemies instead of hating them, you become a candidate for increase. When you turn away from immorality, you're turning toward blessing. When you see things in your life that you know aren't right and you correct them according to the Word of God, you're preparing yourself to handle greater financial abundance.

The book of Proverbs is full of God's wisdom about everyday things and decisions. It will help you learn how to handle your affairs in a way that is pleasing to God. And since it has 31 chapters, by reading a chapter a day along with your other Bible reading, you can finish it in just a month. It will increase you to read Proverbs over and over.

In Proverbs you'll find out, for example, that the quality of faithfulness and the blessing of prosperity are tied together very closely. Wherever you find one, you'll find the other. For as Proverbs 28:20 says, "A faithful man shall abound with blessings." According to Webster's dictionary, a *faithful* man is one who "adheres to duty, of true fidelity, loyal, true to allegiance, and constant in the performance of duties or services."

Luke 16:10 says, "He who is faithful in a very little [thing], is faithful also in much; and he who is dishonest and unjust in a very little [thing], is dishonest and unjust also in much" *(The Amplified Bible)*. So if you want to be trusted with more and be promoted to a better job, be faithful and honest in the job you have right now.

You may think Christian people don't need to hear about honesty and faithfulness, but they do. I know personally of cases where Christians have stolen money from their employers.

They may not have intended to "steal" anything. They may have just thought, *Well, I'll borrow this money for a couple of weeks and then I'll put it back and no harm will be done.* The problem is, you can't borrow something from someone without their permission. That's stealing and you can't be blessed and steal.

Taking that money may have seemed all right to those people when they did it. They may have made excuses and justified it in their own minds. But if they'd been studying and obeying the Word of God, they wouldn't have fallen for those excuses. That's because the Word discerns the thoughts and intents of the heart (Hebrews 4:12). It teaches you what is right and what isn't.

It reveals not man's way, but God's way of doing and being right. It enables you to lay a firm foundation for godly prosperity.

Build the Whole House

With that foundation laid, you'll be ready to step out in faith and receive the abundance God has in store for you.

Many people who have lived godly lives have failed to do that so they've missed out on God's financial blessings. Although they've continually applied the principles of God's Word and become prime candidates for great prosperity, they've unwittingly passed it by because religious tradition has taught them that God wants them in poverty. Christians like that have great wealth in their spiritual bank account, but because they don't realize it's there, they never tap into it!

Don't let that happen to you. Don't just build the foundation for prosperity and stop there. Go on and build the whole house. Dare to believe that if you'll seek first God's kingdom,

His way of doing and being right, all other things (the food, the clothes, the cars, the houses, everything!) will be added to you as well.

Build your foundation, then dare to believe—and you will surely prosper!

Money Really Matters

Chapter 3

"If you are willing and obedient, you shall eat
the good of the land."
— ISAIAH 1:19, *The Amplified Bible*

Gloria Copeland

"Well, I'm not rich...but in the eternal scheme of things
money doesn't really matter. Right?" Wrong. In this day and
hour, financial prosperity isn't simply a luxury. It's a responsibility. For the committed believer who cares about the eternal
destiny of others, money really matters.

I want to talk to you about a subject that is vital to the
kingdom of God. A subject that will have a tremendous
impact, not only on your life in these days but also on the
lives of others.

I want to talk to you about money.

I realize you may not think money is a very spiritual issue.
You may have been taught that as far as God is concerned, it
doesn't matter if you're rich or poor. But I want you to know—it
matters. Your not having enough money to finance the gospel
won't keep you from going to heaven, but it could keep others
from going.

Prosperity is not a frivolous thing with no eternal conse-
quences. It is a serious issue. If you want to know how serious,
consider this: Right now, in areas such as Eastern Europe, there
are people who have never heard the gospel. For years, the
doors of their nations have been locked to it. But at this moment,
the Body of Christ has the opportunity to preach the Word of
God from one end of that area to the other.

What will we need to take full advantage of that opportunity? Money.

That's right. Money, or the lack of it, can determine whether
someone in an area like that hears the gospel...or not. In my
eyes, that makes our prosperity as born-again believers an
important issue—extremely important.

If we prosper, we'll have enough not just to meet our own little needs, but to send the Word of God around the world. If we don't, we won't. It's that simple.

"Oh, but Gloria, you know we can't all be rich."

Yes, we can. Prosperity is not an accident. It's not a function of circumstances or the economy. According to God's Word, prosperity is a choice. It is a personal decision and a spiritual process.

Most people don't know that. Ken and I didn't either years ago when we first began walking with God. Back then, we were sick some of the time and broke all the time. Our life was one financial disaster after another. It felt like we were living under some kind of curse.

Do you know why we felt that way? Because we were living under a curse! We just didn't realize it.

Failing to prosper is part of the curse that came upon the earth when Adam sold out to Satan in the Garden of Eden. The curse is described in detail in Deuteronomy 28:15-68 and it includes every kind of sickness, sin, tragedy and lack. That passage says that when you're living under the curse "You shall be only oppressed and robbed continually.... You shall carry much seed out into the field, and shall gather little in" (verses 29, 38, *The Amplified Bible*).

Do you ever feel like that? Like every time you try to get ahead, something happens to steal away everything you thought you were going to gain? I know the feeling. I had it for years.

But then, one day Ken and I discovered we had been redeemed from the curse. We found out that according to the Word of God, we didn't have to put up with any of those things listed in Deuteronomy 28:15-68 because: "Christ hath redeemed us from the curse of the law, being made a curse for us: for it is written, Cursed is every one that hangeth on a tree: That the blessing of Abraham might come on the Gentiles through Jesus Christ; that we might receive the promise of the Spirit through faith" (Galatians 3:13-14).

Overtaken—For Better or Worse

Look at the last part of that scripture again. It says the blessing of Abraham has come on the gentiles through Christ Jesus. I know there are many people who say God's blessings are only spiritual and they don't include finances. But that can't be true because the Bible says we have the blessing of Abraham and that blessing brought him great wealth. Genesis 24:35 makes that quite clear.

There Abraham's servant says: "And the Lord [has] blessed my master greatly; and he is become great: and he hath given him flocks, and herds, and silver, and gold, and menservants, and maidservants, and camels, and asses."

God had promised Abraham that He would be his shield and his exceeding great reward (Genesis 15:1). No question about it, that promise caused Abraham to be extremely prosperous in every way and it will do the same for you, if you're a born-again child of God. What is it like to be blessed in every way? (Remember *blessed* means "empowered to prosper.") Deuteronomy 28:1-9 tells us:

And it shall come to pass, if thou shalt hearken diligently unto the voice of the Lord thy God, to observe and to do all his commandments which I command thee this day, that the Lord thy God will set thee on high above all nations of the earth: And all these blessings shall come on thee, and overtake thee, if thou shalt hearken unto the voice of the Lord thy God. Blessed shalt thou be in the city, and blessed shalt thou be in the field. Blessed shall be the fruit of thy body, and the fruit of thy ground, and the fruit of thy cattle, the increase of thy kine, and the flocks of thy sheep. Blessed shall be thy basket and thy store. Blessed shalt thou be when thou comest in, and blessed shalt thou be when thou goest out. The Lord shall cause thine enemies that rise up against thee to be smitten before thy face: they shall come out against thee one way, and flee before thee seven ways. The Lord shall command the blessing upon thee in thy storehouses, and in all that thou settest thine hand unto; and he shall bless thee in the land which the Lord thy God giveth thee. The Lord shall establish thee an holy people unto himself.

Does all that sound too good to be true? Well, it's not. That's the blessing Jesus bought for you on the cross. And it will begin to operate in your life if you'll "hearken...unto the voice of the Lord [your] God."

Notice, I didn't say it will operate just because you're a Christian. Ken and I were Christians for five years before we began to listen to God's Word about prosperity. So during that time, the curse continued to run loose in our lives. It didn't just creep up quietly. It jumped on us and overtook us. No matter how hard we tried, we couldn't outrun it or get away from it.

Then we began to believe God's Word about prosperity—to be willing and obedient—and good things started to happen. First a few. Then a few more. The longer we obeyed God and walked in faith about finances, the more those good things increased.

Just like the curse once overtook us, now the blessings of God overtake us. I like that much better.

The same thing will happen to you if you'll follow the instructions in Deuteronomy 28:1 and "hearken diligently unto the voice of the Lord...." That's because "faith cometh by hearing, and hearing by the word of God" (Romans 10:17). Once faith comes, you can speak to that mountain of financial trouble, command it to be removed, and it will obey you. (See Mark 11:22-24.)

You must realize, however, that faith for finances doesn't come automatically. It doesn't come just because you're a good person and you love God. It comes when you spend time, day after day, listening to and acting on what God's Word says about prosperity.

More Than Enough

As you do that you'll discover, just as Ken and I did, that God doesn't promise just to meet your basic needs, He says He'll give you an abundance. Some religious people would argue about that. But the truth is, there's nothing to argue about because the Word makes it perfectly clear. Look back at what we just read from Deuteronomy 28. It says, "The Lord shall command the blessing upon thee in thy storehouses, and in all that thou settest thine hand unto" (verse 8).

Look at that for a minute. If you don't have abundance, why would you need a storehouse? A storehouse is where you put the extra, the surplus, the "more than enough."

If that's not clear enough, verse 11 says point-blank that, "the Lord shall make you have a surplus of prosperity" *(The Amplified Bible)*. I want you to remember those words—a surplus of prosperity—because that's God's will for you. When you made Jesus Christ the Lord of your life, God's blessing came upon you not so you could just "get by," but so that you could have a surplus of prosperity!

That shouldn't really surprise you. After all, if you look at God's history with man, you'll see that when He had His way, man was abundantly supplied. Everything in the Garden of Eden, for example, was good. The temperature was just right. The food was right there on the trees. All you had to do was pull it off and eat it. Talk about fast food! Adam and Eve lacked nothing in the garden.

All through Israel's history, God supplied their every need, even if He had to bring down manna from heaven. As long as they obeyed Him and honored Him, their families prospered, their livestock prospered, their crops prospered, and no enemy could stand before them. On top of that, there was no sickness in the midst of them.

God has always promised, "If you are willing and obedient, you shall eat the good of the land" (Isaiah 1:19, *The Amplified Bible)*. Understand, though, that being willing means more than just saying, "Well, Lord, if You want me to prosper, I'll prosper." Being willing means that you apply the force of your will and determine to receive by faith what God has promised, no matter how impossible the circumstances may seem to be.

Get Aggressive!

That's what Ken and I had to do. When we saw in God's Word that prosperity belonged to us, we were so deep in debt it looked like we would never get out. But we applied our will anyway. We said, "We will prosper in the Name of Jesus. God says He has provided abundance, so abundance belongs to us!"

That's the kind of aggressive faith you need to believe for prosperity. I didn't understand that for years so, without realizing it, I allowed the devil to come in and give me a hard time over finances. Then one day, God revealed to me that I needed to use the same kind of faith for finances I used to receive healing.

That changed my believing and my actions. You see, I had learned early on to be aggressive about healing. Once Ken and I found out that Jesus bore our sickness, we refused to put up with it anymore. We absolutely wouldn't tolerate it. We considered sickness an enemy and when it would try to come into our house, we'd stand against it.

We'd tell it, "No! You get out of here. We've been redeemed from the curse of the law and that includes every sickness and disease. So get out!"

Sure enough, it would leave. Never in all the time my children were at home did I have to take them to the doctor for sickness. (We certainly would have if it had been necessary.) They'd get symptoms now and then, but we'd just pray and believe God, and they always got healed. Sometimes it took a day or so, but the healing always came.

One day God said to me, *Why don't you treat lack that same way? Why do you put up with it? You say you've been redeemed from it, but you haven't resisted it like you do sickness and disease.*

When I heard that, I determined to make a change. I began to actively, aggressively resist lack and to cultivate my faith for prosperity as diligently as I had cultivated my faith for healing. And I can tell you, it made a big difference in our lives.

Start Where You Are

I must warn you though, it wasn't easy. It takes effort and perseverance in the Word of God to develop that kind of faith. If you want to believe for divine prosperity, you'll need to keep a constant dose of the Word of God in your heart. You'll need to meditate on it all the time.

You can't just grab a verse once in a while and then run out and prosper. You have to let the Word of God renew your mind and teach you how to think differently and you'll have to let that Word take root in your heart. That doesn't happen overnight.

I've heard people say, "Well, we've been tithing and obeying God and we're not out of debt yet. Is there any way to hurry this thing up?"

Yes. You can double up on the Word, spend more time with God, and be sure to give every time God tells you. That's in addition, of course, to tithing 10 percent of your income that belongs to God—offerings come after that. But even so, you still have to start where you are.

When Ken and I were first learning to walk in faith for prosperity, we didn't know very much of God's Word yet. We got our revelation piece by piece. Every time we'd learn something new, we'd put it into practice.

Actually, it's much easier for us now to walk in prosperity than it was back then. Today, we have to believe for millions of dollars just to pay our TV bills. But that's not nearly as challenging as it was to believe God back then for food on the table. During those days I often had to pray in the spirit just to pay my way out at the grocery store. That was the hardest time of all because we were just learning.

You have to grow in these things. If you're just now hearing that God wants you to prosper, you probably won't be able to get a million dollars in cash by this time next week.

Why? Because your faith isn't up to that yet. What you need to do is start right where you are. Start believing God for rent money. Start believing God to buy groceries. Start believing, and then increase.

That's what we did. We believed for rent. Then we believed for a car. Then one day we believed for a house. The first time it took us six years to get it. The next time it took three weeks.

We just kept growing. We kept listening to God and walking in the faith that we had and it got bigger. And we kept tithing and giving!

No Time to Waste

What's important is to start now. Don't wait until next month. Start believing God for the things you need today. Start thanking Him for them. Tell the devil you're out from under his curse. Grab hold of the Word of God and don't let go.

If you'll do that and stay with it, and continue to do what God tells you, you'll eventually have a surplus of prosperity so that you can not only pay your bills, but also have the capacity to give into every good work! (2 Corinthians 9:6-11).

So get out the Word and get busy. There's no time to waste. We're rapidly coming to the end of this age. We have opportunities today we've never had before. Nations are allowing us to preach the gospel on television that never allowed it before. But it takes money to do that.

Who's going to provide that money? You and I and every other member of the Body of Christ who will dare to rise up and reject lack as a lifestyle. Every believer who will be bold enough to say, "Prosperity belongs to me. I will believe it and I will receive it in Jesus' Name! I will stand up to the devil and fight the fight of faith for it!"

It's time we realized it's not just our own personal needs that are hanging in the balance. It's more than that. It's the eternal destiny of other people. It's the work of the kingdom of God.

Prosperity is not a frivolous matter. It's serious. More hinges on it than you have realized. So get aggressive. Take a stand on the Word of God and take what belongs to you as His child. I won't kid you, you'll have to fight some battles. But I can tell you in advance, if you'll do it in faith, you'll win. It will be well worth the fight.

Chapter 4

Prosperity—
It's Not an Option

Markus Bishop

"Let them shout for joy, and be glad, that
favour my righteous cause: yea, let them say
continually, Let the Lord be magnified, which
hath pleasure in the prosperity of his servant."
— PSALM 35:27

Have you ever noticed how sensitive people are about their
money? You can talk to them about the way they look, the way
they talk, even about their family. But when you start talking
about their money—watch out!

Money seems to be where people really live. The truth is,
they are that way about money because that's the way the devil
is about money.

When you start talking about money, you really stir up
the devil! You have to understand that he is the god of this
world (2 Corinthians 4:4). But he is not God of the earth.
Scripture says, "...the earth is the Lord's, and the fullness
thereof" (1 Corinthians 10:26).

The devil is the god of the world's system. When you start
talking about the prosperity of believers, you are talking about
money being taken out of the devil's pocket. That money comes
from his operation—his kingdom—and it's put over into the
kingdom of God to help pay for the gospel being preached
throughout the world. That makes him mad!

Satan's Lie About God

That's why he has promoted the lie that money is evil, even
though Scripture says, "The love of money is the root of all evil"
(1 Timothy 6:10). That's why by his deception, there is some
perverted preaching going on in the pulpits of America and all
over the world that says God wants His people to be poor.

As a result, many people's minds have been so cluttered
with garbage that they can't even think straight. They think,

Well, I'm having a financial difficulty. God must be trying to teach me something.

They read Psalm 35:27 this way: "Let them shout for joy, and be glad, that favor my righteous cause: yea, let them say continually, God wants me broke."

That's not what this verse of Scripture says. It says: "...let them say continually, Let the Lord be magnified, which hath pleasure in the prosperity of his servant."

God wants to see His people prosper. Under the Old Covenant, the Israelites were servants of God who brought pleasure to the heart of God through their prosperity. How much more today do we as believers, as sons and daughters of God, as children of the Most High God, bring pleasure to the heart of God when we do well financially?

Bringing Pleasure to the Heart of God

Jesus asked, "If ye then, being evil, know how to give good gifts unto your children, how much more shall your Father which is in heaven give good things to them that ask him?" (Matthew 7:11).

Those of us who are parents are always trying to help our children and bless them. If we, falling so far below God's goodness, do this for our children, how much more does our heavenly Father give good things to those who ask Him?

As children of God and joint heirs with Jesus Christ, we have been given the blessing of the Lord.

According to Proverbs 10:22, "The blessing of the Lord... maketh rich, and he addeth no sorrow with it." As believers, we become enriched in our souls when we know the Lord. The word *rich* here has only one meaning, and that is for financial prosperity. It is a word that describes wealth, money, income. We could quote Proverbs 10:22 this way: "The blessing of the Lord, it maketh financial prosperity." There is a prosperity that can come from the world. But the world's system is vicious, and the prosperity it offers brings sorrow with it. You are a child of

God. Your heavenly Father longs to pour out on you, as His child, blessings that bring no sorrow with them.

When you receive a bill in the mail, your first question should not be, "How am I going to pay it?" Your first question should be, "I wonder how my heavenly Father is going to bring it to me this time?"

You Have to Know What's Yours

Sometimes I am asked, "If it's God's will for every believer to prosper, then why are so many dear Christian brothers and sisters still experiencing poverty and lack?" Because their souls have not been trained in this truth. Their understanding of the Scriptures has not been renewed to include all the promises of God.

In 3 John 2, God's Word clearly promises financial prosperity as a blessing from God for every believer: "Beloved, I wish [or will] above all things that thou mayest prosper and be in health...." Notice what the rest of that verse says: "even as thy soul prospereth."

You will prosper in proportion to the prosperity of your soul—and that comes in accordance with your understanding of the Word and your obedience to that Word. God's Word says, "And this is the confidence that we have in him, that, if we ask any thing according to his will, he heareth us: And if we know that he hear us, whatsoever we ask, we know that we have the petitions that we desired of him" (1 John 5:14-15).

Knowledge of the will of God is essential for you to have faith in your prayers. I remember some wonderful words shared by Kenneth E. Hagin in a meeting several years ago. They were so powerfully true I can't improve upon them. He said, "Faith can never rise above the known will of God."

You can't believe for something when you don't know if it's God's will for you to receive it. It's not just having a covenant with God; it's being a doer of the Word that releases these blessings. But if you don't know the Word, how can you be a doer of the Word? You will only prosper in proportion to the prosperity of your soul, or your understanding of the Scriptures.

When you know it's God's will for you to be saved, you have faith to be saved. When you know it's God's will for you to be healed, you can feed your spirit with promises of divine healing from God's Word and have faith to be healed. Prosperity is just like any promise, any blessing or any other provision of your redemption in God through Christ Jesus.

Prosperity—God's Perfect Will

Let yourself see financial prosperity for what it scripturally and actually is—a part of your redemption, which Jesus Christ died and paid for. You have to see prosperity in that light.

Prosperity is not an option. It's not something God just tolerates or allows you to have in His permissive will. Prosperity is one of the things the precious blood of Jesus was shed to purchase for you. Renew your mind to this truth. Prosperity was bought and paid for by Jesus Christ. It is the perfect will of God for your life.

As soon as you become convinced of that, divine prosperity will become more than a right. It will become a daily reality in your life.

That's when you will begin praying with the aggressiveness necessary to actually transfer wealth out of the kingdom of darkness and into the hands of God's people in these last days. That's what the devil is fighting.

God wants you to prosper. He absolutely takes pleasure in you "always having all sufficiency in all things" so that you "may abound to every good work" (2 Corinthians 9:8).

Are you willing to please God by being prosperous?

10% of Your Income...
100% of Your Heart

Chapter 5

Gloria Copeland

"Bring ye all the tithes into the storehouse, that there may be meat in mine house, and prove me now herewith, saith the LORD of hosts, if I will not open you the windows of heaven, and pour you out a blessing, that there shall not be room enough to receive it. And I will rebuke the devourer for your sakes, and he shall not destroy the fruits of your ground; neither shall your vine cast her fruit before the time in the field, saith the LORD of hosts. And all nations shall call you blessed: for ye shall be a delightsome land, saith the LORD of hosts."
— MALACHI 3:10-12

Are you ready to take the limits off your income? I am! And the Lord has been showing me how we can do it.

I'm excited about it because this is the day when we as believers need to prosper. We need to have enough not just to meet our own needs, but to see to it that the gospel is preached around the world.

Jesus is coming back soon! We don't have time to sit around wishing we had enough money to go through the doors God is opening before us. We don't have time to say, "Well, one day when finances aren't so tight, I'll give to this ministry or that one so they can buy television time in Eastern Europe, or print books in Spanish." We need to increase so we can give—and we need to do it now!

How do we get on that road to increase? I can tell you in two simple words: through tithing. In the plan of God, tithing and wealth are so closely connected that in the Hebrew language, they both come from the same root word.

Tithing is the covenant transaction that opens the door for God to be directly involved in our increase. It is a two-way exchange in which we honor God by giving Him 10 percent of our income and He, in return, provides us with a "surplus of prosperity" (Deuteronomy 28:11, *The Amplified Bible*). You can see how that transaction works in Malachi 3:10-12. There the Lord says:

> Bring all the tithes—the whole tenth of your income—into the storehouse, that there may be food in My house, and prove Me now by it, says the Lord of hosts, if I will not open the windows of Heaven for you and pour you out a blessing, that there shall not be room enough to receive it. And I will rebuke the devourer...for your sakes, and he shall not destroy the fruits of your ground; neither shall your vine drop its fruit before the time in the field, says the Lord of hosts. And all nations shall call you happy and blessed; for you shall be a land of delight, says the Lord of hosts *(The Amplified Bible)*.

More Than a Religious Routine

"But Gloria," you may say, "I know Christians who have been tithing for years and they're not wealthy!"

Actually, you don't. You just know people who have put 10 percent of their income into the offering bucket. They went through the motions, but they weren't really tithing. We've all done that at times.

You see, tithing isn't just a matter of the pocketbook. It is a matter of the heart. That's the way it is with everything as far as God is concerned. He always looks on the heart. So when we tithe as a religious routine, not in faith, just because we're supposed to and not as a genuine expression of our love for God, we miss out on the blessings of it.

That's what happened to the people in Malachi's day. They were bringing sacrifices to the Lord. They were going through the motions of tithing. But they were not being blessed. In fact, they were living under a financial curse because the attitude of their heart was not right.

In Malachi 1, we can read what the Lord had to say to them:

A son honors his father, and a servant his master. If then I am a father, where is My honor? And if I am a master, where is the [reverent] fear due Me? says the Lord of hosts to you, O priests, who despise My name. You say, How and in what have we despised Your name? By offering polluted food upon My altar. And you ask, How have we polluted it and profaned You?... When you priests offer blind [animals] for sacrifice, is it no evil? And when you offer the lame and the sick, is it no evil? Present such a thing...now to your governor [in payment of your taxes, and see what will happen]. Will he be pleased with you? Or will he receive you graciously? says the Lord of hosts (verses 6-8, *The Amplified Bible*).

What was missing from the tithes and offerings of these people? Honor! They weren't giving God their best. Because they didn't love and reverence God in their hearts, they were offering Him their leftovers. They were fulfilling religious requirements by keeping a formula with no worship.

As tithers, we should learn a lesson from them. When we find ourselves suffering financial lack and failing to enjoy the supernatural increase God has promised, we should check our attitude—fast! We should make sure we're giving God our best (not our leftovers) and honoring Him with all our heart.

Stick With God's Plan

If you're not sure whether your heart is right, here is one good way to tell. Check your attitude at offering time. Malachi 1:13 tells us what the Israelites' attitude was. They said, "Behold, what a drudgery and weariness this is!"

Have you ever had that thought when you were writing out your tithe check? Have you ever wanted to hide your pocketbook from God so you wouldn't have to give? If so, you need to change your attitude or it will prevent you from receiving your financial harvest. It will stop your increase.

Refuse to harbor such dishonorable thoughts toward God in your heart. Rebuke them and say, "No! I will not have that attitude. I love God and I love to give my tithe!"

Actually, we ought to be like little children when it comes to giving. Have you ever noticed how excited children get when their parents give them some money to put in the offering? They can hardly wait to give it.

We ought to be the same way. We ought to look forward to giving our tithes and offerings all week long.

"Well, it's hard to have that attitude now," you might say. "After all, I'm not a child anymore. No one is giving me any money."

God is! He is the One who gives you everything you have. He owns everything on this earth because He made it. He will give you possessions if you will honor Him in joy with the first-fruits of your increase.

Of course, some people try to come up with their own plan. They'll say, "I can't really afford to give a full 10 percent, so I'll just give five." But that won't work because the Bible says the first tenth already belongs to the Lord. If we give Him anything less, we're robbing Him (Malachi 3:8). Leviticus 27 says it this way: "...no thing that a man shall devote to the Lord of all that he has, whether of man or beast or of the field of his possession, shall be sold or redeemed; every devoted thing is most holy to the Lord...And all the tithe of the land, whether of the seed of the land or of the fruit of the tree, is the Lord's; it is holy to the Lord" (verses 28, 30, *The Amplified Bible*).

Just as tithing opens the door to increase and the blessings of God, stealing God's tithe and using it on yourself opens the door to decrease and the financial destruction the devil brings. You'll never come out ahead by keeping the tithe.

Ken and I know that from personal experience. Right after we were born again, before we had much revelation of the Word, we'd try tithing for a few months. Then we'd decide we needed the money more than God did, so we'd stop. As a result, we just kept on decreasing financially. We kept on getting deeper in debt.

When we began to learn and obey God's Word, we made up our minds to tithe first, no matter what. That's when our finances turned around. We began to increase and we've been increasing ever since, praise God! Today if I had to choose between paying my tithe or having food to eat—I'd skip the food and pay my tithe because I know the blessings tithing in faith will bring.

Don't Forget Faith

When you really understand what a great deal tithing is, you'll have a hard time not getting excited about it! You'll want to jump and shout and praise God every time you think about it. You won't begrudge God His 10 percent, you'll thank Him for letting it flow through your hands.

He didn't have to do that, you know. He could have just given us the 90 percent and withheld the 10. He could withhold 90 and give us 10! But He didn't. He gave it to us so we could use it to keep the door of prosperity open. He gave it to us so we could return it and establish a covenant of blessing with Him.

Do you realize what a wonderful privilege it is to have a financial covenant with Almighty God? Do you understand what it means to be connected to His heavenly economy?

It means we don't have to worry about depression or recession—there is no recession or depression in heaven. It means we can sleep peacefully at night when the rest of the world is tormented by fear of financial failure. It means when the devil comes to steal our increase we can stand firmly on that covenant and say, "Get out of here, Satan! You're rebuked! We're tithers and the Word of God says you cannot devour our money. You can't devour our children. You can't devour our health. We've given God the firstfruits of all our increase so we are blessed. And what God has blessed, you can't curse!"

Oddly enough, there are some Christians who shrink back at such bold words. "Well, I just don't know if I could say that," they protest. "I'm a tither, but I'm still not as rich as the sinner down the street. So I'm not sure tithing does that much good."

The people in Malachi's day said exactly the same thing. They said, "...It is useless to serve God; and what profit is it if we keep His ordinances?...And now we consider the proud and arrogant happy and favored; evildoers are exalted and prosper..." (Malachi 3:14-15, *The Amplified Bible*).

God didn't like those words. He said they were hard and stout against Him. Why? Because they were words of unbelief instead of words of faith.

You see, God not only wants us to tithe in honor and love, He also wants us to tithe in faith! It takes faith to please Him (Hebrews 11:6).

If you don't have faith that God will prosper you, then get your Bible and study the promises He has made to you as a tither. For "faith cometh by hearing, and hearing by the word of God" (Romans 10:17). Meditate the Word so you can tithe believing that God will keep His end of the covenant and bless you abundantly.

God loves it when you tithe with that kind of confidence. He enjoys it when you give with an attitude of reverence and gratitude, trusting Him to take care of you.

In fact, Malachi 3:16-17 says:

Then those who feared the Lord talked often one to another; and the Lord listened and heard it, and a book of remembrance was written before Him of those who reverenced and worshipfully feared the Lord, and who thought on His name. And they shall be Mine, says the Lord of hosts, in that day when I publicly recognize and openly declare them to be My jewels—My special possession, My peculiar treasure. And I will spare them, as a man spares his own son who serves him *(The Amplified Bible)*.

Don't you want to be counted as one of God's special treasures? I certainly do! First of all, because I love God and I want to be pleasing to Him. Second, because I know how I treat special treasures. I keep my eye on them. I take good care of them, and if I'm God's special treasure, that's exactly how He'll treat me!

"Lord...Bless Me!"

The fact is, God has already treated us with overwhelming kindness. He has already given us all more than we ever dreamed possible. He has saved us. He has provided healing for us. He has blessed us in a thousand different ways. And that's what we should remember every time we tithe. We should come before the Lord and thank Him for bringing us into our promised land. Tithe with an attitude of gratitude.

If you'll read Deuteronomy 26, you'll see that's what He instructed the Israelites to do. He didn't want them to simply plunk their tithe without putting their heart into it. He commanded them to come very purposefully and worship Him with it, saying:

...A wandering and lost Aramean ready to perish was my father [Jacob], and he went down into Egypt, and sojourned there, few in number, and he became there a nation, great, mighty, and numerous. And the Egyptians treated us very badly, and afflicted us, and laid upon us hard bondage. And when we cried to the Lord, the God of our fathers, the Lord heard our voice, and looked on our affliction, and our labor, and our (cruel) oppression; And the Lord brought us forth out of Egypt with a mighty hand, and with an outstretched arm, and with great (awesome) power, and with signs, and with wonders; And He brought us into this place, and gave us this land, a land flowing with milk and honey. And now, behold, I bring the first fruits of the ground, which You, O Lord, have given me (verses 5-10, *The Amplified Bible*).

We would do well to say much the same thing each time we tithe. To say, "Father, once I was lost, a prisoner of sin with no hope and no covenant with You. But You sent Jesus to redeem me. You sent Him to shed His precious blood so I could be free. Thank You, Lord, for delivering me out of the kingdom of darkness and translating me into the kingdom of Your dear Son. Thank You for receiving my tithe as an expression of worship to You."

But we shouldn't stop with that. We should also say as the Israelites did, "Now, Lord, I have brought the tithe out of my house. I haven't kept it for myself. But I've given it just as You have commanded. So look down from Your holy habitation, from heaven, and bless me!" (see verses 13-15).

Does that kind of talk make you nervous? Do you think God will be offended if you tell Him to bless you? He won't! He'll be delighted. After all, blessing us was His idea. It's what He has wanted to do all along.

So don't be shy. Tithe boldly! Tithe gladly! Give God 10 percent of your income and 100 percent of your heart. Then rejoice in faith and say continually, "Let the Lord be magnified, who takes pleasure in the prosperity of His servant!"

Begin to expect!

Take the limits off God and let Him have a good time prospering you!

Chapter 6

The Tithe— Is It for Today?

Kenneth Copeland

"Bring ye all the tithes into the storehouse, that there may be meat in mine house, and prove me now herewith, saith the LORD of hosts, if I will not open you the windows of heaven, and pour you out a blessing, that there shall not be room enough to receive it."
— MALACHI 3:10

It amazes me how many believers waste their energies arguing whether or not tithing is a New Testament doctrine. I've heard people say, "Tithing is under the law! We're not under the law, we're under grace. That's why I don't tithe. Oh, I give offerings, but I don't tithe." People who think this way are self-deceived.

Tithing didn't begin with the law! According to Genesis 4:1-4, before the law was ever given to Moses, Abel and Cain brought the firstfruits of their labor to God.

And again in Genesis 14, we find that Abraham tithed— **before the law!** Abraham and 318 of his armed servants had conquered a group of enemy kings, slaughtered them, and took the spoils. And the very first thing Abram did was tithe the spoils. Melchizedek, the priest, blessed Abram and said, "Blessed be Abram of the most high God, possessor of heaven and earth: And blessed be the most high God, which hath delivered thine enemies into thy hand. And he gave him tithes of all" (verses 19-20). So tithing didn't begin with the law. The law only explained the tithe, gave it procedure, and demanded it.

But, is tithing under the New Covenant as well? To answer this question, let's first read Hebrews 7:1-8.

For this Melchisedec, king of Salem, priest of the most high God, who met Abraham returning from the slaughter of the kings, and blessed him; to whom also Abraham gave a tenth part of all; first being by interpretation King of righteousness, and after that also King of Salem, which is, King of peace; without father, without mother, without descent, having neither beginning of days, nor end of life; but made like unto the Son of God; abideth a priest continually. Now consider how great this man was, unto whom even the patriarch Abraham gave the tenth of the spoils. And verily they that are of the sons of Levi, who receive the office of the priesthood, have a commandment to take tithes of the people according to the law, that is, of their brethren, though they come out of the loins of Abraham: But he whose descent is not counted from them received tithes of Abraham, and blessed him that had the promises. And without all contradiction the less is blessed of the better. And here men that die receive tithes; but there he receiveth them, of whom it is witnessed that he liveth.

What do these verses mean? Simply this, that Melchizedek was a man whose birth was not on record. His genealogy could not be traced back to Levi (or the tribe of the priesthood). Nevertheless Melchizedek was made a priest by God and received Abraham's tithes. You cannot argue that tithing is just under the law because this happened 400 years before the law.

Hebrews 5:6 tells us that Jesus is a High Priest after the order of Melchizedek. He has all the rights that Melchizedek had, which included the right to bless the tithe. Under the New Covenant, Jesus not only receives our tithes, He blesses them and then blesses us just as Abraham was blessed. Why? Because as Galatians 3:14 says, "...the blessing of Abraham [has] come on the Gentiles through Jesus Christ"! The day that Melchizedek blessed Abraham, that very blessing was handed to you and me through Jesus Christ—our High Priest after the order of Melchizedek! If Melchizedek blessed Abraham, then how much more will Jesus bless us!

How do we activate that blessing? By placing our faith in the Word of God, and faith without actions of obedience to back it up is dead (James 2:17, *The Amplified Bible*). Since true faith is acting on what you believe, if you believe that you are blessed with faithful Abraham, you will do what he did—tithe to your Faithful High Priest!

Tithing activates the blessing of God in your finances. Read Malachi 3:10-12. There God promises that when you tithe, He'll rebuke the devil and command him to keep his hands off your finances. And that promise is as good today as it ever was because when God rebukes the devil, he stays rebuked!

So if you want to involve Almighty God in your finances,

Bring ye all the tithes into the storehouse, that there may be meat in mine house, and prove me now herewith, saith the Lord of hosts, if I will not open you the windows of heaven, and pour you out a blessing, that there shall not be room enough to receive it. And I will rebuke the devourer for your sakes, and he shall not destroy the fruits of your ground; neither shall your vine cast her fruit before the time in the field, saith the Lord of hosts. And all nations shall call you blessed: for ye shall be a delightsome land, saith the Lord of hosts.

Yes! Tithing is part of the New Covenant. Don't wait until your back is against the wall before you use your faith in the financial realm. Begin tithing while things are going well. Learn to act on the Word now, and when Satan tries to pin you against the wall, you can smile and know that you have it made. His power over you financially has been stopped! When you stand on the covenant of God and exercise your rights as a tither, Satan has no chance against you.

Chapter 7

The Power to Prosper

"Christ hath redeemed us from the curse of the law, being made a curse for us: for it is written, Cursed is every one that hangeth on a tree: That the blessing of Abraham might come on the Gentiles through Jesus Christ; that we might receive the promise of the Spirit through faith."

— GALATIANS 3:13-14

Kenneth Copeland

A little sickness here...a pinch in the finances there...that's how the devil tries to bully you out of your blessings. Don't let him do it! Stand firm in the faith and kick a little sand in his face for a change. After all, you're no weakling. You've been given—the power to prosper.

"You were blessed."

"You are blessed."

"You will be blessed."

Do you recognize what these sentences represent? They are the past, present and future tenses of the verb "to bless."

Don't worry, I'm not going to give you a grammar lesson. I'm going to give you a lesson in living! You see, if you're going to enjoy the full and prosperous life God has made available to you, you're going to have to realize that His blessings cover the past, present and future! The following story from Luke 13 perfectly illustrates this point.

And he [Jesus] was teaching in one of the synagogues on the sabbath. And, behold, there was a woman which had a spirit of infirmity eighteen years, and was bowed together, and could in no wise lift up herself. And when Jesus saw her, he called her to him, and said unto her, Woman, thou art loosed from thine infirmity. And he laid his hands on her: and immediately she was made straight, and glorified God. And the ruler of the synagogue answered with indignation, because that Jesus had healed on the sabbath day, and said unto the people,

There are six days in which men ought to work: in them therefore come and be healed, and not on the sabbath day. The Lord then answered him, and said, Thou hypocrite, doth not each one of you on the sabbath loose his ox or his ass from the stall, and lead him away to watering? And ought not this woman, being a daughter of Abraham, whom Satan hath bound, lo, these eighteen years, be loosed from this bond on the sabbath day? (verses 10-16).

First of all, I want you to notice that Jesus called this little lady a daughter of Abraham. By using this terminology, He was pointing out that she had a very special relationship with Almighty God. She had a covenant relationship with Him, a bond, a pact, and because of this, she could be set free from her infirmity.

I want you to also notice that Jesus didn't tell her that maybe some day she might be loosed from her infirmity. No, He said, "You are loosed," present tense. Jesus knew that she was a covenant woman. In His mind, her healing was already provided.

God is always operating in the present tense. He never forgets what He has provided for His children. His covenant is ever close to His heart.

In order to receive from God, you must realize that His Word is His bond, and regardless of how much time passes, the depth of His commitment never wanes. It remains fresh in the mind of God regardless of whether His people remember it or not.

That is why Jesus could tell that little woman, "You are loosed from this infirmity." Because God was still mindful of His Word to Abraham. And the day He spoke to Abram, 700 years before she was born, that little lady was in Abraham's loins. If the promises were made for anyone, they were made for her!

In fact, the covenant was made to everyone in that synagogue. They just didn't know it. They were so mindful of their traditions they didn't even know what the Master was talking about. They became angry with Him for healing on the Sabbath!

As a Christian, you have a covenant with Almighty God. It is just as binding as the one Abraham had, only it is a better covenant with better promises (Hebrews 8:6). To get an understanding of your covenant provisions, let's look at Galatians 3:6-14:

> Even as Abraham believed God, and it was accounted to him for righteousness. Know ye therefore that they which are of faith, the same are the children of Abraham. And the scripture, foreseeing that God would justify the heathen through faith, preached before the gospel unto Abraham, saying, In thee shall all nations be blessed. So then they which be of faith are blessed with faithful Abraham. For as many as are of the works of the law are under the curse: for it is written, Cursed is every one that continueth not in all things which are written in the book of the law to do them. But that no man is justified by the law in the sight of God, it is evident: for, The just shall live by faith. And the law is not of faith: but, The man that doeth them shall live in them. Christ hath redeemed us from the curse of the law, being made a curse for us: for it is written, Cursed is every one that hangeth on a tree: That the blessing of Abraham might come on the Gentiles through Jesus Christ; that we might receive the promise of the Spirit through faith.

I want you to notice how many times the word "bless" is used in this passage of Scripture. Unfortunately, this word is too often heard as merely a religious term, and very few people understand the real meaning of it. But God is very exact in His usage of this word; He doesn't take it lightly.

The phrase "to bless" is used mainly in a covenant relationship. You begin to understand its meaning when you study the covenant that God has entered with us. When He joined Himself irrevocably to us, we had nothing to give Him. We were totally spiritually bankrupt with nothing to offer Him while He, on the other hand, is Almighty God, all-powerful and the possessor of heaven and earth. He took our spiritual bankruptcy and exchanged it for His life and nature. He took our sinfulness and exchanged it for His righteousness. He took our sicknesses and carried our diseases and gave us divine healing. Hallelujah!

And you'll notice that in verses 13-14, He took the curse for us so that we might be blessed with faithful Abraham through Jesus Christ. What does that mean? The best way I know to describe the term *to bless* is to "empower one to prosper." To *prosper* means "to excel in something that is desirable as well as good."

To be spiritually blessed would be to be empowered to prosper spiritually. To prosper spiritually would first of all mean being born again. You could not excel spiritually if you still had the sin nature. But on the other hand, once you are born again, you can excel to the point of being baptized in the Holy Ghost, hearing the voice of the Lord, exhibiting the nature and character of God in your daily life, and operating in the gifts of the Spirit. To be spiritually blessed according to the Bible means to be empowered to excel in that which is desirable to the Holy Spirit. If you are spiritually blessed, there is no limit to how much you can prosper in the spirit realm.

To be blessed physically means to be empowered to prosper in your physical body, to be healthy and vibrant and able to accomplish the will of God for your life. It is not God's will for the devil to hinder you and keep you bound by sickness and disease.

To be blessed mentally means to be empowered to prosper in your mind. It includes being emotionally sound. It also means being able to understand the Word and spiritual things. It means having your mind renewed with God's Word.

Now, what do you think it means to be cursed? That is also a covenant term, and its true meaning is "to empower to fail."

Let's read Galatians 3:13-14 again in this new light. Using our definitions, let's see how the meaning of these verses expands our understanding of our covenant with God. "Christ has redeemed us from being empowered to fail by being empowered to fail for us: for it is written, Empowered to fail is every one who hangs on a tree: That the empowerment to prosper from Abraham might come on the Gentiles through Jesus Christ; that we might receive the promise of the Spirit through faith." (You can go to Deuteronomy 28:1-13 and find out exactly what the blessings of Abraham are. Rather than reading them the way they are written in the *King James Version,* read them with the Bible definition of the word *bless.)*

With this in mind, consider the following statement God made to Abraham. "And I will bless them that bless thee, and curse him that curseth thee: and in thee shall all families of the earth be blessed" (Genesis 12:3). Again, using our definition, let's read it this way, "I will empower those to prosper who empower you to prosper. And I will empower those to fail who try to cause you to fail."

In other words, "Anyone who has your best interest at heart, I will empower to prosper. And anyone who does not have your best interest at heart, I will cause their efforts to fail." If you are in covenant with God, you are destined to succeed! Anyone who comes against your success is coming against your covenant. God will stop their efforts to hurt you, not because He doesn't love them, not because He prefers you, but because He is bound by His Word. God loves everyone equally and wants everyone to be blessed.

So what will keep you in a state of always being empowered by God to prosper? Seek to empower those around you to prosper in every area of their lives—spiritually, mentally, physically, financially and socially. If you bless others, God will bless you!

Galatians 3:29 promises that the blessings of Abraham are yours in Christ. "And if ye be Christ's, then are ye Abraham's seed, and heirs according to the promise." Notice again that this is in the present tense. If you are in Christ, you are Abraham's seed and an heir according to the promise made to Abraham.

Just like the little lady in Luke, you are loosed from your infirmity. You are empowered to prosper in every area of your life—right now! Don't put it off to the future—some day in the sweet by-and-by—or think that it passed away with the first disciples. You are empowered to prosper today!

Better Than Miracles

Chapter 8

"The LORD shall increase you more and more,
you and your children."
— PSALM 115:14

Jerry Savelle

How many Christians do you know right now who are just barely hanging on financially? How many do you know who are looking for a miracle to get them through a critical time of shortage and lack? Unless I miss my guess, you know quite a few. You may even be among them yourself.

If so, I know what you're going through. Financially speaking, several years ago, I went through the toughest years of my life and ministry. During that time it seemed the pressure never ceased. It's not that God didn't deliver us. He did! He rescued us from disaster over and over again.

Yet as soon as one financial miracle came—another impossible situation rose up right behind it. We literally lived from one financial miracle to the next.

I don't mind telling you that, even though I was grateful for those miracles (and this ministry wouldn't have survived without them), I got tired of living that way.

"Well, Brother Jerry, isn't that just part of living by faith?" you ask. "Isn't it God's plan for us to believe Him every day for enough to get by?"

No, it isn't.

God has impressed on me that His will for us is much higher than that.

A Covenant of Increase

You see, God's covenant with us isn't a "just get by" covenant. It's a covenant of supernatural increase. That's proven again and again throughout the Bible. Psalm 115 says:

O Israel, trust thou in the Lord: he is their help and their shield. O house of Aaron, trust in the Lord: he is their help and their shield. Ye that fear the Lord, trust in the Lord: he is their help and their shield. The Lord hath been mindful of us: he will bless us; he will bless the house of Israel; he will bless the house of Aaron. He will bless them that fear the Lord, both small and great. The Lord shall increase you more and more, you and your children (verses 9-14).

God has made a solemn, covenant vow to increase you. How much will He increase you? More and more! In other words, His increase is unlimited. That means no matter how much increase you have experienced up to now, you still haven't seen all the increase God has in store for you.

I know material wealth makes religious people nervous, but God has no problem with it. It wouldn't bother Him at all if it took every bank in town to hold all your increase, as long as you remembered and honored Him as the God of increase. (See Deuteronomy 8:11.) In fact, Psalm 35:27 says the Lord "hath pleasure in the prosperity of his servant"!

No Interruptions, Please

God's kind of prosperity isn't sporadic, either. It doesn't just come occasionally to get you out of a financial jam. No, we've already seen that it increases you "more and more." The *R.K. Harrison Translation of Hebrew Into Current English* says it like this: "May the Lord give you continual prosperity."

Continual prosperity! Continual means without interruption. If there's no interruption in my prosperity, I won't have to live on financial miracles!

God gives us a picture of that kind of prosperity in Deuteronomy 8:6-9. There, He tells the Israelites:

Therefore thou shalt keep the commandments of the Lord thy God, to walk in his ways, and to fear him. For the Lord thy God bringeth thee into a good land, a land of brooks of water, of fountains and depths that spring out of valleys and hills; a land of wheat, and barley, and vines, and fig trees, and pomegranates; a land of oil olive, and honey; a land wherein thou shalt eat bread without scarceness, thou shalt not lack any thing in it.

Continual prosperity is a lifestyle without scarceness. A lifestyle without lack. What's more, Deuteronomy 28:11 says, "The Lord shall make you have a surplus of prosperity..." (*The Amplified Bible*). A surplus means there's more than enough!

Most of us have thought, if we could just get our needs met, we'd be prosperous. But that's a shallow version of what God calls prosperity. He says prosperity is having a surplus. He says, "A good man leaveth an inheritance to his children's children" (Proverbs 13:22).

Notice how much higher His thoughts are than our thoughts. In His estimation of increase, not only are all your needs met, but also you have enough left over to help somebody else and enough in store for two generations after you!

How do we walk in that kind of increase? The first step is to begin to expect it. We'll never experience continual, supernatural prosperity until we elevate our thinking to God's level and enlarge our capacity to receive.

We must be able to see it happen with the eyes of our heart. When we have that image on the inside of us, God will be able to deliver it to us. Our only limitation is our own thinking.

A Reward for the Diligent

Let me warn you, though, this kind of increase is not something you're going to experience overnight. It's not something that will happen after just a week or two. It takes commitment.

God told Moses in Deuteronomy 28:1, "...it shall come to pass, if thou shalt hearken diligently unto the voice of the Lord thy God, to observe and to do all his commandments...that the Lord thy God will set thee on high above all the nations of the earth." *Diligence* means to "make a steady effort to accomplish." A diligent person never backs off. Never quits. Never gives up.

As I've studied the Word, I've found that supernatural increase comes to faithful and diligent people. People who have a determination to hold fast to God's Word no matter how impossible the circumstances may seem.

Galatians 6:9 says, "And let us not be weary in well doing: for in due season we shall reap, if we faint not." There is a due season for those who are diligent and faithful. There is a set time, a designated moment when God rewards those who diligently seek Him (Hebrews 11:6).

Time for a Change

I want you to know, I've come to my "due season" and I'm enjoying it. I've enlarged my thinking and set my sights on the good land where there is no scarceness or lack. I intend to live in continual prosperity.

Since November 1992, when God began to deal with me about His covenant of supernatural increase, the financial blessings that have come in my ministry are as overwhelming and hard to keep up with as the pressure was previously. Our increase is so great, we can hardly contain it!

I've made up my mind, I'm not going to live from one financial miracle to the next anymore. If I can believe God to bail me out when I'm almost at rock bottom, then I can believe God for continual prosperity so I won't have to go through that kind of mess!

Praise God, I am blessed of the Lord, and as Proverbs 10:22 says, "The blessing of the Lord, it maketh rich, and he addeth no sorrow with it."

Now don't misunderstand. I'm not telling you to get your eyes on riches. I'm telling you to be faithful to God and simply expect Him to fulfill the covenant of increase.

If you'll do that, you won't have to get your eyes on riches and wealth. In fact, you won't even have to pursue them. They'll chase you down!

God said, "...all these blessings shall come on thee, and overtake thee, if thou shalt hearken unto the voice of the Lord thy God" (Deuteronomy 28:2). He didn't say you'd come on the blessings and overtake them.

If you're pursuing the blessings, you have it backward. Jesus said, "...seek ye first the kingdom of God, and his righteousness; and all these things shall be added unto you" (Matthew 6:33).

Please note, however, that He did say, "all these things shall be added." I believe it's time for that "addition" to come. It's time for supernatural increase in the Body of Christ. We've been financially overwhelmed in the past—not only individually, but collectively. But that's about to change.

Due season has come. It's time for us to tear down the fences of limitation in our lives and believe God to enlarge our borders. It's time to stop living from financial miracle to financial miracle and start living in continual prosperity.

I'm ready, aren't you?

Name Your Seed!
Sow It...Don't Throw It!

"Be not deceived; God is not mocked: for whatsoever a man soweth, that shall he also reap."
— GALATIANS 6:7

Jesse Duplantis

I'm going to catch me a thief!

Satan stole my harvest for years, but I found out why and I
know how to stop him.

Let me explain. One of the very first things I began to do as
a new believer was to give. I wasn't giving to get. I was giving
because I wanted to do the kinds of things God did. Giving was
the first thing I noticed about God. It's His nature to give. I
picked that up immediately: "For God so loved the world, that
He gave" (John 3:16).

From my first day as a new Christian, I was doing a good
job of fulfilling the first part of Malachi 3:10: "Bring ye all the
tithes into the storehouse, that there may be meat in mine
house...." There was meat in my house and I was blessed as a
giver. But then I discovered God wanted even more for me. I
began to get excited every time I heard the second part of that
verse: "and prove me now herewith, saith the LORD of hosts, if
I will not open you the windows of heaven, and pour you out a
blessing, that there shall not be room enough to receive it."

But despite the fact that I was a faithful giver, I could not
say I had been blessed to the point that I didn't have room for
more. Why?

One day when I was jogging, the Lord began to deal with
me about that.

You know, what you sow is what you reap, He said. *You
know you've always had everything met—your needs have
always been met.*

"That's right," I said.

But are you at the point in your life where you cannot receive any more blessing?

"No," I answered.

Let Me tell you something, Jesse. For years you never named your seed.

He was right. I didn't know how many times I had given gifts—sometimes quite large gifts for me—in obedience to the Lord. Then months later, I would be walking past great fields of harvest that I didn't know were mine. I would see harvests everywhere and think, *God, this is what I need for my ministry.*

Because I didn't know what kind of seed I had sown, I didn't know what kind of harvest to expect. I didn't know I was walking past my harvests. As a result, the devil was able to control what belonged to me. He was standing by those harvests with his guards saying, "That's not yours. This is the wealth of the wicked. You are the just."

Satan was able to do it because I never named my seed. I didn't know what I put in the ground, so how was I to know when it came back thirty-, sixty-, a hundredfold?

Sown or Thrown?

I was not operating according to a basic principle—sowing and reaping. Galatians 6:7 says, "Be not deceived; God is not mocked: for whatsoever a man soweth, that shall he also reap."

"Whatsoever" you put in the ground is going to come up. "Whatsoever" encompasses all human activity. All our acts are forces. Every time we think, every time we feel, every time we exercise our will, we are sowing. So we have to consider our ways and give thought to what we are sowing. If you consider what you are sowing, then you will recognize your harvest.

What you sow is what you reap is the law of Genesis 1:12, that every seed reproduces after its kind: "And the earth brought forth grass, and herb yielding seed after his kind, and the tree yielding fruit, whose seed was in itself, after his kind: and God saw that it was good."

All of life, everything you do, is a process of sowing. You sow clothes, you get clothes. You sow healing, you get healing.

I told a lady one time, "I want to pray for you so I can feel better."

"No, you mean so I can feel better."

"No, so I can feel better," I said. After I prayed for her, I said, "Oh, I feel better."

"So do I," she said.

"Go sow. Go sow," I said. "More health will come to you."

Understand what tithing does. It meets the general operating expense of the church, such as salaries, light bills and upkeep. When you brought meat to God's house, that meat met the necessities of God's house. Because you met the necessities of God's house, you harvested provision to meet the necessities of your house.

But when you gave an offering above the tithe without naming it, you were throwing it instead of sowing it, and you lost it before you got out the door. You would see a need and throw money at it, not even thinking about naming the type of seed you were sowing or naming your harvest. That seed would land on top of the ground and before you got out the church door, the devil would steal it.

So, you were eating and paying the light bill, but you continued to face the loan payments.

That's not what God wants. He wants His people to be blessed. He wants His Church to be out of debt. The Church will be out of debt when the people are out of debt. Deception has kept God's people without their full entitlement.

Sow Specific Seed

I don't care if it's 2 cents, name your seed. When you give your child $3, $2, a quarter and you say, "Put this in the Sunday school offering," ask him what he's believing for.

Out West not long ago I had a little 7-year-old boy walk up to me wearing a big, silver belt buckle, starched and creased jeans and a western shirt. With tears in his eyes he said, "I want to give to your television ministry."

He gave me $7. Now that's a lot of money for a 7-year-old. I almost went, "No, little fellow." But the Lord said, *What are you doing? Ask him what he's believing for.*

So I told him, "You have given me a seed. If you don't name this seed you're going to lose this money. And seven bucks is a lot of money to lose."

"That's right," he said.

"What are you believing for?" I asked. "Name your seed, little fellow."

"A four-wheeler wouldn't be bad."

"Anything else? This is a big seed."

"And a horse."

I said, "Fine. Now this is a horse and a four-wheeler. Isn't that wonderful? The devil can't rob you, son. You have planted your seed. You're motivated by love. You've named it. You're not deceived. You're not mocking God. You've got it coming."

"Thank you," he said. Then he asked me if he could hug me. He hugged my leg and off he went.

That was in the basement of the church. Right after that I met the boy's father in the foyer of the church and he told me how proud he was of his son, how his son was a hard worker and had never asked for a dime.

"It's kind of strange," he said. "I don't know if I know the voice of God as much as some of you ministers, but let me just ask you a question. This morning I was driving to church and the Lord...I don't know if it was the Lord or not...my wife and I were talking, and we thought about maybe buying the kid a four-wheeler...."

"Has your son ever asked you for a four-wheeler?" I asked.

"He never asks me for anything. He's a hard little worker... he delivers papers. He does all kinds of things. And my wife said, 'Let's get him a horse, too.'"

"When are you planning on doing that?" I asked.

"I'm thinking about doing it this afternoon."

I told him, "You know, you ought to obey God."

Now, if I had said to that little boy, "Thank you, brother, for blessing the ministry. Come here, little fellow, let me bless you," that would have been a thoughtless gesture on my part. That little boy would not have named his seed, and you will never make me believe, if he hadn't named his seed, he would have gotten his horse or his four-wheeler.

Leaving a Money Trail

Thoughtlessness is the beginning of great loss. Thoughtlessness can result in giving that is not properly motivated. It can also result in failure to name your seed.

Haggai 1:4-6 warns believers to be thoughtful givers: "Is it time for you, O ye, to dwell in your cieled houses, and this [God's] house lie waste? Now therefore thus saith the LORD of hosts; Consider your ways. Ye have sown much, and bring in little...he that earneth wages earneth wages to put it into a bag with holes."

You may be a faithful giver and yet be a thoughtless giver. You pay off your monthly obligations but never have anything left over. How does the devil always know where you are? You're leaving a trail of money for him to follow.

Haggai says you have "sown much, and bring in little"...and the bag into which you put your wages has holes in it. Throwing seed on top of the ground is like putting money in a bag full of holes. Satan will walk right behind you picking up that thrown seed so he can invest it in his people.

Don't be a thoughtless giver. Purpose in your heart what you will give. Second Corinthians 9:7 says, "Every man according as he purposeth in his heart, so let him give; not grudgingly, or of necessity: for God loveth a cheerful giver." Regard your giving as an act of worship. Make sure you are motivated by love—by the desire to bless, rather than the desire to get. Then name your seed. If you do, you will be in line for a blessing.

You don't have to let the devil control what belongs to you. I asked the Lord one time about Proverbs 13:22: "...the wealth of the sinner is laid up for the just." That sounded like Robin Hood stuff to me. Why would He take from those people and give to me? Rob from the rich and give to the poor?

Jesse, your ancestors for centuries have been giving and throwing seed instead of sowing seed, He said. *The reason why the wealth of the wicked is laid up for the just is that's your ancestors' seed that they never named. That's My money, and if it's My money, it's your money because you're an heir with Me—a joint heir.*

That's why it's coming back. That's why He can go to get the wealth of the wicked and give it to you. God is very interested in your being out of debt. When He pulled the nation of Israel out of Egypt and set them free, He said, "Take My money. Get My money. Be not deceived." He's not letting the devil keep His money. Egypt owed Israel 400 years of labor. God said, "Get My money. Bring it out with you."

If you have named your seed, next time you pass your harvest, you can tell the devil, "Hey, that's my harvest. That's mine. Get off my property."

The Sector of Optimum Yield

Once you've named your seed, cultivate it. Think about it. You want it to come up. If you'll put fertilizer on it, keep the weeds away from it, and cultivate it, you'll get a higher yield— an optimum yield. Cultivation is the very act of thinking, "Now faith is the substance of things hoped for, the evidence of things not seen" (Hebrews 11:1).

I've given seed for my television ministry. I cultivate that seed. I tell Cathy, "Bless God, we gave this money over here, gave this money over there. That's coming in the Name of Jesus." I'm cultivating.

I'm not asking God to give me my money back. No. I want my harvest. It's going to happen, too. You can take it to the bank. The devil stole from me for too long. I tell you, I'm catching that thief and I'm getting back what's mine. I'm going back in my canceled check records and finding records of seed I planted and I'm naming it and calling it mine.

The Bible says if you catch the thief, he's got to return it sevenfold. I'm going to get too expensive for the devil to mess with.

I've only been to one Kenneth Hagin convention, but it was the most expensive pit stop I ever made in my life. The Lord told me what He wanted me to give, and I had trouble believing it. I leaned over to the guy next to me and asked, "Did you say anything?" Sweat was coming off his cheeks and he said the Lord had just told him to give that same amount. "I heard it, too," I said. "That must be yours. That's not mine."

But the Lord said, *I told you, too.*

"God."

What Jesse?

"That's all I got."

That's all I asked for.

I'll never forget that, but you know I lost my return on that seed. I don't mean it didn't get used for the Lord's work. I didn't get my return, because I never named it.

But you know what I did? I went back to those 1983 and '84 check records and found that Hagin seed. I went back in those bank records. I've gone to catch a thief. And every time I find a canceled check for a gift I've given, I say, "Aha, devil. You owe me seven times. You've got to pay me, boy!"

I'm not claiming it because it's money, praise God, but because it's my seed. It's my harvest.

I'm not looking for money.

Money's looking for me.

God says the wealth of the wicked is laid up for Jesse. When they come with my money, I'm going to say, "Bring it on in. Just bring it on in. Put it over here, bless God."

Miraculous Provision
Is on the Way

"...Go, borrow thee vessels abroad of all thy neighbours, even empty vessels; borrow not a few."

— 2 Kings 4:3

Chapter 10

Mark Brazee

One day while I was praying, asking the Lord about things to come—both in my ministry and in the Church overall—I heard one word in my spirit just as plain as could be.

Miracles.

I meditated on that for a while, thinking primarily about healing miracles—when the blind see, the deaf hear, the lame walk and the maimed are made whole. Then I decided to start studying what the Word has to say about miracles. What I discovered really jarred my thinking. And it gave me insight into not only *how,* but *why* God will cause miracles to be increasingly commonplace before Jesus returns.

Four Types of Miracles

Miracles—extraordinary events demonstrating divine intervention in human affairs—can be traced from Genesis to Revelation and divided into four main categories. There are physical miracles, such as the man at the gate called Beautiful, who went walking, leaping and praising God when Peter and John commanded him to be made whole. There are also provisional miracles, like when Jesus provided money for Peter to pay taxes. Peter found the money in the mouth of the fish.

Then, there are miracles of protection or deliverance—like when Peter was delivered out of prison by an angel, or when an angel appeared to Paul and told him all lives on board his sinking ship would be saved. Finally, there are signs and wonders that God performs—miracles that simply prove His power or existence—like when God caused the sun to move backward 10 degrees for Hezekiah.

Elijah, Elisha, Jesus

The first thing I noticed when I began to study miracles was that there were three main people in the Bible through whom God worked miracles: Elijah, Elisha and Jesus. They shared a striking similarity: They began and ended their ministries with provisional miracles.

Elijah's first miracle is recorded in 1 Kings 17, when he prayed and the rain stopped. Three years later, he prayed and it rained. That's provision. His last miracle occurred when he parted the Jordan River. He needed to get across and he didn't have a boat. He had to catch up with the chariot of fire that took him up to heaven. So Elijah parted the waters by striking them with his mantle, and provided himself access to the other side. That, too, was a provisional miracle.

Elisha began his ministry with a provisional miracle—the same kind that concluded Elijah's ministry. He needed to get across the river to enter into the fullness of his ministry, and it took divine intervention, in the ordinary course of nature, to transport him there.

He took the mantle that fell from Elijah, rolled it up, hit the waters of the Jordan River with it and said, "Where now is the Lord, the God of Elijah?" (2 Kings 2:14, *New International Version)* and the river parted.

What about Elisha's last miracle? That, too, was provisional.

We find the account of it in 2 Kings 6. After the Syrians had surrounded Samaria and cut off all its supplies, the people of the city were starving to death. People were paying just about all the money they could get their hands on for an ass's head or a cab of dove's dung (2 Kings 6:25). They were even eating their own children. In the midst of this crisis, Elisha said by the Spirit of God, "Tomorrow at this time, you can find anything you want." In a miraculous act of provision, God used four lepers to plunder the enemy's camp and take everything they needed—silver, gold, food and clothing. This was Elisha's last miracle.

Jesus also began and ended His ministry on the earth with provisional miracles. At the wedding feast in Cana, He turned water into wine. Multiplying the loaves and the fish was a provisional miracle. Jesus' last miracle before His ascension took place after He arose from the dead. He was on the shore, watching Peter and some others fishing, when he called out to Peter, "Throw your net out the other side." When Peter did as he was told, his net caught 153 fish. Divine intervention prospered Peter's business tremendously, causing him to recognize the Lord immediately.

The Spirit of Elijah on the Church

When I began to study provisional miracles carefully, I discovered that God almost always performs provisional miracles first—before He performs the physical miracles. Now, that really jarred my thinking because I had always thought a physical miracle, such as healing, took priority over other miracles. But the Lord drew my attention to the beginning of all things—the book of Genesis.

The very first miracle recorded in Genesis is provisional. God created the world and everything in it *before* He created man. God didn't physically create man first and then temporarily suspend him in space while He made provision for him. No. God made provision for man *first*, then He created him.

Once I caught the revelation of that order—first the provisional, then the physical miracle—I saw the significance of it throughout Scripture. Physical miracles always produce an increase. If no provision is made for that increase first, then the increase will be lost.

Do you see how that pertains to the harvest? In Acts 3:7, one man was healed. As a result, 5,000 people were added to the Church (Acts 4:4). Physical miracles produce increase. But what would happen if you had physical miracles without the proper provision to handle that increase?

As we come into the last days, the spirit of Elijah is going to fall upon the Church collectively, and not just on one individual singularly. The "spirit of Elijah" is the spirit of preparing for the coming of the Lord Jesus. As that anointing comes upon the Church we will experience the same flow of the miraculous that Elijah and Jesus experienced.

I find it interesting that when Elisha picked up Elijah's mantle, Elisha received a double portion of Elijah's anointing and operated in a continual flow of provisional miracles. Amazing things happened in his ministry. For instance, there was the widow woman who came to Elisha for help. Her husband had died, she couldn't pay her bills and her two sons were to be sold into slavery.

Her situation was serious. She needed provision, and asked the prophet what to do.

I like his response: "What do you have?"

What she had wasn't even a dime's worth of oil. But he sent her out to gather vessels to make provision for the increase she was about to receive. God miraculously increased her oil and it didn't stop pouring until she no longer had vessels to contain it.

Then Elisha told her to sell the oil, pay her bills, and she and her sons could live off the rest.

Her miracle was in her own house. And so is yours.

God will work a miracle with what you have, not with what you don't have. Just give Him what you have. He'll multiply it and keep it pouring as long as you have a place for Him to fill.

You may not have what you need, but you do have seed. The amount you have may not cover your bills, but you can sow something as seed for God to meet your need. You have what it takes to set your miracle in motion.

The whole kingdom of God works on farming principles. A farmer isn't going to run all over the community saying, "Would somebody please give me some corn." Of course not. He's going to take the corn he has, plow a field and plant his seed. And then the harvest will come.

The harvest you desire in your own life will come the same way—by seeding, not by pleading.

Miraculous Provision for the Harvest

The Church is standing on the verge of the greatest move of God to reach and rescue the souls of men that the earth has ever seen. To reap that kind of harvest will require the miracle power of God. But God isn't looking to pour out His power in places where the people will get stuck inside four walls because they can't afford to get out of town. What's the use in having a flow of physical miracles if you don't have the provision to take that power to people around the world? You can have power and you can have prayer, but if you don't have prosperity to propel you along, you won't get very far.

Recently, we were having a service and many Bible school graduates were in attendance. I asked, "How many of you are called to the nations?" Immediately, about 80 percent of the people in the room raised their hands. I thought, *Well, then why are you sitting here? You need to go. We love having you with us, but we'd rather you would be ministering on the mission field.*

Most of the people who acknowledged the calling on their lives that night didn't have the money to go and fulfill that call. But I'm telling you, those days are over. Some may hate the prosperity message, but God loves it. And everywhere prosperity is preached, God will accompany and confirm that message with miraculous provision. Why? So He can send His Body out equipped to reach the nations!

The religious community gets fighting mad when you preach prosperity. But they don't realize that *GOD* is the One preaching prosperity. The reason is simple: In these last days God is looking to pour out His power on people who can afford to get that power out to a world that needs it.

The purpose for prosperity is not to take care of the Church. God can give us water out of a rock and feed us with manna from heaven. But He has to provide prosperity for the Church to reach the world. The world doesn't accept "manna" to fly airlines to the nations. They want dollars. So, since it takes dollars, God will give us dollars.

Provisional miracles. We must have them for this hour. It's no wonder John said, "I [pray] above all things that thou mayest prosper..." (3 John 2). Religion will fight prosperity to the end. But before it's all over, the Body of Christ will experience a flood of miracles. And that flood will begin with a tidal wave of provisional miracles and great prosperity.

This Gospel Must Be Preached

It's no wonder the devil has fought prosperity for so many years, because more people need a financial miracle than a physical miracle. That's because for 2,000 years the Church didn't have the backbone to preach prosperity. But this message must be preached. We're not going to reach the nations for God preaching a poverty message.

If you didn't preach salvation, how many people would get saved? If you didn't preach healing, how many people would get healed? Well, if you don't preach prosperity, how many people are going to walk in it and receive their needs met? You don't get the blessings of God without faith, you don't get faith without hearing, and you don't get hearing without preaching. And if somebody doesn't preach prosperity, people aren't going to have prosperity.

The Church will have to move in provisional miracles before we move into a flood of physical miracles. Then, God is going to unload some big dollars into the Church to help us reach the world and reap the harvest. Angels are working to bring the money in. And the time we have left before Jesus' return will be marked by notable miracles, many of provision.

Some people think the only people God will be able to use are those who have great business minds or who have had money behind them for generations. Not so. When God was ready to take care of the prophet in 1 Kings 17, He said first,

"I've commanded a raven to take care of you." Then He said, "I've commanded a widow woman to take care of you."

You can be a bird, or even be broke, and God will use you! He's not looking for great ability. Just start out giving into the work of God. What you have is the seed of your miracle. Don't be surprised if God takes what you can do, and what you already have, and turns it into something a whole lot bigger than you can dream.

Think Like God—BIG!

Hanging around God and spending time with Him in the Word, in prayer and in fellowship with His Spirit will cause your spiritual capacity to increase. That's one reason why God is moving by His Spirit in this hour to get people filled and refilled with the Holy Ghost. Because the more you become filled to all fullness with God Himself, the more you think and act like Him. And God thinks BIG!

I started hanging around God so much that He stretched my vision and expectations further than I ever imagined possible. He's still stretching me. Today, we give as seed what we used to believe for as income.

I used to think if we preached from one end of the United States to the other, we'd really be doing something. Then when God dropped Europe in my heart—a continent of 750 million to a billion people—I thought that would keep us busy until halfway through the millennium. But recently God told me, *Expand the plan. What works in Europe will work in Asia.*

God thinks big. He has big plans. And it's going to take big dollars for us to put those plans into action.

That's why it's so important to be continually "being filled." The more full you become of God, the more you will think like Him. God is yanking the Church out of the confines of small, mediocre thinking because He has a big job for us to do. You may have a limited paycheck, but you don't have to have a limited income. You can have whatever you dare to believe. Let

God expand your vision until your paycheck looks like seed for what He has for you down the road.

A poverty message is not going to reach and win the centers of the world, where the greatest harvest lies waiting for the Church. The gospel has never been bad news. The gospel of Jesus is good news. And good news to a poor person is that you don't have to be poor anymore!

God is pooling resources in preparation to reach the nations. He's finding people He can trust as His channels for provisional miracles. They are the men and women who will obey Him and give so He can multiply their investment.

God is going to dramatically multiply seed sown into the gospel. He does it with every other seed, certainly He can do it with financial seed. In fact, He must do it for the sake of the harvest. The nations of the world, the last great frontiers, are about to open up so the gospel can be preached to all the ends of the earth. Smith Wigglesworth said that before Jesus returns, the last part of the world to see a major move of God would be Australia, New Zealand and the islands of the sea. We're almost there.

So whatever it takes to get the job done—anointing, books, tapes, printed materials, aircraft, buildings—God will see to it that we have whatever we need to reach out and bring in that wonderful harvest.

Even if it takes a miracle.

The ABCs of Abundance

"(As it is written, I have made thee a father of many nations,) before him whom he believed, even God, who quickeneth the dead, and calleth those things which be not as though they were."
— ROMANS 4:17

Kenneth Copeland

Right now many of us are facing needs. Big needs. Needs so great that without the direct intervention of God, they can't possibly be met.

Because of that, we need to be more certain than ever before that we understand—and abide by—God's laws of abundance. Those laws are extremely important—but, praise God, they're not complicated. In fact, they're as simple as ABC.

A: Decide to Plant

In Mark 4, Jesus compared the workings of the kingdom of God to planting seeds in the earth. "When the seed is sown," He said, "it grows up and becomes greater" (verse 32).

Notice, He didn't say that when the seed is sown it occasionally grows up and becomes greater. Or it grows up and becomes greater if it's God's will. He said, "It grows up and becomes greater." Period.

God's economy isn't like ours. It isn't up one day and down the other. It's always the same and it always works perfectly. If you have good earth, good seed and good water, you will have growth. It's inevitable. The laws of God will produce that increase every single time.

So, if you're facing a need, don't panic—plant a seed!

That seed may take the form of money, time or some other resource you have to give. But no matter what form it takes, you need to understand that the gift itself isn't really your seed. There's no life in it. It's just the husk.

There are people who've planted husks for years. But, because they didn't put any life in them, nothing ever came up. So don't just plunk a husk in the offering bucket when it goes by. Put life in it first. Praise and worship God over it. Say, "Lord, I'm offering You my goods to do Your work with, and as I bring You my goods, I bring myself. I give myself to You, spirit, soul and body."

Pray over that seed. Fill it with faith, worship and the Word. Then it will be ready to plant.

B: Find Good Ground

Out in West Texas on my grandfather's farm, there were big, white patches of caliche. It's the most worthless dirt in the world when it comes to planting seed. It won't grow anything. I don't care how fine your seed is, if you plant it in caliche, you won't get a crop.

There are some ministries that, spiritually, are just like caliche. They aren't good ground for your seed. So before you give, pray about where that gift should go.

Don't rely on your own judgments. Don't reason it out and say, "Well, this preacher over here is screaming and crying and saying he's going under, so I guess I'll give to him." You go to the Lord of the tithe and find out where He wants you to put your money. He's the only One who can direct you to truly good ground every time.

C: Water!

Once Your good seed is in good ground, keep watering it with the Word of God. Speak faith over it all week long. Call forth the growth of that seed by "calling things that be not as though they were" (Romans 4:17). It may just be a little seed, but you need to start calling it grown.

You may say, "Well, brother, I believe in telling things like they are."

You won't ever see any growth in your life then because spiritual things grow as words are released. That's God's way.

Charles Capps says the one who "tells things like they are" is like the guy who went out on the porch to give his dog a bone. When he got out there, he found the dog wasn't there—just the cat. So he started saying, "Here, kitty, kitty, kitty."

His neighbor said, "I thought you wanted to give that bone to the dog."

"I did," answered his friend, "but I like to say it like it is—and the cat, not the dog, is the one that's here."

Don't be like that guy. Call the dog. He'll come. Water your seed with words of faith. Don't call poverty if you don't want poverty. Call yourself prosperous. Call that need met. Before long, you'll be so full of joy and so full of expectancy that even the watering will be fun!

Plant the seed. Find good soil. Water it. Then as Mark 4:27 says, all you have to do is "sleep, and rise night and day, and the seed will spring and grow up."

"But I don't understand how that works!" you say.

It doesn't matter. Just do it. Plant and water. Sleep and rise. Sure enough, one of these mornings you'll wake up to an abundant harvest!

Why Is My Harvest So Small?

"Give, and it shall be given unto you; good measure, pressed down, and shaken together, and running over, shall men give into your bosom. For with the same measure that ye mete withal it shall be measured to you again."
— LUKE 6:38

You can't figure it out. From the time you first learned about the principle of sowing and reaping, you have given offerings and sown seed into the kingdom of God. Although you've experienced a measure of blessing, you know you haven't reaped the thirty-, sixty-, hundredfold return Jesus said could be yours. Oftentimes you wonder, *Why is my harvest so small? I thought it would be bigger than this! What's wrong?*

There are reasons why people reap a small harvest. If your own harvests don't compare to the quality of increase you see in the Word of God, you can do something about that. The Bible gives us clear insights that, when followed, guarantee we will reap a plentiful harvest—every time.

Sow as Much as You Can

The first reason people only reap a small harvest can be found in 2 Corinthians 9:6: "...He which soweth sparingly shall reap also sparingly; and he which soweth bountifully shall reap also bountifully."

Jesus said, "with the same measure that ye mete withal it shall be measured to you again" (Luke 6:38).

That's such a basic principle, it seems obvious, but people overlook it. They'll put a dollar or two in the offering and when they don't receive much of a return they say, "I guess God just ordained me to have a small harvest." What they fail to realize is that God didn't determine the size of their harvest. They determined the size of their harvest the moment they decided how much seed to sow! If you don't sow much seed, you won't have much of a harvest.

"But, Brother Keith, I can't give any more than a few dollars," you say. "That's all I have!"

That's all right. Plant it and it will increase. Then take that increase and (instead of spending it on yourself) plant it again. You'll be amazed how fast it will grow.

I once read about a flour mill operator in Tecumseh, Michigan, who experimented with this process. After hearing a sermon on the principles of sowing and reaping, he set aside one cubic inch of wheat, which is 360 kernels. Then he committed to the Lord that for six years, he would take the harvest from that ground, tithe 10 percent of it, and then sow the remaining 90 percent back into the ground.

The first year it took a 4-foot by 8-foot plot of ground to contain the harvest from that first cubic inch of wheat. The next year it took a 24-foot by 60-foot plot. By the sixth year, it took 2,666 acres because those first 360 kernels of wheat had multiplied to become 55 *billion!*

That testimony impacted me so strongly with the belief that, if you plant as much of your harvest back into the ground as you can, your harvests will increase until you'll have more than you could possibly eat. And you'll have much to give!

One big temptation people face, however, is when their harvest comes in, they want to spend it on themselves to immediately elevate their standard of living. They don't realize they're delaying their own prosperity by doing that. So don't eat your seed. Make giving a priority and then believe God to be able to give even more because "A man's harvest in life will depend entirely on what he sows" (Galatians 6:7, *J.B. Phillips Translation).*

Sow Into Good Ground

The second reason people have small harvests is they don't sow their seed into good ground. Some ground is average. Some ground is poor. Some is tremendous! The quantity of your harvest is directly affected by the quality of the ground where you have sown.

"How do I determine what is good ground?" you may ask.

First of all, Jesus said, "Ye shall know them by their fruits" (Matthew 7:16). If a ministry is yielding solid, scriptural fruit—such as getting people born again, edifying believers, preaching the unadulterated Word of God or helping the poor—then it's probably a good place to plant your seed.

Second, the Holy Spirit will not lead you to waste your seed by planting it in ground that's not strong and good enough to nourish it and produce a harvest. It's possible to waste seed by sowing money or things into certain people or works. That's why you need to be led by the Holy Spirit about where to and not to sow. Don't waste anything by haphazardly making decisions just off the top of your head. Listen. Stay open to the Spirit of God to direct your giving. Then follow that inward witness, knowing that He's leading you to sow in good ground.

Tithing Creates a Climate of Blessing

Natural seed needs the right amount of rain and sunshine to grow. The same is true of spiritual seed. It needs the blessing of God to produce a big harvest.

Tithing is the key to your harvest being blessed.

Although tithing does not qualify as sowing, it opens the windows of heaven and creates the right climate for your seed to flourish. Furthermore, if you're a tither, God says He will "rebuke the devourer for your sakes, and he shall not destroy the fruits of your ground" (Malachi 3:11).

Boll weevils, bugs and other insects will totally devour a crop. But you can be assured that when the devil sends spiritual bugs into your field, God Himself will say, "Get back, bugs! You can't eat that crop! It belongs to a tither. Because he puts Me first, I take care of him and his, personally!"

Discern Your Harvest

If you want to reap a bumper crop, in addition to planting plenty of seed, choosing good ground and creating a climate of blessing, you have another very important job to do. You have to discern when, where and how much or what size your harvest will be.

You probably have never thought about needing to discern your harvest. But that is why many of us have reaped only a little when we should have reaped a lot. We failed to discern our harvest!

Consider the importance of each of these elements, starting with the crucial element of timing. Scripturally, you know that you're not going to plant today and reap tomorrow. The Bible says we must wait until "due season" (Galatians 6:9). But the only way you can possibly tell when due season comes is by the witness of the Holy Spirit in your heart. First John 2:20 says, "... ye have an unction [or anointing] from the Holy One, and ye know all things." That unction will enable you to sense when you're getting close to your harvest.

One of the key indications that your harvest is due is that joy will rise up within you (see Isaiah 9:3). You'll have a sense of excitement in your heart. Your head may not be able to figure it out, but if you pay attention to what's inside you, you'll know that the time is near!

The Obedience of Faith

The next thing you need to know is where your harvest will be. Practically speaking, you have to locate where the cornfield is before you can reap the corn. The Lord knows that, and you can trust Him to help you find it.

But let me warn you, once He shows you where the field is, you'll have to take steps of faith to get to it. Romans 16:26 calls such steps the "obedience of faith." And if you don't take them, you won't receive the increase God has in store.

Read Luke 5 and you'll see that Peter faced that very situation. He sowed into Jesus' ministry by lending Him his boat and letting him preach from it. When Jesus was finished, He said to Peter, "Launch out into the deep, and let down your nets for a draught" (verse 4).

Peter was tired and hungry. He'd already fished all night without success. He knew there were no fish out there! What Jesus was actually doing was showing Peter where his harvest was. The problem was, now his nets were all washed and put away.

Peter had to take a step of faith to launch back out in that boat.

But, thank God, he took that step! If he hadn't, he would have missed his harvest. He would have missed the biggest catch of fish he'd ever seen in his life.

How many times have people tithed...and sowed...and waited? Then harvest time came and God said, *Take this step of expansion. Start this new business.* They were excited because they could see huge potential. But for whatever reason, they became afraid, yielded to unbelief and decided to play it safe. They didn't want to take on the extra contracts or do the necessary work.

As a result of not taking that step of obedience, they missed the blessings of God because they failed to discern their harvest. Their own lack of faith caused them to miss the place, the timing and the increase of harvest God had prepared for them.

Think *Big*

When it comes to discerning your harvest, you also need to know the size of your harvest. When the Lord first spoke to me about this, He asked me a question. (I don't mean I heard a voice or saw a vision. I just knew in my heart what He was communicating to me.) *Keith,* He said, *do you know how much you sowed above your tithe last year?*

"Yes, Lord, I do," I answered. He had already taught me to be diligent to know the state of my flocks (see Proverbs 27:23).

He asked me further: *Have you thought about what even a fiftyfold return would be? Are you really expecting that much to come in?*

I whipped out the calculator, did the math and my eyes got big. It was a startlingly large figure! I had to say, "No, Lord. I'm not expecting that much."

Then stir up your faith! He said.

I don't mind telling you, I obeyed Him. And if you want to enjoy your full harvest, you should too because you don't just reap according to what you've sown, you reap according to your faith.

If your faith is smaller than your harvest, you'll be like the farmer who planted 500 acres, got a full crop, then went out and harvested only 50 acres. You'll end up leaving most of your crops in the field.

We have a big God. Make a decision to spend enough time in His Word that He can expand your "expecter"! Learn to think *big*, to claim *big* and to believe *big things*. Then stay with it until your increase reflects the greatness of our God!

Keep on reaping...and reaping...and reaping...until you realize you have more than you can possibly use. Then call your brothers and sisters in the Lord and say, "Hey, let me give you some of what God has given me, I have plenty to spare!"

They'll be blessed. Your heavenly Father will be well pleased. And you'll have more fun giving it away than you ever dreamed possible.

Now that's what I call a harvest!

What Happened to My Harvest?

Chapter 13

"...Whatsoever a man soweth, that shall he also reap."

— GALATIANS 6:7

Keith Moore

It's frustrating. You've been confessing that God supplies all your needs, but you're still broke. What's even more puzzling is that you're a tither and a giver. You know that God's Word is true and He promised to open the windows of heaven and pour out blessings you wouldn't have room enough to receive. But...you still have plenty of room. You can't figure it out. You're wondering, *Where is my abundant supply? What happened to my harvest?*

When God began teaching me about the laws of increase, He showed me there are reasons why some people fail to reap a harvest and why others reap only a small one. If we'll give attention to those reasons—and make adjustments accordingly—we can enjoy a bumper crop of God's blessings every time!

First Things First

The first reason people fail to reap a harvest is simple and obvious. But we can't pass over it because it's the most common mistake people make.

When the Lord initially pointed it out to me, He said, *Keith, did you notice that I set up laws of sowing and reaping, not reaping and sowing?*

I realize that's very basic, but it's amazing how many people want to reap a harvest when they haven't even sown yet. Jesus said, "Give, and it shall be given unto you" (Luke 6:38). The Apostle Paul wrote, "...he which soweth bountifully shall reap also bountifully" (2 Corinthians 9:6). Again and again in the Scriptures, we see that sowing must come before reaping. Yet the No. 1 reason why people fail to receive a harvest is because they haven't sown!

They'll make confessions. They'll turn in prayer requests. They'll call hot lines. But when all that is said and done the fact remains, if they haven't planted anything, if they haven't given anything, they're not going to reap a harvest.

"But Brother Keith," you may say, "I don't have anything to give!"

No problem. Second Corinthians 9:10 says God will provide seed for the sower. So if you have absolutely nothing, just say, "God, I need some seed to sow," and He'll give it to you.

When He does, don't just plant it haphazardly. Sow it in the particular area in which you want to reap. Here's why.

Genesis 1:11-12 plainly tells us that every seed produces after its own kind. That's not only true in the natural, it's true spiritually, too. Galatians 6:7 says it this way, "Whatsoever a man soweth, that shall he also reap." If you sow money, you'll reap money. If you sow jewelry, you'll reap jewelry. Whatever you sow is what will grow into a harvest in your life.

As soon as my wife and I started practicing this principle, things began to happen in our life. For example, we helped someone pay off their car. We made a payment for them every month for a year. Just a few months later, we were able to pay off our own car. We sowed a $3300 debt repayment and reaped a $15,000 debt repayment in return!

Right now you may be thinking, *That's great! I'll take part of my tithe and pay off someone's car!* If so, let me warn you: Tithing is not sowing—there's a difference. When you tithe, you're giving back to God what already belongs to Him. The Bible says the firstfruits (that's the first and best 10 percent of your increase) belong to the Lord. Sowing implies giving something that belongs to you, so you're only sowing when you give something over and above your tithe.

Your tithe does affect your sowing, however. In fact, it's the key to your sowing being blessed. Malachi 3:10-13 says, when you tithe, God will open the windows of heaven, rain on the seed you've sown and multiply it many times over.

Don't Faint

The second reason why people don't reap is that they get tired of waiting for their harvest and give up. God warns us about that in Galatians 6:9. He tells us not to "be weary in well doing: for in due season we shall reap, if we faint not."

We have, however, a hard time waiting for "due season" because it almost always comes later than we want! Our flesh is impatient. It expects to plant a seed today and reap a harvest tomorrow. But that just doesn't happen.

Spiritual things work just like natural things. A farmer knows it will take a certain amount of time for his crop to grow. He doesn't try to rush the ground. He doesn't get on his tractor and drive around yelling, "Hurry up, crops. I need a harvest *now!*" He just waits patiently because he knows his harvest will come in due season.

Many charismatic Christians, on the other hand, seem to think that the moment they sow, the ground will quake, lightning will flash from the sky, and suddenly a massive harvest will shoot up from the ground. When that doesn't happen, they just shrug their shoulders and say, "Well, I guess I'm not going to get anything."

So they go on about their business and never give another thought to the seed they planted. As a result, they faint and miss their due season by forgetting what and where they sowed. Many times this happens because people don't take their giving seriously enough to even expect a harvest. They view their giving as a loss instead of as an investment.

Take your sowing seriously. Remember when and where you planted seed. Every time you think about it say, "I've sown in that area and I'm expecting a harvest!" Then constantly watch for it. Proverbs 10:5 says, "He that gathereth in summer is a wise son: but he that sleepeth in harvest is a son that causeth shame." Don't be a sleeping son at harvest time. Stay awake and reap the rewards!

Reaping Is *Not* Automatic

"If I plant good seed in faith, won't my harvest just automatically come in?"

No. It won't. Reaping is no more automatic than sowing. Read the parable Jesus told in Mark 4 and you'll see what I mean:

> ...So is the kingdom of God, as if a man should cast seed into the ground; and should sleep, and rise night and day, and the seed should spring and grow up, he knoweth not how. For the earth bringeth forth fruit of herself; first the blade, then the ear, after that the full corn in the ear. But when the fruit is brought forth, immediately he putteth in the sickle, because the harvest is come (verses 26-29).

God didn't sow the seed in this parable. The man did. God gave the increase. Then it was the man who reaped the harvest by putting in the sickle.

Reaping takes work. It requires action on our part. Just as a farmer doesn't sit around at harvest time expecting his crops to march out of the field and into the barn all by themselves, we cannot expect our harvest to come in without our help. Maybe you were hoping God would take the responsibility for it all. But He won't.

If you'll read the Bible, you'll see that even when God supplied spectacular, miraculous provision, He still required His people to go out and gather it. When the Israelites were in the wilderness, for instance, God poured food down on them from the sky. But they couldn't just sit in their tents and wait. It fell in little flakes like snow and they had to take their pot and pick up these little specks until they had collected enough to make bread. They had to reap the harvest!

Spiritually speaking, you will have to do the same thing. You have to thrust in your sickle of faith and lay claim to the provision that's yours by right of the seed you've sown. You have to say, "I believe I receive my harvest in Jesus' Name. Now go, ministering spirits, and cause my money (or whatever it is) to come in!" (see Hebrews 1:14).

In other words, you must reap by faith just like you sow by faith. Instead of just sitting around "waiting on the Lord," you must become aggressive. You have to go after what's yours.

Mark 11:24 tells us how to do that. It says, "What things soever ye desire, when ye pray, believe that ye receive them, and ye shall have them."

Look again at that verse. It says you're to believe. Believe what? Believe that you receive.

It's not enough for you to believe God is good and wants you to prosper. It's not enough for you to believe that your harvest is out there. You must believe that you receive. In this passage, the word translated *receive* literally means "take." You can't be a timid soul and be successful in the Christian life. The Apostle Paul told Timothy, "Fight the good fight of faith, lay hold on eternal life..." (1 Timothy 6:12). When it comes to enjoying the blessings of God that are provided for you, you have to wade in and lay hold—you have to be bold to possess what God said belongs to you.

So get busy. Plant some seed in the specific area where you need a harvest. Stand strong, stay alert and awake until due season comes. Then put in the sickle and take what God has given you.

Chapter 14

Faithful Over Little—
Ruler Over Much

Gloria Copeland

"Well done, thou good and faithful servant:
thou hast been faithful over a few things, I will
make thee ruler over many things: enter thou
into the joy of thy lord."
— MATTHEW 25:21

You may not realize it, but if you're a born-again believer,
you have a quality within you that is in great demand in the
world today.

It's a quality employers prize so highly that they'll promote
people who have it—and often pay top dollar for it. It's a
quality so valuable it can make you a success in every area of
your life.

What one quality could possibly be so precious?

The quality of faithfulness.

According to the dictionary, *faithfulness* is "firmly adhering
to duty, of true fidelity or loyalty, true allegiance, constant in
performance of duties or services." A faithful person is steadfast,
dependable and trustworthy. He's consistent.

A faithful person keeps his word. When he says he'll do a
job, you can count on him to get it done and done well. If he is
being paid by the hour, he doesn't steal from his employer by
wasting his time. He works diligently even when his boss isn't
watching. He's honorable, treating others with the same kindness and integrity with which he would like to be treated.

Spiritually, a faithful person is exactly what that word
implies—full of faith. He trusts consistently in the Word of God
and acts consistently on that Word. He doesn't have faith in
God one moment and doubt Him the next. He steadily believes
God and does what He says.

"Certainly faithfulness is a wonderful quality," you may say. "But I have to be honest. I just don't have it!"

You do if you have made Jesus the Lord of your life and been born again. Because Galatians 5:22 says, "...the fruit of the Spirit is love, joy, peace, patience, kindness, goodness, faithfulness, gentleness and self-control" *(New International Version)*. That's the fruit of your reborn spirit.

When you were born again, God re-created your spirit in His own image. He put His own character within you, and one of God's most outstanding character traits is His faithfulness. As 1 Corinthians 1:9 says, "God is faithful—reliable, trustworthy and [therefore] ever true to His promise, and He can be depended on" *(The Amplified Bible)*.

Actually, the kind of faithfulness God has put within us is more than just a character trait. It's a supernatural force that comes to our rescue in times of trouble. It gives us the ability to keep going when things get tough.

The force of faithfulness is what enables us to continue living by faith even when our fleshly inclination is to throw down the Bible and say, "I quit!" It's the force that causes us to go to work, and smile, and do our best—even on days when we'd rather stay in bed.

The Sure Path to Promotion

Of course, even though the supernatural force of faithfulness is within you, for it to operate in your life, you have to yield to it. You have to develop it and exercise it. But it's worth the effort because the Bible promises that the "faithful man shall abound with blessings!" (Proverbs 28:20).

That holds true in every area of life. When you're faithful spiritually, you abound with spiritual blessings and that opens the door for blessings in every other area. When you're faithful on your job, you abound with financial blessings. When you're faithful at home, you're blessed with a good, strong family.

What's more, Jesus told us that those who would be faithful over little would be made ruler over much (see Matthew 25:21). So faithfulness is a sure path to promotion!

Employers, for instance, are desperate for faithful people. The world is full of employees who will just do enough to keep from getting fired. It's full of people who will slack off the moment the boss isn't looking. It's full of people who may come to work—and may not. That's how worldly people are!

But it's a treasure for employers to find a person who works wholeheartedly at his job, who is trustworthy and dependable and honest. So when an employer finds a person like that, he's usually eager to promote him.

The fact is, every believer ought to be that kind of person. Each one of us should live a lifestyle of faithfulness. As Ken says, in every situation we should make it a lifestyle to do what's right, do it because it's right and do it right. Anything less is disobedience to God's Word.

In the workplace, we should be following the instructions in Colossians 3:22-24:

> Servants, obey in everything those who are your earthly masters, not only when their eyes are on you, as pleasers of men, but in simplicity of purpose (with all your heart) because of your reverence for the Lord and as a sincere expression of your devotion to Him. Whatever may be your task, work at it heartily (from the soul), as [something done] for the Lord and not for men, Knowing (with all certainty) that it is from the Lord [and not from men] that you will receive the inheritance which is your (real) reward. [The One Whom] you are actually serving [is] the Lord Christ, the Messiah *(The Amplified Bible).*

Ken and I have seen some of the employees at this ministry take that attitude and, as a result, be promoted again and again. One man started out with the simple job of duplicating tapes for us, but over the years he was so faithful that he eventually became director over the business affairs of the entire ministry.

You may think, *Well, that wouldn't work in my case. My boss is an unfair man. He wouldn't reward my faithfulness.*

That's no problem. The scripture doesn't say your reward will come from your employer. It says your reward will come from the Lord!

You see, God has established a principle of sowing and reaping in the earth—and that principle is always at work. As Galatians 6:7 says, "Be not deceived; God is not mocked: for whatsoever a man soweth, that shall he also reap." If you plant faithfulness in your job, you will receive blessing in return—even if that blessing means a different but better job. Granted, that blessing may not come overnight, but if you will not be weary in well doing, in due season you shall reap, if you faint not (verse 8).

So make up your mind to put your whole heart into your work, no matter how menial or unpleasant it may seem to be. Do it well. Do it with a smile and an attitude of enthusiasm and say, "Lord, You know this is not where I want to be. But I am sowing faithfulness into this job as seed for a better job." I guarantee you, a better job will soon come along.

Recently, the Lord has impressed me that it is important for us as believers to obey these principles of faithfulness right now, especially in the area of finances and employment. Why is that? I'm not sure. I don't know what is going to happen to the economy of this world between now and the time Jesus catches us away. But there may come a time when jobs are more scarce than they are now. If so, we'll definitely want to be reaping the blessings of faithfulness. And we can be, if we'll start sowing right now. Besides that, it's the right thing to do!

Lions Don't Eat Faithful Men

Some Christians get nervous when they hear things like that. It scares them to think that difficult times might be ahead.

But it shouldn't, because Psalm 31:23 tells us "the Lord preserveth the faithful."

It doesn't matter how dark the world around us may become. It doesn't matter how hard the devil tries to bring us down, if we're steadfast, dependable and trustworthy—constantly serving the Lord and doing what's right—God will bring us through in victory.

If you have any question about that, just take a look at what He did in the life of Daniel. When Daniel was just a young man, his nation was besieged and defeated by the nation of Babylon. He was taken captive from his own country and brought to serve in the palace of the Babylonian king.

Even though Daniel was an alien in Babylon, he was eventually promoted to one of the highest positions in the nation. He served as one of three presidents directly under the king himself. Daniel did his job so faithfully that he "was preferred above the presidents and princes, because an excellent spirit was in him; and the king thought to set him over the whole realm" (Daniel 6:3).

When the other presidents and princes found out that Daniel was about to be promoted and given power over them, they were jealous. So they looked for some accusation to bring against him.

You know how it is at election time. Each candidate tries to find something bad they can say about the other. Sometimes, they don't have to look too hard, either.

In Daniel's case, however, it was different. His opponents "could find none occasion nor fault; forasmuch as he was faithful, neither was there any error or fault found in him. Then said these men, We shall not find any occasion against this Daniel, except we find it against him concerning the law of his God" (verses 4-5).

They couldn't dig up any real dirt on Daniel, so they came up with a scheme to trap him. Since he was faithful to God and prayed every day, they talked the king into signing a decree "that whosoever shall ask a petition of any God or man for thirty days, save of [the]...king, he shall be cast into the den of lions" (verse 7).

Do you know what Daniel did when he heard about that decree? The same thing he had always done. He just kept on being faithful. "...he went into his house; and his windows being open in his chamber toward Jerusalem, he kneeled upon his knees three times a day, and prayed, and gave thanks before his God..." (verse 10).

Of course, Daniel's opponents immediately informed the king that Daniel had broken the law and must be thrown to the lions. The king was grieved and tried to figure out a way to deliver Daniel from his death sentence. But because the king himself had signed the law, it could not be changed.

As they cast Daniel into the den of lions, the king said to him:

> ...Thy God whom thou servest continually, he will deliver thee.... Then the king went to his palace, and passed the night fasting...and his sleep went from him. Then the king arose very early in the morning, and went in haste unto the den of lions. And when he came to the den, he cried with a lamentable voice unto Daniel: and the king spake and said...O Daniel, servant of the living God, is thy God, whom thou servest continually, able to deliver thee from the lions? (verses 16, 18-20).

Notice that both times the king spoke to Daniel, he mentioned the fact that Daniel continually served God. In other words, what stood out about Daniel was his faithfulness. He spiritually wasn't up one day, and down the next. He wasn't believing God on Sunday and then crying on Monday about how depressed he was. He was faithful—both in spiritual things and in natural things.

So what happened? God preserved him! God sent His angel and shut the lions' mouths so they couldn't hurt him. Just think,

Daniel slept better in the lions' den that night than the king did in the palace!

The next morning, the king brought Daniel out of the lions' den and then commanded that his accusers be thrown in it along with their families. The lions devoured them before they hit the floor. After all, they had missed dinner the night before!

That just goes to show you, it never pays to try to destroy a faithful man. If you do, you'll end up being destroyed yourself—and he'll end up not just being preserved, but being promoted.

That's what happened to Daniel. He "prospered in the reign of Darius, and in the reign of Cyrus the Persian" (verse 28). He went through these two kings and was abundantly blessed under both of them.

Make a Change!

Will God do for you what He did for Daniel? He certainly will! Jesus left no question about that for He said: "Who then is a faithful and wise servant, whom his lord hath made ruler over his household, to give them meat in due season? Blessed is that servant, whom his lord when he cometh shall find so doing. Verily I say unto you, That he shall make him ruler over all his goods" (Matthew 24:45-47).

God gives us certain responsibilities in His kingdom. He gives us assignments. Our first assignment might be nothing more than to weed the flower bed at the church or to wait tables at a restaurant. But if we'll be faithful over that assignment, the next assignment He gives us will be bigger and better.

So start being faithful with what God has given you right now. Be faithful spiritually by diligently attending to the Word every day. Follow the instructions in Proverbs 4 and let God's Word "not depart from thine eyes; keep them in the midst of thine heart.... Keep thy heart with all diligence; for out of it are the issues of life" (verses 21, 23).

Put yourself in position to increase in the natural realm by being faithful with the material things God has given you. For example, if you're living in a rent house and you want a house of your own, treat that rent house as if it belonged to you. Don't tear it up and be careless with it. For Jesus said, "...if ye have not been faithful in that which is another man's, who shall give you that which is your own?" (Luke 16:12).

Until now, you may have acted like the most unfaithful person around. You may feel like you've made disastrous mistakes in your life by being undependable and untrustworthy. You may have always been a quitter. But you can start changing that today because as a child of God, you have inside you His very own force of faithfulness. So start yielding to it.

Begin to strengthen that force by meditating on God's Word. Read and study what it says about faithfulness. Since faith comes by hearing, and hearing by the Word of God, you can build your ability to believe you are faithful by turning your attention away from who you've been in the past, and focusing instead on who the Word says you are today.

And who does the Word say you are today?

It says you are among those who have sided with Jesus. You can be among those who "are called, and chosen, and faithful" (Revelation 17:14)! The Holy Spirit will help you.

Remind the devil of that next time he pressures you to quit. Remind him of it when he tempts you to do less than your best. Then determine to be the kind of person God can trust to follow through, no matter what the inconvenience or discomfort. Say, "Lord, I am a faithful person. I will get my job done and do it well. I will trust You to help me, energize me and create in me the power and desire. And I'll stay with it at any cost."

Step out in faithfulness and you shall abound with blessings!

Do You Know What Time It Is?

Chapter 15

"Now unto him that is able to do exceeding abundantly above all that we ask or think, according to the power that worketh in us."
— Ephesians 3:20

Gloria Copeland

If you're a born-again child of God and you've been struggling financially—scraping along with just barely enough—it's time for that to change. It's time for you to wake up to the riches that belong to you in Jesus, kick the limits off your faith and receive your financial inheritance.

Even if you haven't been struggling, even if your bills are paid and your major needs are met, you need to step up to greater abundance. We all need to do that, because God has more in store for every one of us than we possess right now. He "is able to do exceeding abundantly above all that we ask or think, according to the power that worketh in us" (Ephesians 3:20).

What's more, we are now closer than ever to the end of the age. Jesus is coming soon. God is desiring to pour out His glory in greater measure than ever before, not just in our hearts, lives and church services, but in our finances as well.

Some time ago, the Lord began to speak to me about that. *Do you know what time it is?* He said. *It's exceeding-abundantly-above-all-that-you-can-ask-or-think time!*

I don't mind telling you, I was thrilled when I heard those words! And I've gotten even more excited about them as the months have passed, because the Holy Spirit has continued to say them to me. I believe it, too! I believe it with all my heart!!

We are in the days of the end-time transfer of wealth about which the Bible prophesies. In these days, God is teaching us how to draw great riches from our heavenly account so we can glorify Him and get the gospel preached to the world. He is revealing to us how we can have more than enough to give to every good work and have plenty left over to enjoy!

God's Financial Safeguard

The very idea of that kind of wealth scares some Christians. They think having a lot of money is ungodly—but that's not what the Bible says.

God doesn't object to us having money. On the contrary, He "takes pleasure in the prosperity of His servant" (Psalm 35:27, *The Amplified Bible*). What God doesn't want us to do is covet money. He doesn't want us to love money and make it our God.

So He gave us a safeguard. He gave us in His Word a foundational instruction about prosperity that enables us to be wealthy and godly at the same time. "Seek for (aim at and strive after) first of all His [God's] kingdom, and His righteousness [His way of doing and being right], and then all these things taken together will be given you besides" (Matthew 6:33, *The Amplified Bible*).

That is the foundation of biblical prosperity. It's based on God's way of doing and being right. It comes to those who operate in this earth according to His system of economy instead of the world's system.

The world's system has money for its god. It loves and seeks after money. But the kingdom of heaven has the Father for its God. And in His economy, you can't prosper unless you put Him and His ways first place in your life.

Granted, there are times when godly people begin to prosper and then get off track. Those people pass the poverty test, but fail the prosperity test. They start out seeking first God's kingdom. But when they begin to experience the financial blessings of that kingdom, they become overly occupied with the things that have been added to them. Their hearts begin to grow cold toward God because they don't continue to give Him first place in their lives.

God doesn't want that to happen to His people. That's why He told the Israelites not to forget Him when they entered the Promised Land, started living in goodly houses and enjoying material abundance. "But you shall (earnestly) remember the Lord your God; for it is He Who gives you power to get wealth..." (Deuteronomy 8:18, *The Amplified Bible*).

Your Heavenly Account

Notice God didn't say, "Since you might forget Me if you get rich, I'm going to keep you poor." No, He said, "Always remember that I'm the One who gives you the power to get wealth." Remember where you got it!

Hallelujah! As born-again believers, you and I are God's people just as surely as those Israelites were. Since we are Christ's, then we are "Abraham's seed, and heirs according to the promise" (Galatians 3:29). Therefore, we can expect God to anoint the work of our hands. We can expect Him to bless us and give us the power to get wealth!

"But Gloria," you may say, "I know people who have served God and put Him first all their lives, yet, they were always broke. God didn't give them the power to get wealth!"

Yes, He did. They just didn't know how to use it.

You see, God's abundance doesn't just fall out of heaven and hit us on the head. He has designated ways for us to receive it. If we don't know how to operate in those ways, we will miss out on what is ours.

That's really not surprising when you think about it. Even things on earth work that way. For example, you can have a million dollars in a bank account, but if you don't know it's there or if you don't know how to make a withdrawal on your account, you won't be able to enjoy that money.

The same thing is true in the kingdom of God. The Bible says you have a heavenly account. The Apostle Paul referred to it when he wrote to his partners and thanked them for giving into his ministry. "Not because I desire a gift," he said, "but I desire fruit that may abound to your account" (Philippians 4:17).

Your heavenly account is much like an earthly bank account in that you can make deposits in it. Not only is it possible to make deposits there, Jesus told us it is very important for us to do so. In Matthew 6:19-21, He said: "Lay not up for yourselves treasure upon earth, where moth and rust doth corrupt, and where thieves break through and steal: But lay up for yourselves treasures in heaven, where neither moth nor rust doth corrupt, and where thieves do not break through nor steal: For where your treasure is, there will your heart be also."

It's a wonderful thing to have an account in heaven! It's a wonderful thing to know like Paul's partners did, that "...God will liberally supply (fill to the full) your every need according to His riches in glory in Christ Jesus" (Philippians 4:19, *The Amplified Bible*).

Headquarters for heaven's economy is not in the impoverished system of this world, but in glory! The government of heaven has for its source El Shaddai, the One who is more than enough!

That's good news because the governments of this world are, for the most part, broke. They print money that doesn't have gold to back it up. They borrow money from other governments. They even borrow it from you.

But God doesn't have to print money He can't back up. His streets are gold. He owns everything. God has the greatest real-estate conglomerate that ever existed. He has a lot of land leased out, but He can repossess it whenever He wants.

That's what He did for the nation of Israel. He repossessed the land of Canaan, the Promised Land, from the wicked. He said to the Israelites, "Here, you can have this land. I'm giving it to you. All you have to do is go in there and take it." (Other times, He told them they couldn't have certain places because He had already given it to "so-and-so.")

Think about that! The Canaanites had dug wells and built houses on that land. But God gave it away right out from under them. He had a right to do it. It all belonged to Him. As Psalm 50:10 says, *He* owns "the cattle upon a thousand hills." ("And the 'taters under them, too!" as one fellow added.)

The Bottom Line

Once you understand you have a heavenly account into which you can make deposits, the next question you need to answer is this: How do I make those deposits?

You make them by giving to God's work.

The foundation for that giving is the tithe. When you give the first tenth of your income to the Lord, you open the door for God to come into your finances and move supernaturally. Proverbs 3:10 says that when you honor the Lord with the first-fruits of your increase, "so shall your storage places be filled with plenty" *(The Amplified Bible)*.

In addition to your tithe, you can also deposit to your heavenly account by giving offerings into the work of the gospel. Be sure, however, when you give, you are truly giving into a work of God. You have to put your money in good ground if you want to get a return.

If you're like me, you're already getting eager to get to the bottom line here. You're saying, "OK, I know that I have an account. I know where it is, and I know how to make deposits. But when can I get the money? When can I write a check on this account?"

You find the answer to that question in Mark 10:29-30. There, Jesus was answering the disciples who had asked Him what they were going to get in return for the giving they had done for the gospel's sake. He said: "Verily I say unto you, There is no man that hath left house, or brethren, or sisters, or father, or mother, or wife, or children, or lands, for my sake, and the gospel's, but he shall receive an hundredfold now in this time, houses, and brethren, and sisters, and mothers, and children, and lands, with persecutions; and in the world to come eternal life."

Jesus says we can receive a hundredfold return from our heavenly account today, in this time! Although our deposits are going to be bringing us rewards for eternity, we don't have to wait until we die and go to heaven to draw on those resources. We can make withdrawals on our heavenly account here and now!

Don't Let Tradition Cheat You

How do you make those withdrawals? You make them by faith. You believe in your heart and speak with your mouth that "my God supplies all my need according to His riches in glory by Christ Jesus" (Philippians 4:19).

You reach out with the hand of faith and claim what's yours!

Many Christians seem reluctant to do that. They remind me of the elder brother in the story of the prodigal son. Do you remember him? His younger brother had asked for his share of the inheritance, so the boys' father divided his estate between them.

The younger brother ran off and squandered his share of the estate on a sinful lifestyle. The elder brother stayed home and faithfully served his father. When the younger brother repented and returned home asking only to be treated as a servant in his father's house, the father received him with open arms. He killed a calf for him so they could celebrate with a feast. He put a robe on his back and a ring on his finger.

The older brother was furious and said to his father, "Lo, these many years do I serve thee, neither transgressed I at any time thy commandment: and yet thou never gavest me a kid, that I might make merry with my friends: But as soon as this thy son was come, which hath devoured thy living with harlots, thou hast killed for him the fatted calf" (Luke 15:29-30).

The father's answer is very important to us and we need to consider it carefully. He said, "Son, thou art ever with me, and all that I have is thine" (verse 31).

That father had divided his estate between his two boys. Therefore, after the younger brother had taken his goods and departed, everything that was left belonged to the elder son. Everything! He could have eaten a fatted calf every day if he'd wanted. Every cow on the estate belonged to him, but he didn't take advantage of his inheritance!

A multitude of Christians are going to find themselves in the same situation when they get to heaven. They're going to find out after they get there what belonged to them down here.

They're going to realize too late that they were cheated and swindled out of their earthly inheritance by religious tradition.

They're going to find out then what you are finding out right now, and it's this: God has always wanted His people to live in abundance, and all He has is ours. He put every good thing in this earth for His family. He didn't put riches here for the devil and his family. He put them here for us.

God wants you to live in a good house. He wants you to have the car you need. He wants you to be so blessed you don't even have to think about those things. He wants you to be able to think about Him instead of thinking about how you're going to buy your next tank of gas.

Listen, God isn't anywhere near broke! He has enough wealth to richly supply all of His children. Lack is not His problem. His problem has been getting His people to believe what He says about their prosperity in His Word. His problem has been getting us to be kingdom-of-God minded in our finances.

God's Hand Is Not Short

One thing that has kept us from becoming kingdom-of-God minded is our own human reasoning. Instead of just trusting God to do for us what He promised, we try to figure out how He is going to do it. And if we can't see how it can happen, all too often, we won't believe.

Don't do that. Get out beyond what you can reason. God is not reasonable! Don't base your praying and your faith on what you can see in this natural realm. Base your praying and your faith on what the Word says.

For example, stop being content just to believe God for the money to make your house payment each month. Start believing Him for the money to pay off the entire mortgage!

"But, Gloria, I just don't know how God would ever get that kind of money to me."

So what! Moses didn't know how God was going to bring in enough meat to feed over a million Israelites for a month, either. So when God said He was going to do it, Moses said, "It would take all our herds and flocks to feed this bunch! It would take all the fish in the sea! It's impossible!"

"And the Lord said unto Moses, Is the Lord's hand waxed short?" (Numbers 11:23). Then He proved He was able to do what He said by raining so much quail out of heaven the Israelites actually got sick of it!

When you have a need in your life that seems impossible to meet, think about that. Remember the question God asked Moses. "Is the Lord's hand waxed short?"

No! It wasn't short then and it isn't short now. God knows how to get the job done. He knows how to get you everything you need. So look to Him as your Source. Become expectant. Become miracle minded, blessing minded, supernatural increase minded.

God knows how to do things. You don't have to worry about that. You just focus on your part—believe, speak the Word and walk in the ways of God. Stop limiting God just because you don't understand how He is going to do the things He has promised. If we had to depend on what we could understand, we'd be in great trouble. But we don't! All we have to understand is that God is God and He has all power. He is able to do exceeding, abundantly above all we can ask or think!

That means if you can think of it, God is able to do more than that. If you can dream of it, God is able to do more than that. If you can hope for it, God is able to do more than that.

Whatever needs or godly desires you might have, God is able to satisfy them—and then do much, much more. And as I said before, these are the days when we will see that superabundance. This is the time.

"What time is it?" you ask.

It's *exceeding-abundantly-above-all-you-can-ask-or-think time!*

I plan to make the most of it. Don't you?

Chapter 16

How to Prosper From the Inside Out

"Beloved, I wish above all things that thou mayest prosper and be in health, even as thy soul prospereth."

— 3 JOHN 2

Kenneth Copeland

Whether they admit it or not, a great many believers have trouble believing—really believing—they'll ever be financially prosperous. You can show them what the Word of God says. You can load them up with scriptures that prove God's will for them is prosperity—and they'll agree with every word. But they'll still go home and live poor. When they look around them at their mountains of bills, the faltering economy, and their dead-end job, they just can't see how God could possibly prosper them. *After all, what's He going to do?* they wonder. *Start floating $20 bills down from the trees?*

How does God prosper His people? It's a good question. One that deserves an answer, and you can find it in 3 John 2. There the elder Apostle John writes by inspiration of the Holy Ghost: "Beloved, I wish above all things that thou mayest prosper and be in health, even as thy soul prospereth."

I want you to notice something. That scripture doesn't say I pray you prosper even as the economy prospers or even as your employer decides to promote you. It says I pray you prosper as your soul prospers.

That's where most believers miss it when it comes to receiving financial prosperity. They keep looking at situations outside them, thinking that's where their hope lies. But God doesn't work from the outside in. He works from the inside out.

He blesses you materially as your soul prospers on His Word. Then, as the seeds of prosperity are planted in your mind, in your will and in your emotions, and as you allow those seeds to grow, they eventually produce a great financial harvest—no matter how bad the conditions around you may be.

Read the story of Joseph in Genesis 37 through 41 and you can see exactly what I'm talking about. When Joseph was sold as a slave to the Egyptians, he didn't have a dime to his name. He didn't even have his freedom. But, right in the middle of his slavery, God gave Joseph such wisdom and ability that he made his owner, Potiphar, rich. As a result, Potiphar put Joseph in charge of all his possessions.

Later, Potiphar's wife got mad at Joseph and he ended up in prison. Talk about a dead-end job! There's really not much chance for advancement in prison, is there? But God gave him insight that no other man in Egypt had. He gave him such great wisdom that he ended up on Pharaoh's staff—not as a slave but as the most honored man in the entire country next to Pharaoh himself. From prison to prime minister.

He rode along in a chariot and people literally bowed down before him. During a worldwide famine, Joseph was in charge of all the food. Now that's prosperity!

How did God accomplish that? By prospering Joseph's soul. No matter how dismal Joseph's situation became, no matter how impossible his problems, God was able to reveal the spiritual secrets that would open the door of success for him.

That's what makes God's method of prospering so exciting. It works anywhere and everywhere. It will work in the poorest countries on the face of this earth just like it will work here in the United States. I've seen it happen.

A few years ago, for instance, we received an amazing firsthand report from an African village called Rungai. I'll never forget the story. There had been such a long drought in the countryside surrounding Rungai that the village was in terrible shape. The reservoir that had once supplied it with water had been empty for so long that the dam was broken and crumbling.

There didn't seem to be any hope. Then a local pastor latched onto God's Word concerning prosperity. He began to pray and seek God's guidance. Sure enough, it came.

God told him to get the believers in the village together and rebuild the dam. I'm sure it looked like a ridiculous thing to do. There hadn't been any rain for months and there wasn't a cloud in the sky. But God had given them the secret to success and, in faith obedience, they acted on it.

Not long after the job was done, a rain cloud formed right over their little reservoir, filling it with water. But that's not the end of the story.

You see, the soil at Rungai had been so parched, so full of alkali and poison, that nothing much would grow in it. Yet, after that rain, the pastor called all the people together and told them to start planting around that water hole. He knew God was going to prosper those crops. He also knew that the crops belonging to the believers would be especially blessed. So when he parceled out the land, he interspersed the believers' plots among those of the unbelievers so that the miracle of God could be clearly seen.

During that first season, everybody's crops flourished. Sinners and believers alike. Then the season for harvesting ended. All the sinners' crops died as they were supposed to. But all the believers' crops produced another harvest. Then another. Then another. The believers' crops just kept producing all year long.

Now you may say, "Brother Copeland, God did more than just prosper their souls there. He worked some miracles."

Yes, He did. But how much good would those miracles have done if He hadn't prospered that pastor's soul first? How much good would that rain have been if the pastor hadn't heard from God and patched up the dam before it came? How much good would it have done for God to bless the soil if that pastor hadn't heard God's instructions to plant there?

Those miracles wouldn't have helped those people one bit if God hadn't prospered their souls first! It was because they believed His Word and were willing to listen to His voice that He could reveal to them the secrets of success for their particular situation.

Deuteronomy 29:29 says this: "The secret things belong unto the LORD our God: but those things which are revealed belong unto us and to our children for ever, that we may do all the words of this law."

Secret things! How many times have you racked your brain, trying to figure out the solution to a problem? You knew there was an answer, but you just couldn't figure out what it was. In other words, the answer was a secret—a secret that only God knew. It didn't belong to you.

But if you'd gone to the Word and really searched it in prayer and meditation, that secret would have been revealed! God would have shown you precisely what the solution to that problem was.

In Mark 4:21-22, Jesus says, "Is a candle brought to be put under a bushel, or under a bed? and not to be set on a candlestick? For there is nothing hid, which shall not be manifested; neither was any thing kept secret, but that it should come abroad."

God doesn't want you groping around in the dark. He wants to reveal His secrets to you, secrets that will prosper you and make you successful in every area of your life—including your finances.

That's why He's given you the Holy Spirit. Do you have any idea what a tremendous resource He is? Most believers don't. They get in church and say, "Oh, yes, amen, brother. Thank God for the Holy Spirit. Praise God. Hallelujah." Then they go home and forget about Him.

It's not that they aren't sincere on Sunday. They are. They genuinely appreciate the little bit they understand about the Holy Spirit. But they haven't learned how to tap into the unlimited wisdom and power He can make available to them in their daily lives.

Jesus said, "Howbeit when he, the Spirit of truth, is come, he will guide you into all truth: for he shall not speak of himself; but whatsoever he shall hear, that shall he speak: and he will show you things to come" (John 16:13).

Read that verse again and think about it.

Jesus said the Holy Spirit would guide us into all truth! Not just enough truth to get by on. Not just an occasional truth to help us teach our Sunday school classes. All truth!

If you're a businessman, that means the Holy Spirit will show you how to increase your profits and reduce your expenses. If you're a mother, it means the Holy Spirit will show you how to settle arguments between your children. If you're a student, it means the Holy Spirit will show you how to excel in your classes.

In fact, if you know Jesus Christ as your Lord and are baptized in the Holy Spirit, somehow inside you is the answer to every financial problem, every spiritual problem and every physical problem that exists. You have answers for problems you don't even know about yet.

There's a story that came out of World War II that illustrates that perfectly. The United States Navy had run into some serious trouble. Their ships were being sunk by the enemy faster than they could build new ones, a process which at the time took an entire year.

Finally, they came up with a way that made it possible to build a ship in a single day. But there was one hitch. The process involved building the ship upside down and when the ship was turned upright, the welds would pop and the ship would come apart.

The problem was presented to a deeply spiritual man who was a famous industrialist at the time. "I'll find out how to do it," he said. After days of prayer and fasting, God showed him the welding formula that would hold the ship together.

One idea! Just one idea made it possible to go from building a ship a year, to building a ship a day.

Can you begin to see now how God could prosper you?

There are so many people standing around wringing their hands and worrying. "God could never prosper me," they say. "All I get is this little paycheck...and my company's losing money, so I know they're not going to give me a raise. How on earth is God going to prosper me?"

Maybe He'll give you an idea that will take your company's loss and turn it into a profit. Maybe He'll give you an idea for a new product and you'll start your own company.

God has probably already given you idea after idea that would have made you rich if you'd just had spiritual sense enough to recognize them. But you didn't even know they were there because you weren't paying attention to the things of God. You weren't seeking revelations of the "secret things." You were probably too busy watching TV and listening to some announcer tell you which brand of toothpaste to buy or how bad the economy is.

Listen to me. The Holy Spirit isn't going to be able to get through to you while you're lying around watching television. He's a gentleman. He just isn't going to come, grab the remote control out of your hand, and say, "Listen to Me, dummy! I have some important things to tell you."

No. He'll wait quietly for you to shut off all that other junk that's been occupying your mind and tune in to Him.

Right here is where most believers miss it. They're so involved in life, and even so involved in church activities and religious organizations that they don't ever have any time to spend with the Lord. They never just stop and fellowship with Him. All He gets is a few moments with them as they drive down the freeway or a few minutes between television commercials, and most of that is filled with "poor ol' me."

There are believers God has wanted to put into high political offices. He would have shown them how to solve some of their nation's problems. But He couldn't get their attention. So He just left them where they were, spinning their wheels in a dead-end job. There are others God would have promoted until they became chief executives of major corporations, but they were too busy working toward their own little goals to find out what His goals were.

Don't miss out on God's plans of prosperity for you. Spend time with Him. Listen to Him and learn to recognize His voice.

It's going to take more than a couple of Bible verses and a five-minute prayer to tap into the revelations the Holy Spirit has for you. You'll have to get serious about it.

If you think you don't have time to do that, think again.

How many hours a day do you spend in front of the television? How many hours a week do you spend reading the newspaper? How many hours reading novels and looking at magazines? How much time thinking about your problems?

Replace those things with the Word of God. Use that time to meditate on the Scriptures. Get in prayer and say, "Holy Spirit, I need to know what to do regarding this situation I'm in." Then listen. He'll start giving you the wisdom of God concerning your finances (or any other part of your life).

Will He really? Sure He will. James 1:5-6 says: "If any of you lack wisdom, let him ask of God, that giveth to all men liberally, and upbraideth not; and it shall be given him. But let him ask in faith, nothing wavering. For he that wavereth is like a wave of the sea driven with the wind and tossed."

Again, though, let me warn you. We're talking about more than reading a few quick scriptures a day and wishing for prosperity. We're talking about digging into the Word and staying there until you begin to hear from the Holy Spirit and until you develop a faith that doesn't waver.

That's not something that happens overnight. Like a spiritual farmer, you must plant and weed and water the Word within you. It will take some time and some work, but believe me, the harvest will be well worth the effort.

Chapter 17

Heaven's Economics: "Laws of Abundance"

"But my God shall supply all your need according to his riches in glory by Christ Jesus."
— PHILIPPIANS 4:19

Kenneth Copeland

If, in spite of all the Bible's promises about prosperity...in spite of all the prayers you've prayed...you are still struggling financially today, I want you to consider this question: Where do you think God is going to get the resources to meet your needs?

Without even realizing it, many believers limit God because they have their eyes trained on the limited resources of this world rather than the unlimited riches of God's kingdom. Their faith fails when they think of the troubled economy on the earth, of the shortages and the scarcity that surrounds them. They wonder, *How is God going to bless me in the middle of all this?*

If that's what you've been thinking, here's some news that will turn those thoughts around!

The Bible says in Colossians 1:13 that God has "delivered us from the power of darkness, and hath translated us into the kingdom of his dear Son." To be translated means to be taken out of one place and put over into another. In other words, your citizenship is not primarily of this earth. You are not primarily American or Canadian or Australian—you are first and foremost a citizen of the kingdom of God.

That means this planet doesn't have any right to dictate to you whether your needs are met or not. The Bible says God will meet your needs according to His riches in glory (Philippians 4:19)! You need to learn to live by heaven's economy, not earth's economy—and in heaven there is always more than enough.

A friend of mine was born and raised in Eastern Europe about the time of World War II. For years all he and his family knew were persecution and scarcity. They lived on the run, first from the Germans, then from the Communists. They ate out of trash cans until they were finally caught and sent to a concentration camp.

Finally through some miracles of God and the prayers of a couple of grandmothers, they were able to get away and come to the United States. The first place they went when they got to this country was a grocery store. Can you imagine what it was like coming out of a concentration camp and going into a grocery store? They just walked up and down the aisles of that store and wept for joy at the abundance that was available.

If you and I would only wake up to the abundance of heaven that's been made available to us, that's how we'd feel too. We'd realize we've been translated out of the world of poverty into a kingdom that flows with milk and honey.

You know, God meant for us to come to that realization every time we tithe. He meant for us to give our tithe as a way of activating heaven's economy in our lives, to give it in gratitude and faith expecting our needs to be met abundantly.

In Deuteronomy 26, God told the Israelites exactly what to say when they brought their tithes. He instructed them to acknowledge the fact that He had brought them out of the bondage of Egypt and to say: "The Lord brought us forth out of Egypt with a mighty hand, and with an outstretched arm, and with great terribleness, and with signs, and with wonders: And he hath brought us into this place, and hath given us this land, even a land that floweth with milk and honey" (verses 8-9).

Hallelujah, God has done the same thing for us! So when you bring your tithe to the Lord, make it a time of rejoicing. Make it a time of realizing anew that you've been translated from a world of scarcity to a heavenly economy of abundance!

Here's a prayer to help you get started.

"Father, I thank You and praise You for translating me from the kingdom of darkness into the kingdom that You have prepared for me. Thank You that it is a kingdom of mercy, a kingdom of joy, a kingdom of peace, and a kingdom of abundance.

"I bring my tithe now to You, Lord Jesus. It is the firstfruits of what You have given me, and I plant it in Your kingdom as a seed of blessing, expecting the rich blessings of heaven to be multiplied to me in return.

"I thank You, Lord, that You've rebuked Satan for my sake, and I stand in agreement with Your Word that he'll not destroy my land. He'll not destroy my blessings, and he'll not destroy my crop in the field. I am a citizen of Your kingdom. I have the rights and privileges of a citizen of that kingdom, and I stand upon them. Thank You, Jesus, that heaven's unlimited resources are mine in Your Name! Amen."

Chapter 18

The Seeds of Your Success

"Except a corn of wheat fall into the ground and die, it abideth alone: but if it die, it bringeth forth much fruit."
— JOHN 12:24

Jerry Savelle

Some time ago I was scheduled to fly to Tulsa, Oklahoma, to speak in a meeting. Before I left home, I tried to talk to the Lord about some critical needs in my life and ministry. Instead of answering the way I had expected, He told me, *When you get to Tulsa, I want you to give away your van.* I dropped the subject.

On the plane I again approached the Lord about my pressing situation. "Father, I really need to talk to You about my needs," I told Him. "It just seems they have become overwhelming."

Again, the Lord spoke to me and said, *When you get to Tulsa, I want you to give away your van.* So again, I dropped the subject.

A while later, I once more took up my "case" with the Lord: "Father, during this meeting in Tulsa, I am going to have a little time between services, and I really need to talk to You about my needs."

Once more there came His response, *When you get to Tulsa, I want you to give away your van.* But this time He went on: *Also, there are five preachers in Tulsa who have become discouraged and are about to give up the ministry. I want you to give each of them a suit of clothes.* So once more I decided not to continue the discussion.

Finally, I just couldn't hold back any longer. I said to the Lord, "Father, I've just got to talk to You! You know we've been building our international headquarters in Fort Worth this year. We have moved into them, but there are still lots of things we need. More land, for instance, and more buildings. But we just don't have the money to get what we need...."

When you get to Tulsa, I want you to give away your van and five suits of clothes.

It was then that it finally hit me what was happening. Every time I tried to talk to God about my need, He talked to me about seed.

Now, that's not deep. As children of God, all of us should understand it. We are seed-planting people. But, if you are like me, you have probably noticed that over the past couple of years, your needs have grown larger and larger. You must be wondering, as I was on that plane, where in the world the money is going to come from to meet those steadily increasing obligations.

I believe the Lord showed me the answer to that important question while I was in that airplane on my way to Tulsa. He told me, *In the days to come, the needs of the Body of Christ are going to become so great that, in the natural, they will appear to be impossible to meet. But I am telling you now, don't wait until then to get busy sowing seed into the kingdom.... Don't wait until you get an answer to your present needs before you begin to prepare for the future needs.*

Then He made a statement that suddenly put the whole subject into perspective for me:

You must become seed-conscious, not need-conscious.

That's how God Himself is—He's seed-conscious. When He had "needs" of His own, He fulfilled those needs by giving. He "needed" the redemption of mankind. He "needed" a family. So what did He do? He planted a seed. He gave Jesus.

Our Lord told us plainly: "Except a corn of wheat fall into the ground and die, it abideth alone: but if it die, it bringeth forth much fruit" (John 12:24). God sowed His "Seed," His only Son, Jesus, into the earth and reaped in return a harvest of sons and daughters. He planted the best seed heaven had to offer, not worthless seed. He didn't look for some old decrepit, worn-out angel to use as seed, someone who was no longer needed. No, He chose and planted the very best He had. And He reaped the best of all harvests—human souls.

God explains that principle of seed planting and harvest clearly in Ecclesiastes 11:1-6. There He says:

> Give generously, for your gifts will return to you later. Divide your gifts among many, for in the days ahead you yourself may need much help. When the clouds are heavy, the rains come down; when a tree falls, whether south or north, the die is cast, for there it lies. If you wait for perfect conditions, you will never get anything done. God's ways are as mysterious as the pathway of the wind and as the manner in which a human spirit is infused into the little body of a baby while it is yet in its mother's womb. Keep on sowing your seed, for you never know which will grow—perhaps it all will *(The Living Bible)*.

Now, in this passage we see a vital principle of godly giving: "Give generously, for your gifts will return to you later."

You might say to me, "I just don't understand that. I don't understand how I can give away something and expect God to give it back to me."

I know you don't understand it. Neither do I. It is not necessary that we understand God's principles to benefit from them. We must simply learn, then believe them, and act upon them.

For example, we don't know how seeds bring forth plants for fruit. We just know they do, so we sow seeds into the ground, patiently tend and nurture them, and then reap an abundant harvest from them. That's what God expects us to do with the good seed of His Word.

It is our job to sow seeds, God's job to meet needs.

But notice that the Bible says only that our godly gifts will come back to us. It doesn't say how or when. I wish I could tell you how and when your gift will be returned to you in multiplied form. I don't know. But I do know one thing: The time between sowing and reaping is the most important and exciting in our lives. It becomes a great adventure in faith. The secret is to sow faithfully, generously, and regularly so that we can expect a continual flow of godly gifts in return.

When my staff and I first began our ministry in Africa, we had to go through a battle royal in that land. At every step we had to battle corruption and opposition. But God had told us to go into that area and pull down the strongholds of Satan, and that was exactly what we intended to do, troubles or no troubles.

Our loyal workers lived under constant threat, in turmoil and stress 24 hours a day, with never a moment to relax. They were never able to let down their guard for an instant. The warfare they were engaged in was not only spiritual, but also natural. Some people were so opposed to the ministry, they had actually hired assassins to kill the members of our staff.

But despite the dangers, obstacles and opposition from both man and Satan, we just kept on planting seeds into that outreach, week after week, month after month. After nine long months of seeming failure, we finally began to see a return on our investment in those precious African lives. Now my staff there can hardly contain their joy because every day brings a new victory over the forces of evil and darkness. All the seed we had been faithfully and consistently planting suddenly began to grow and produce fruit for the kingdom of God.

So don't become discouraged and quit sowing. Don't stop planting seed just because you don't see any immediate results. Keep sowing.

One Word From God
Can Change
Your Health

The Great Exchange

"Surely he hath borne our griefs, and carried our sorrows: yet we did esteem him stricken, smitten of God, and afflicted."
— ISAIAH 53:4

Kenneth Copeland

Your days of sickness and disease are over.

I'll never forget the day God spoke those words to me. It was some of the best news I'd ever heard. I believed it and have been walking in the glorious truth of it for more than 25 years now.

If you're sitting there right now, wishing God would say those same words to you, I have good news for you: He has.

He has said it to every one of us.

He said it with such power and force that it made hell tremble and heaven ring. He wrote it in the covenant blood of His own Son. He shouted it down through the ages through prophets and apostles and preachers.

The problem is, most Christians haven't truly heard it. They haven't let it reach down into their hearts and become truth to them. God has said it...but they haven't yet believed.

If that is the case with you today, I want you to know that what you are about to read can change that forever. If you will take this message, study it out in the Scriptures and see for yourself that it is the truth, if you will dare to believe it and act on it, it will not only change your heart, it will change your body.

This one message will forever alter how you see sickness and disease. It will put to rest every doubt about God's will for your healing and open the door of divine health to you.

A Supernatural Substitution

What message could possibly be that powerful?

Only one. The message of the Cross.

If you're a believer, you've already experienced how life-changing that message can be. When you first received it by faith, the Anointing of God in it snatched you out of the kingdom of darkness and delivered you into the kingdom of the light of God's Son. It changed your eternal destination from hell to heaven. It transformed you spiritually and made you a new creation. Think of the power it released in your life!

Yet the fact is, most of us have understood only a tiny fraction of what was accomplished at Calvary. We have only begun to grasp all that was done for us in that Great Exchange.

I like the phrase, The Great Exchange, because the Spirit of the Lord gave it to me, and it captures what happened during Jesus' death and resurrection. It communicates that Jesus did more than pour out His life to pay the penalty of our sin. He actually was made "to be sin for us, who knew no sin; that we might be made the righteousness of God in him" (2 Corinthians 5:21).

To understand how all-encompassing The Great Exchange truly was, you have to realize that the word *sin* there does not just refer to what we'd normally think of as religious errors. It includes everything in our lives that falls short of the glory and perfection of God's original design (see Romans 3:23).

If you want to see that original design, look back at the Garden of Eden. What you'll find is a man and a woman living in unbroken fellowship with Almighty God, untouched by sickness, grief or poverty, and exercising dominion over the whole earth.

Religion has tried to cheapen what Jesus did for us by teaching that He only brought forth a partial redemption—that He freed us only from the eternal damnation caused by sin and not from its damnable effects in the here and now. But thank God, that is not the case.

Calvary was the most complete event that has ever taken place.

God left nothing out of it. Not one cursed thing that came about through mankind's union with Satan was left standing. Jesus triumphed over it all. By taking upon Himself every foul thing that fallen man has ever suffered, He set us free—spirit, soul and body.

He became our substitute. He became poor, that we might be rich (2 Corinthians 8:9). He became weak so that we might be strong. He endured death so that we might be made alive (1 Corinthians 15:22). He "[bore] our sins in his own body on the tree, that we, being dead to sins, should live unto righteousness: by whose stripes [we] were healed" (1 Peter 2:24).

A Mystery Hidden in God

Notice there that Peter lists redemption from sin and healing in the same breath. So does Psalm 103. It says, "Bless the Lord, O my soul: and all that is within me, bless his holy name. Bless the Lord, O my soul, and forget not all his benefits: Who forgiveth all thine iniquities; who healeth all thy diseases" (verses 1-3).

All through the Bible, healing and forgiveness go together like hand in glove. God does not separate them. The reason is simple. They are not separate!

Just as sickness entered the world through Adam's sin, healing came when Jesus paid the price for that sin. To believe otherwise would be tantamount to saying that what God did in Jesus on the cross was less powerful than what the devil did in Adam in the Garden of Eden. That could not possibly be so! For Romans 5:15 assures us:

God's free gift is not at all to be compared to the tres- pass—His grace is out of all proportion to the fall of man. For if many died through one man's falling away— his lapse, his offense—much more profusely did God's grace and the free gift [that comes] through the unde- served favor of the one Man Jesus Christ [the Anointed One], abound and overflow to and for [the benefit of] many *(The Amplified Bible)*.

In other words, what God accomplished through redemp- tion not only equaled what Satan accomplished through the Fall...it far surpassed it!

I'll admit, judging by the sickness-ridden, poverty-plagued, defeated lives of many Christians, it may not seem like redemption did much more than save us from hell by the skin of our teeth. But that's because for the most part, we don't have any idea what really happened at Calvary. And that lack of knowledge has destroyed many precious Christian lives.

"Well now, Brother Copeland, I know what happened at Calvary. I've read every Gospel account of it."

That may be so, but quite frankly, you can't find out what happened there strictly by reading Matthew, Mark, Luke and John. For one thing, those books contain very little information about the Crucifixion. And for another thing, the men who wrote them had viewed it from a natural perspective. They didn't understand it themselves at the time it happened because it was a mystery hidden in God (see 1 Corinthians 2:6-8).

To see the Crucifixion from God's perspective, you must read what the prophet Isaiah wrote about it. For God revealed to him not just the physical facts, but also the spiritual truths of what actually occurred the day Jesus died for us. You can find what he wrote in Isaiah 53:

> Surely He has borne our griefs—sickness, weakness and distress—and carried our sorrows and pain [of punishment]. Yet we ignorantly considered Him stricken, smitten and afflicted by God [as if with leprosy]. But He was wounded for our transgressions, He was bruised for our guilt and iniquities; the chastisement needful to obtain peace and well-being for us was upon Him, and with the stripes that wounded Him we are healed and made whole (verses 4-5, *The Amplified Bible*).

Some theologians have tried to rob this passage of its full power by teaching that the healing it refers to is merely spiritual healing. But the Gospel writer Matthew makes it clear that they are mistaken. For in Matthew 8:17, he quotes this very passage and applies it to the healing ministry of Jesus in which people were cured of every kind of physical sickness and disease.

With that said, look back at those scriptures again. Do you see there where it says He "was bruised for our guilt and iniquities...and with the stripes that wounded Him we are healed"? If you were to look up the Hebrew words that have been translated *bruised* and *stripes,* you'd find out that they both come from the same word saying He was bruised for our iniquities and with those bruises we are healed.

That means healing and forgiveness of sin were bought by the same blood that poured from the same wounds on Jesus' body. He paid the same awesome price for them both. He took on His own body every sickness and infirmity of every man just as He took on Himself the sin of every man. He suffered the torments of them all so that we could be free of them all.

The very thought of it staggers the mind. Just imagine, for a moment, if someone were to take every illness ever experienced by anyone in your city—everything from hangnails to the measles to cancer—and put them on one person all at once. It's hard to even think of such a thing, isn't it? We've never seen anybody that sick!

Imagine that same person must also take into his spirit every sin ever committed by anyone in your city. Violence, adultery, perversion, murder, hatred, jealousy, resentment—all of it must enter into him at once. Can you imagine what that would do to someone? Sin is powerful! It will change the color of a person's hair. It will twist their countenance. It will darken the light in their eyes.

Now expand that picture to include the sicknesses and sins of every man, woman and child who will ever live on this planet. Of course, you cannot imagine such horror. But if you could, you would be able to see the awful price Jesus paid for us at Calvary.

Isaiah described the sight of it, saying, "[the Servant of God became an object of horror; many were astonished.] His face and His whole appearance were marred more than any man's, and His form beyond that of the sons of men" (Isaiah 52:14, *The Amplified Bible).*

The weight of all that sin and sickness on one man was so heavy it rocked the earth. It was so terrible the sun refused to shine on it. No wonder the Roman centurion who witnessed Jesus' crucifixion said, "Truly this man was the Son of God" (Mark 15:39). He had never seen a man die like that.

"If It Be Thy Will"

In the light of such a sacrifice, it is as grievous to the heart of God for us to pray, "If it be Thy will, heal me," as it is for us to say, "If it be Thy will, save me." God revealed His will once and for all when He laid our sicknesses on Jesus. Giving us that revelation cost Him dearly. Once, when He spoke to me of Calvary, He said, *It is as close to Me as if it had happened today. It is burned into My consciousness.*

How dare we, then, ignore what happened there and tell some sick brother that it is God's will for him to be sick a little longer so he can learn something?

Isaiah 53:10 says, "It was the will of the Lord to bruise Him; He has put Him to grief and made Him sick" *(The Amplified Bible)*. If it was the will of God to bruise Him and make Him carry our sicknesses, how can it be the will of God to bruise us and make us carry those same sicknesses again? It can't be! That would be a travesty of divine justice!

If you want to see just how repulsive such a thought really is, switch things around for a moment. Think what your reaction would be if a fellow believer came to you and said, "Yesterday I got so drunk, I could hardly walk. Then I beat my wife and my kids. After that I robbed a gas station. But don't blame me for it. God put that sin on me to teach me something."

The very concept is revolting, isn't it? You would never tolerate it. You'd shut it down immediately. "Friend," you'd say, "you have the wrong idea. Jesus shed His precious blood to deliver you from sin. So if you choose to let it into your life, don't blame it on Him because it's not His fault!"

You may think that's an absurd example. You may think no one could ever be that foolish. But, the truth is, there were people in the Apostle Paul's day who preached that very thing. They went around saying that Paul's message of grace meant that we ought to sin so that grace could be shown.

That sounds silly to us today because we know that sin is repugnant to God. He hates it.

It's high time we realized that He hates sickness in the same way. Listen, sin, sickness and disease all came out of the same pit at the same time! God hates it when some devilish germ gnaws the life out of the body of one of His precious children. He designed and formed that body with His own hand out of the dust of the earth—and He made it perfect. How do you think He feels when He sees it twisted and tormented, bringing grief not only to the sufferer, but also to all those who love him?

Don't you ever let anyone tell you that God likes that. He is a Father—not a monster! Such suffering could never be His will.

If by some convoluted stretch of the religious imagination we could decide it is His will for us to be sick, then we'll have to put the hospital and the beer joint in the same category. We'll have to condemn every doctor and every nurse for trying to thwart God's will.

"Now, Brother Copeland, that's stupid."

Yes, it is! Religious tradition is always stupid. It makes men believe things in church they'd never believe on the street. It makes them sit in a pew and agree with a preacher who says we learn from sickness and pain. "Oh yes, amen!" they'll say. But if that same preacher were to take a hammer, go down to the school and start knocking kids in the head to help them learn better, those same amen-ers would have him arrested!

Healing Always Comes

Of course, some sincere-hearted believers have gotten confused about healing because they've seen or heard of instances where a good Christian didn't receive it. We've all heard the stories. "Well, healing couldn't be included in redemption because Sister So-and-So who taught Sunday school every week for 65 years got sick, and God didn't heal her."

I want you to know something about those stories: They are lies. Granted, those who tell them usually don't realize it, but they are lies just the same.

I realize that's a shockingly blunt statement, but the Bible itself is just that blunt. It says: "What if some did not believe and were without faith? Does their lack of faith and their faithlessness nullify and make ineffective and void the faithfulness of God and His fidelity [to His Word]? By no means! Let God be found true though every human being be false and a liar" (Romans 3:3-4, *The Amplified Bible*).

God has made His Word plain to us. He has said, "By whose stripes we were healed" (1 Peter 2:24). He has said, "The prayer of faith shall save the sick, and the Lord shall raise him up" (James 5:15). He has said, "[Jesus] Himself took our infirmities, and bare our sicknesses" (Matthew 8:17).

God always keeps His Word. Healing always comes. The problem has been in our receiving, not in God's giving.

Put that over in the realm of the new birth and you can easily see what I mean. The Bible says that by the righteousness of one, the free gift has come upon all men (Romans 5:18). Jesus has already gone to the cross and been raised from the dead. He has reconciled us to God and made righteousness available to every person on the face of the earth.

Therefore, it always comes. To whom? To anyone who will obey the instructions in Romans 10:9-10: "If thou shalt confess with thy mouth the Lord Jesus, and shalt believe in thine heart that God hath raised him from the dead, thou shalt be saved. For with the heart man believeth unto righteousness; and with the mouth confession is made unto salvation."

Healing comes to the same people. It comes to those who will believe in their hearts that Jesus was crucified and raised from the dead to purchase their healing. It comes to those who will open their mouths in faith and say, "Glory to God, I receive it. I am healed!"

Actually, if you could read that verse in the Greek, you'd see that it pertains to healing just as surely as to the new birth because the Greek word *sozo,* which is translated "saved," literally means "to be made sound, to be delivered from every form of sickness and danger, both temporal and eternal."

What Do You Think Would Happen?

"But if receiving healing is as simple as receiving salvation," you ask, "why are so many Christians still sick?"

First and foremost, it's because the truth about healing has not been consistently preached. Since "faith cometh by hearing, and hearing by the word of God" (Romans 10:17), our failure to teach the fullness of the gospel has left many Christians without enough faith to heal a headache—much less cure cancer.

You know, there was a time not so very long ago when it was just as tough to get people born again as it is to get them healed today. It's true! Religious tradition had convinced people that salvation just couldn't be obtained by the average person. But then, praise God, people like Dwight L. Moody came on the scene and started preaching the new birth. They started telling people that Jesus bore their sins and if they'd receive the gift of salvation in simple faith, they'd be born again!

Whole denominations like the Baptists preached that message to everything that would stand still. You'd hear it in every church service. If you walked in the door and admitted you weren't saved, somebody would grab you and say, "Jesus died for your sins, man! You don't have to stay in that condition. Just trust Him, receive Him as your Lord and He'll save you right now. Then He'll take you to heaven when you die!"

Praise God for all those precious Baptists and every other denomination like them! They preached the new birth until getting saved seemed like the easiest thing in the world.

Now what do you think would happen if everyone picked up on the truth about healing in that same way? What do you think would happen if every born-again believer in town started knocking on doors and having testimony meetings and revival meetings and telling everyone they meet a thousand times over, "Hey, man! Jesus bore your sicknesses and carried your diseases! You don't have to suffer with that cancer. Just trust Jesus and He'll heal you. He does it every time!"

I can tell you what would happen. Healing would become as common as the new birth and we'd wonder why we had so much trouble with it for so long!

What's more, in that environment, if someone prayed for healing and then said, "I don't think I got anything. I don't feel any better," do you know what they'd be told? The same thing people are told today when they doubt their salvation because they don't "feel" saved.

Some mature believer would pull them aside and say, "Now listen, here. You can't go by feelings. You have to do this by faith. If you wait until you feel something to believe you're saved (or healed), you'll never be able to receive!"

Start Your Own Healing Revival

If you're sitting there right now wishing such a healing revival would begin, stop wishing and start your own! Dig into the Word. Study and meditate the truth about healing and redemption. Listen to tapes of men and women of God who have the revelation of it.

Then start preaching. Preach it to yourself. Preach it to your children. Preach it to your dog if he's the only one who will listen. It probably won't do much for him, but it will help you—and that's what matters.

If you'll do that, you'll eventually get to the point where you'll fight sickness and disease the same as you do sin. You'll be just as mean to Satan when it comes to standing for the redemption of your body as you are when it comes to the redemption of your spirit.

When he comes at you with symptoms of sickness, you won't crawl up in the bed and whine, "Why does this always happen to me?" You'll stomp your foot and say, "Glory be to God, this body is off limits to you, Satan. I refuse to allow you to put that foul thing on my body after Jesus has already borne it for me. So you might as well pack it up and go home right now!"

I'm not saying it will be easy. It won't be. Not in this life. Not in this world. Just as you don't live in victory over sin without putting forth an effort, you can't bumble along in life and have God just drop healing in your lap.

No, you'll have to stand for it. You'll have to fight the good fight of faith.

But don't let that scare you. It's a fight you can win. I know you can because 2,000 years ago, Jesus gave you everything you'd ever need to win it. He took your weakness and gave you His strength. He took your sin and gave you His righteousness. He took your sickness and gave you His health. He took your every defeat and gave you His victory in its place.

You are the heir of the Greatest Exchange ever made.

Begin to live like it and this world will never be the same again.

God's Prescription for Divine Health

Gloria Copeland

Chapter 2

"My son, attend to my words; incline thine ear unto my sayings. Let them not depart from thine eyes; keep them in the midst of thine heart. For they are life unto those that find them, and health to all their flesh. Keep thy heart with all diligence; for out of it are the issues of life. Put away from thee a froward mouth, and perverse lips put far from thee."
— PROVERBS 4:20-24

There is a medicine so powerful it can cure every sickness and disease known to man. It has no dangerous side effects. It is safe even in massive doses. And when taken daily according to directions, it can prevent illness altogether and keep you in vibrant health.

Does that sound too good to be true? It's not. I can testify to you by the Word of God and by my own experience that such a supernatural medicine exists. Even more importantly, it is available to you every moment of every day.

You don't have to call your doctor to get it. You don't even have to drive to the pharmacy. All you must do is reach for your Bible, open to Proverbs 4:20-24 and follow the instructions you find there: "My son, attend to my words; incline thine ear unto my sayings. Let them not depart from thine eyes; keep them in the midst of thine heart. For they are life unto those that find them, and health [Hebrew: medicine] to all their flesh. Keep thy heart with all diligence; for out of it are the issues of life. Put away from thee a froward mouth, and perverse lips put far from thee."

As simple as they might sound, those four verses contain the supernatural prescription to divine health. It's a powerful prescription that will work for anyone who will put it to work.

If you have received healing by the laying on of hands, following this prescription will help you maintain that healing. If you have believed for healing, but are experiencing lingering symptoms, it will help you stand strong until you are completely symptom-free. And if you are healthy now, it will help you stay that way—not just for a day or a week, but for the rest of your life!

Powerful Medicine

To understand how this prescription works, you must realize that the Word of God is more than just good information. It actually has life in it. As Jesus said in John 6:63, "It is the spirit that quickeneth [or makes alive]; the flesh profiteth nothing: the words that I speak unto you, they are spirit, and they are life."

Every time you take the Word into your heart, believe it and act on it, that life of which Jesus spoke, the very *life* of God Himself, is released in you. You may have read the healing scriptures over and over again. You may know them as well as you know your own name. Yet every time you read them or hear them preached, they bring you a fresh dose of God's healing power. Each time, they bring life to you and deliver God's medicine to your flesh.

That's because the Word is like a seed. Hebrews 4:12 says it is "alive and full of power—making it active, operative, energizing and effective..." *(The Amplified Bible).* It actually carries within it the power to fulfill itself.

When you planted the Word about the new birth in your heart, then believed and acted on it, that Word released within you the power to be born again. By the same token, when you plant the Word about healing in your heart, believe and act on it, that Word will release God's healing power in you.

"But, Gloria," you may say, "I've met people who know the Bible from cover to cover and still can't get healed!"

No doubt you do. But if you'll look back at God's prescription, you'll find it doesn't say anything about "knowing" the Bible. It says, attend to the Word.

When you attend to something, you give your attention to it. You make it top priority. You set aside other things so you can focus on it. When a nurse is attending to a patient, she constantly looks after him. She doesn't just leave him lying alone in his hospital room while she goes shopping. If someone asks her about her patient, she doesn't feel it's sufficient to say, "Oh, yes. I know him."

In the same way, if you're attending to the Word, you won't leave it lying unopened on the coffee table all day. You won't spend your day focusing your attention on other things.

On the contrary, you'll do what Proverbs 4 says to do. You'll continually incline your ear to God's Word.

Inclining your ear includes more than just putting your physical ears in a position to hear the Word being preached (although that, in itself, is very important). It also requires you to actively engage with God's Word, to believe it and obey it.

In fact, *The Amplified Bible* translates Proverbs 4:20, this way: "My son, attend to my words; consent and submit to my sayings." Submitting to the Word means making adjustments in your life. Say, for example, you hear the Word in Philippians 4:4 that you are to "rejoice in the Lord always." If you've been doing a lot of griping and complaining, you'll have to change in order to submit to that Word. You'll have to repent and alter your behavior.

Take as Directed

In addition to inclining your ear to the Word of God, the Proverbs 4 prescription also says you must keep it before your eyes and not let it depart from your sight. In Matthew 6:22-23, Jesus reveals why that's so important. He says, "The light of the body is the eye: if therefore thine eye be single, thy whole body shall be full of light. But if thine eye be evil, thy whole body shall be full of darkness. If therefore the light that is in thee be darkness, how great is that darkness!"

Your eyes are the gateway to your body. If your eye (or your attention) is on the darkness, or the sickness that is in your body, there will be no light to expel it. If, however, the eyes of your heart are trained strictly on the Word, your whole body will eventually be filled with light, and healing will be the result.

Granted, it isn't easy to keep your attention centered on the Word like that. It takes real effort and commitment. It may require getting up a little earlier in the morning or turning off the television at night. But I urge you to do whatever it takes to take God's medicine exactly as directed.

It won't work any other way!

That really shouldn't be so surprising. After all, we wouldn't expect natural medication to work for us if we didn't take it as prescribed.

No rational person would set a bottle of pills on the night stand and expect those pills to heal them. No one would call the doctor and say, "Hey, Doc! These pills don't work. I've carried them with me everywhere I go—I keep them in the car with me, I set them on my desk at work, I even have them next to me when I sleep at night—but I don't feel any better."

That would be ridiculous. Yet, spiritually speaking, some people do it all the time. They cry and pray and beg God to heal them, all the while ignoring the medicine He's provided. (They might take a quick dose on Sunday when they go to church, but the rest of the week they don't take time for the Word at all!)

Why do people who love God and believe the Bible act that way? I think it's because they don't understand how putting the Word in their hearts can affect their physical bodies. They don't see how something spiritual can change something natural.

If you'll read the Bible, however, you'll see that spiritual power has been affecting this physical world ever since time began. In fact, it was spiritual power released in the form of God's Word that brought this natural world into existence in the first place.

When you realize that God's Word is the force that originally brought into being everything you can see and touch—including your physical body—it's easy to believe that the Word is still capable of changing your body today. It makes perfect sense!

Faith in Two Places

"I'd have no problem at all believing God's Word would heal me if He'd speak to me out loud like He did in Genesis," you might say, "but He hasn't!"

No, and He probably won't, either. God no longer has to thunder His Word down at us from heaven. These days He lives in the hearts of believers, so He speaks to us from the inside instead of the outside. What's more, when it comes to covenant issues like healing, we don't even have to wait on Him to speak.

He has already spoken!

He has already said, "By [Jesus'] stripes ye were healed" (1 Peter 2:24). He has already said, "I am the Lord that healeth thee" (Exodus 15:26). He has already said, "The prayer of faith shall save the sick, and the Lord shall raise him up" (James 5:15).

God has already done His part. So we must do ours. We must take the Word He has spoken, put it inside us and let it change us from the inside out.

You see, everything—including healing—starts inside you. Your future is literally stored up in your heart. As Jesus said, "A good man out of the good treasure of the heart bringeth forth good things: and an evil man out of the evil treasure bringeth forth evil things" (Matthew 12:35).

That means if you want external conditions to be better tomorrow, you'd better start changing your internal condition today. You'd better start taking the Word of God and depositing it in your heart just like you deposit money in the bank. Then you can make withdrawals on it whenever you need it. When sickness attacks your body, you can tap into the healing Word you've put inside you and run that sickness off!

Exactly how do you do that?

You open your mouth and speak—not words of sickness and disease, discouragement and despair, but words of healing and life, faith and hope. You follow the last step of God's divine prescription and "put away from thee a froward mouth, and perverse lips put far from thee" (Proverbs 4:24). In short, you speak the words of God and call yourself healed in Jesus' Name.

Initially, that may not be easy for you to do. But you must do it anyway because for faith to work it must be in two places—in your heart and in your mouth. "For with the heart man believeth unto righteousness; and with the mouth confession is made unto salvation" (Romans 10:10).

Some people say faith will move mountains. But, the scriptural truth is, faith won't even move a molehill for you unless you release it with the words of your mouth.

The Lord Jesus told us that "whosoever shall say unto this mountain, Be thou removed, and be thou cast into the sea; and shall not doubt in his heart, but shall believe that those things which he saith shall come to pass; he shall have whatsoever he saith" (Mark 11:23). Notice the word *say* appears three times in that verse while the word *believe* appears only once. Obviously, Jesus wanted us to know that our words are crucial.

It's also important to note that He did not instruct us to talk about the mountain, He instructed us to talk to it! If we're going to obey Him, we must talk to the mountain of sickness and cast it out of our lives. The Lord told Charles Capps, *I have told My people they can have what they say, but they are saying what they have!* Instead of saying, "I'm healed," most Christians say, "I'm sick," and reinforce the sickness or disease.

"But, Gloria, it bothers me to say I'm healed when my body still feels sick!"

It shouldn't. It didn't bother Abraham. He went around calling himself the Father of Nations for years even though he was as childless as could be. Why did he do it? Because "he believed...God, who quickeneth the dead, and calleth those things which be not as though they were" (Romans 4:17). He was "fully persuaded that, what [God] had promised, he was able also to perform" (verse 21).

You see, Abraham wasn't "trying" to believe God. He wasn't just mentally assenting to it. He had immersed himself in God's Word until that Word was more real to him than the things he could see. It didn't matter to him that he was 100 years old. It didn't matter to him that Sarah was far past the age of childbearing and that she had been barren all her life. All that mattered to him was what God said, because he knew His Word was true.

If you don't have that kind of faith for healing right now, then stay in the Word until you get it! After all, "faith cometh by hearing, and hearing by the word of God" (Romans 10:17). Read, study, meditate, listen to tapes, watch videos of good, faith-filled teaching, and watch our Sunday and daily television broadcast *every day* until God's Word about healing is more real to you than the symptoms in your body. Keep on keeping on until, like Abraham, you "stagger not at the promise of God through unbelief, but grow strong in faith as you give praise and glory to God." (See Romans 4:20, *The Amplified Bible*).

Having Done All...Stand!

As you put God's prescription for health to work in your life, don't be discouraged if you don't see immediate results. Although many times healing comes instantly, there also are times when it takes place more gradually.

So don't let lingering symptoms cause you to doubt. After all, when you go to the doctor, you don't always feel better right away. The medication he gives you often takes some time before it begins to work. But you don't allow the delay to discourage you. You just follow the doctor's orders and expect to feel better soon. Really, you are "treating" your spirit, which is the source of supernatural life and health for your physical body.

Release that same kind of confidence in God's medicine. Realize that the moment you begin to take it, the healing process begins. Keep your expectancy high and make up your mind to continue standing on the Word until you can see and feel the total physical effects of God's healing power.

When the devil whispers words of doubt and unbelief to you, when he suggests that the Word is not working, deal with those thoughts immediately. Cast them down (see 2 Corinthians 10:5). Speak out loud if necessary and say, "Devil, I rebuke you. I bind you from my mind. I will not believe your lies. God has sent His Word to heal me, and His Word never fails. That Word went to work in my body the instant I believed it, so as far as I am concerned, my days of sickness are over. I declare that Jesus bore my sickness, weakness and pain, and I am forever free."

Then, "having done all, to stand. Stand" until your healing is fully manifested (see Ephesians 6:12-14). Steadfastly hold your ground. Don't waver. For as James 1:6-8 says, "He that wavereth is like a wave of the sea driven with the wind and tossed.... let not that man think that he shall receive any thing of the Lord. A double minded man is unstable in all his ways."

Above all, keep your attention trained on the Word—not on lingering symptoms. Be like Abraham who "considered not his own body" (Romans 4:19). Instead of focusing on your circumstances, focus on what God has said to you. Develop an inner image of yourself with your healing fully manifested. See yourself well. See yourself whole. See yourself healed in every way.

Since what you keep before your eyes and in your ears determines what you will believe in your heart and what you will act on, make the Word your No. 1 priority. Keep taking God's medicine as directed and trust the Great Physician to do His wonderful healing work in you!

More Than a
New Year's Resolution

Chapter 3

Marty Copeland

"Commit thy way unto the Lord; trust also in him; and he shall bring it to pass."
— PSALM 37:5

At the same time every year many people make New Year's resolutions. For most, these resolutions are earnest attempts to change. Unfortunately, most people don't realize they're setting themselves up for failure.

A New Year's resolution promises gain, but lacks the substance to produce it. Any resolution that tries to bring about a transformation by fleshly effort instead of by the power of God sets you up for failure. It has no substance.

Lasting victory is never won by our own might or power. True change and total victory occur only when we exercise our faith in the transforming power of God alone.

As a certified personal trainer and aerobics instructor, I'm regularly involved with people who battle overeating or other compulsive behaviors. In their determination to break free from the grip of destructive habits, they often make desperate resolutions. My heart goes out to them because I used to be trapped in that same struggle. For over half my life, I was in bondage to overeating. I was obsessed with diets and exercise. I lost close to a total of 700 pounds through years of gaining, then losing weight. Today, I'm totally, 100 percent free and experiencing the joy that comes with that freedom. But there was a time when I, like so many others, began each New Year with noble resolutions. I always hoped that this year my resolution would be "The Solution"—only to find myself failing and feeling miserable...again.

In theory, resolutions sound good. In practice, however, they fall short. Desperate resolutions are just carnal methods that play right into Satan's deceptive strategy to keep us frustrated and failing until finally we lose all hope that we'll ever be free.

If Satan can keep you in the arena of the flesh, using carnal weapons to fight a spiritual warfare, he can defeat you. But if you'll take the weapons of your warfare which are not carnal but mighty through God, you can defeat the devil and overcome destructive habits in every area of your life.

Jesus said if we continue in His Word, we shall know the truth and the truth shall make us free (John 8:31-32). So don't let the devil lure you into another cycle of failure and disappointment with the temptation of a "quick fix." There is a way out. But you'll need more than a New Year's resolution—you'll need to make a quality decision to put your hope and faith in God.

As you continue in the Word and trust God to conform you to the image of His Son, that burden-removing, yoke-destroying power of Jesus the Anointed One and His Anointing will set you free from the bondage of weight and the weight of bondage. You can confidently put your hope and trust in Him because when the Son makes you free, you are free indeed (John 8:36)!

Harvest of Health

Chapter 4

"So shall my word be that goeth forth out of
my mouth: it shall not return unto me void, but
it shall accomplish that which I please, and it
shall prosper in the thing whereto I sent it."
— Isaiah 55:11

Gloria Copeland

I have some revolutionary news for you. God wants you
healthy! Every day!

Oh, I know that, you may quickly think, *I know God will heal
me when I get sick.*

Yes, that's true, He will. But that's not what I'm saying. I'm
telling you God's perfect will is for you to live continually in divine
health. His will is for you to walk so fully in the power of His Word
that sickness and disease are literally pushed away from you. Isn't
that good news?

You've probably heard a lot about God's healing power but
there is a difference between divine healing and divine health. Years
ago, the powerful preacher John G. Lake put it this way, "Divine
healing is the removal by the power of God of the disease that has
come upon the body. But divine health is to live day by day, hour by
hour in touch with God so that the life of God flows into the body
just as the life of God flows into the mind or flows into the spirit."

I agree that it is wonderful to get healed when you're sick, but
it's more wonderful to live in divine health. And that's what God
has always intended for His people. Even under the Old Covenant
God promised His people immunity from disease. Exodus 23:25
says, "And ye shall serve the Lord your God, and he shall bless thy
bread, and thy water; and I will take sickness away from the midst
of thee."

That promise is even stronger under the New Covenant. Isaiah,
looking forward to what Jesus would accomplish on the cross
wrote, "Surely he [Jesus] hath borne our griefs, and carried our
sorrows...he was wounded for our transgressions, he was bruised
for our iniquities: the chastisement of our peace was upon him; and
with his stripes we are healed" (Isaiah 53:4-5).

The Apostle Peter, looking back at that same event wrote, "Who his own self bare our sins in his own body on the tree, that we, being dead to sins, should live unto righteousness: by whose stripes ye were healed" (1 Peter 2:24).

"*Were healed!*" That's past tense. Jesus finished your healing on the cross. He paid the price for you to be whole. He bought righteousness for your spirit, peace for your mind and healing for your body.

As far as Jesus is concerned, you're not the sick trying to get healed. You're the healed and Satan is trying to steal your health. I remember when Ken and I realized that, it changed everything for us. We quit trying to talk God into healing us and began instead resisting sickness and disease the way we resisted sin.

No Third Story on a Vacant Lot

Once you understand God's will really is for you to live in divine health, you can't help but question why so many believers live sick. It seems puzzling at first. But the answer is very simple. Many of them just aren't willing to do what it takes to be well.

People want to be well. No one wants to be sick. But to be well, you have to make choices. How often have you seen someone with a hacking cough still smoking a cigarette? Or an overweight person eating an ice cream cone?

Our fleshly nature likes to take the easy way. And it's much easier to give in to habits than to break them. It's easier to give in to your flesh and watch television every night like the rest of the world, than to spend your time putting God's healing Word into your heart.

I recently heard Charles Capps say that some people try to build the third story of a building on a vacant lot. That sounds funny, but spiritually speaking it's true. A lot of people want to enjoy the benefits of healing without building the foundation for it from the Word of God.

It can't be done. If you want a building, you have to start below ground level. If you want a harvest, you're going to have to plant something first.

Everything in the natural world works that way. Ken calls it the law of genesis. This law of planting and reaping works in the spirit realm too. It governs health, prosperity—in fact, everything in God's kingdom is governed by the law of planting and reaping.

Jesus taught about it in Mark 4:26-29. There, He said:

> So is the kingdom of God, as if a man should cast seed into the ground; and should sleep, and rise night and day, and the seed should spring and grow up, he knoweth not how. For the earth bringeth forth fruit of herself; first the blade, then the ear, after that the full corn in the ear. But when the fruit is brought forth, immediately he putteth in the sickle, because the harvest is come.

According to the law of sowing and reaping, if you want health, you need to do more than just want it. You even need to do more than believe in healing. You need to plant seed that will eventually grow up and yield a harvest of health.

What kind of seed produces physical health? Proverbs 4:20-22 tells us: "My son, attend to my words; incline thine ear unto my sayings. Let them not depart from thine eyes; keep them in the midst of thine heart. For they are life unto those that find them, and health to all their flesh."

That word *health* in Hebrew means "medicine." God's Word has life in it. It is actually spirit food. As you feed on it, you become strong spiritually and physically.

"Let them not depart from thine eyes." Read the Word. Meditate on the Word. That's taking God's medicine. If you will be faithful to take it continually, it eventually will be as hard for you to get sick as it ever was for you to get well.

But it's a process. You can't just read the healing scriptures once and then go on about your business. You must continually feed on the Word of God to keep the crop of healing coming up in your life.

What Did You Say?

Isaiah 55:11 says the Word of God prospers (or succeeds) in the thing for which it is sent. That means His Word about healing will produce healing. It may not produce it right away, but the more you let the Word work in you, the greater your results will be.

In other words, the size of your harvest will depend on how much seed you plant. How much time and attention you give to the Word of God will determine how much crop you will yield.

You see, your heart is actually your spirit. Its capacity is unlimited. You can plant as much seed in your heart as you have hours in a day.

If you'll build your life around the Word, you can have a full return. Jesus called it a hundredfold return (Mark 4:20).

Now some people will argue about that. They'll say, "Well, it didn't work for me! I put God's Word about healing into my heart and I'm still sick!"

But do you know what? They give themselves away the minute they say such things. Jesus taught, "Out of the abundance of the heart the mouth speaketh" (Matthew 12:34). If those people had actually planted God's Word in their hearts in abundance, they'd be talking about healing, not sickness! They would be saying, "By His stripes I am healed!"

The same is true for you. The more you put God's Word in your heart, the stronger you'll become. And eventually that Word inside you will begin to come out of your mouth in power and deliverance.

Don't wait until you have a need to start speaking the Word. Start speaking it now.

I'll never forget the first time I realized the importance of speaking God's Word. It was years ago when Ken had just started preaching and I was staying at home with our children. We were in a desperate situation financially and I was eager for answers.

One day as I was sitting at my typewriter, typing notes and listening to tapes, I read Mark 11:23. "For verily I say unto you, That whosoever shall say unto this mountain, Be thou removed, and be thou cast into the sea; and shall not doubt in his heart, but shall believe that those things which he saith shall come to pass; he shall have whatsoever he saith."

Suddenly, the truth of that last phrase just jumped out at me. And the Lord spoke to my heart and said, *In consistency lies the power.*

He was telling me that it's not just the words you speak when you pray that change things, it's the words you speak all the time!

If you want to see your desire come to pass, you need to make your words match your prayers. Don't try to pray in faith and then get up and talk unbelief. Talk faith all the time!

Romans 4:17 says God "calleth those things which be not as though they were." So if you want to receive something from God, follow His example. Speak it. That's the way faith works. You speak the Word of God concerning what you want to happen.

If what you're looking for is health, then go to the Word that tells you, "By His stripes you were healed," and put that in your mouth. Don't talk sickness. Talk health. Don't talk the problem. Talk the answer.

What You Plant Always Grows

"But Gloria," you say, "all that sounds so simple!"

It is simple! Sometimes I think that's why God chose me to teach it. Because I'm simple. When I read the Word of God, I just believe it is speaking to me personally. I don't worry and fuss and say, "Well, I wish that would work for me, but I don't think it will because of this or that...." I just expect God to do what He says.

You can do the same thing. You can come to the Word like a little child and say, "Lord, I receive this. I believe Your Word above all and I trust You with my life." If you will, you'll never be disappointed.

How can you get that kind of simple, childlike faith? By hearing the Word of God.

Romans 10:17 says, "faith cometh by hearing, and hearing by the word of God." But you need to know something else: Doubt comes by hearing also. That's why Jesus said, "Be careful what you are hearing" (Mark 4:24, *The Amplified Bible*).

What you're hearing can be a matter of life and death when you're dealing with healing. If you're going to a church, for example, that teaches healing has passed away or that God uses sickness to teach you something—and you keep hearing that Sunday after Sunday—what do you think will grow in your heart? Doubt, not faith.

What you plant inside your heart grows—always. Doubt will grow and keep you bound. Truth will grow and make you free. So be careful what you're hearing. Listen to the Word of God. As Proverbs 4:21 says, "Let them [that Word] not depart from thine eyes; keep them [it] in the midst of thine heart."

Read the Word every day. Make note cards for yourself using the healing scriptures and tape them to your mirror.

Play teaching tapes. Listen to them in your car. Listen to them while you dress in the morning. If you'll listen to the Word while you're driving back and forth to work every day, you'll be surprised how fruitful that time will become. It will change your life. I challenge you to try it!

Don't Let Them Throw You

God's words have power in them. When you keep them in the midst of your heart, they become life and healing and health. They're medicine. God's medicine.

But beware. People will try to discourage you and keep you from taking that medicine. They'll tell you things like, "If God wants us to live in divine health, why did Sister So-and-So suffer so much sickness? And she was a fine Christian."

Don't let them throw you off track. Instead, just remember this: You don't live in divine health because you're a fine Christian. No one does. You live in divine health because you take the Word of God, and you keep it in front of your eyes. You keep it going in your ears. You keep it in the midst of your heart and you apply it to your life.

You live in divine health because you believe God for it, because you talk about it, and because you act on it—day, after day, after day.

Don't wait until an emergency comes. Don't wait until your body is weak and sick to start feeding on healing scriptures. Start now. Plant God's Word of healing in the good faith-soil of your heart daily—and then, get excited. Your harvest of health is on its way!

Stop Those Fits of Carnality!

"To be carnally minded is death; but to be spiritually minded is life and peace."
— ROMANS 8:6

Jesse Duplantis

My blood was boiling!

There I was on my way to a spiritual meeting. Born again, Spirit-filled and anointed of God for ministry—I was on a mission and late for my plane. With my wife, Cathy, in the passenger seat and our 6-year-old daughter in the back, I had been making good time.

Then another car came flying out on the road. From a fast rate of 60 miles an hour, the car slowed to 35. I tried to pass, but the driver thought both lanes belonged to her. You've probably been behind a man or woman who drove like that. I went to the left—she went to the left. I went to the right—she went to the right.

Soon Tabasco™ sauce was coming up my legs: "God, *do* something with this woman!"

I began to shout through the windshield to her. "Hey, if you can't drive the car, park it!" Finally, I thought, *Brother, if she just goes to the right a half inch, I'm going to put my foot in the carburetor, slam to the left, hit the grass, ride the median— whatever—I'm going to pass that woman!*

I fussed. I fumed. But before I got my chance to pass her, the muffler fell off her car. I was too close to miss it. Boom, boom, boom, boom, boom. Two of my tires were destroyed.

As she puttered off across the horizon, I shouted, "Why you...if I could catch you...."

Then out of the mouth of babes....

"You'd tell her that Jesus loves her, huh, Daddy?" my daughter interrupted.

What had I done?

I had a fit—a fit of carnality.

Had Any Fits Lately?

You've had your fits, too. Don't try to tell me you haven't!

It may have happened after you watched a dessert commercial on television—and before you knew it you were in the kitchen stuffing cake in your mouth as fast as you could. It may have happened when an anointed church service went past lunch. It may have happened with someone you love—one day you were saying, "I love my wife so much. I can't live without her." The next day you were saying, "How'd we get together? Get out of my way!"

These are fits of carnality—fits where you let your flesh take over. Jesus knew what they were. Paul knew too. He'd had his share. In Romans 8:6-8 he tells us very clearly about fits of carnality: "For to be carnally minded is death; but to be spiritually minded is life and peace. Because the carnal mind is enmity against God: for it is not subject to the law of God, neither indeed can be. So then they that are in the flesh cannot please God."

What was Paul saying? That "your fits of carnality have almost cost you your life." Any time we get out of the realm of faith, we get into the realm of carnality, or flesh and death. We get into a realm where we cannot please God, because without faith it is impossible to please God (Hebrews 11:6). Any time we get out of faith and into the carnal realm, we have set ourselves up for a fit of carnality.

A Dead Cat and a Disobedient Woman!

Soon after I was saved, the pipes froze and broke in our little house in Southern Louisiana. I had been a rock musician, not a handyman, so I was not looking forward to this chore. I pulled on my coveralls and dragged myself through a sea of cold water and mud in 30-degree weather. I was aggravated, uncomfortable and needed a helper.

So I asked Cathy, "Cathy, I need some help."

"Oh, I can't come underneath that house," she said. "There's spiders under there."

That made me so mad. "*I need some help!*"

"I can't crawl underneath that house...it's dirty," she said. "But I'll help you."

How? I wondered.

"All right," I said, but I just got madder. Then I cut myself on a piece of broken glass. And I busted my knuckles trying to break the old piece of pipe out. But finally, I got the cold line fixed.

"Cathy," I hollered through the floor, "there's two knobs, one on the left and one on the right. Don't touch the left knob. That's the hot water. Turn on the right knob, because the cold line's fixed."

"OK."

An instant later I was being scalded with hot water. She had turned on the left knob!

"Cathy, turn it off. I am being burned!"

Cathy turned it off, and came to apologize. As she looked down under the house, she said, "Oh, Jesse, don't move! There's a dead cat by your head."

I had smelled a strange odor, but only then did I see it—a cat with its brains hanging out.

"*Grab it!*" I told her.

"I don't touch dead cats," she squealed.

And then I had a fit.

"Woman, when I get out from under this house...."

As I pushed the cat, a thorn jabbed me in the back.

"What is this?" I wailed.

"Oh, I threw some cactus underneath the house," Cathy said.

Cactus...dead cat...scalding water. Did I ever have a fit of carnality. With cuts in my body and a cat in my hand, I was tearing out from underneath that house ready to tell Cathy what I thought, when I was greeted by my unsaved neighbor.

"How you doing, preacher?" he asked. "You know I wouldn't touch that dead cat if I were you. What's the problem anyway?"

I'd been witnessing to this man. Suddenly, I didn't know what to say. But he surmised things pretty quickly.

"Your wife won't help you, huh?"

I said, "How'd you know that?"

"Well, I busted a pipe earlier this morning and tried to get my wife to help. She wouldn't do it, either. You want me to give you a hand?"

While I'd been telling this man, "Jesus is the greatest thing in the world. My God gives. Jesus can handle anything..." my actions were adding..."except a broken pipe, a dead cat and a disobedient woman!"

You can take this to the bank: Every time you have a fit of carnality, somebody is going to see you do it. So how do we stop ourselves from having these fits?

Sound Words Are Salvation Words

First, do what Paul told Timothy to do: "Hold fast the form of sound words, which thou hast heard of me, in faith and love which is in Christ Jesus. That good thing which was committed unto thee keep by the Holy Ghost which dwelleth in us" (2 Timothy 1:13-14).

That day, years ago, as I was driving to the airport, I had a choice. I could have prayed this: "Lord, I'm kind of in a hurry. Would You mind moving that little lady over to the side?"

But it seemed like it was much easier to holler through the windshield. I didn't hold fast to the form of sound words. Instead, I gave myself over to "no" words—words that had no power to bring God on the scene of my need.

Sound words are salvation words. They are the words that can change your situation. They are words that feed and strengthen your spirit.

You will not overcome fits of carnality by focusing your efforts on the flesh. There's no good thing in the flesh. If you think in your finite mind that you're going get this flesh to become holy, you have missed it by 100 miles. First Corinthians 2:14 tells us that "the natural man receiveth not the things of the Spirit of God: for they are foolishness unto him: neither can he know them, because they are spiritually discerned."

But if you will feed and strengthen your spirit on sound words, you will become no longer conformed to this world, but transformed by the renewing of your mind (Romans 12:2). Sound words will turn your spirit into a dynamo that totally regenerates the thought processes of your soul (mind, will and emotions). And then from that mind, will and emotions (soul) will come a cross that crucifies your flesh on a daily basis. If the weight of the Cross is on your mind, will and emotions, you will speak words of faith. Any time you are speaking soundly, a fit will not take place.

Submit Yourself to God

Second, when you see a fit of carnality coming on, "Submit yourselves therefore to God. Resist the devil, and he will flee from you" (James 4:7). What we typically want to do first is to deal more with our anger than with our submitting. We want to start rebuking the devil. But that's the wrong order. Before the devil is ever mentioned, before we have our full-blown fit of carnality, we must first submit ourselves to God.

To submit to God, we must first know what God has said. If we know what He has said, then we should be repeating what He has said. We should speak sound words, and submit ourselves to what we are speaking.

The Bible prophet Elijah spoke God's Word boldly in the presence of the people, challenging the prophets of Baal. When he did, God confirmed those words with a mighty demonstration of His power.

Then Queen Jezebel threatened to kill him, and Elijah took off running. He had a fit of carnality. Why? Because he didn't submit to the sound words that he was speaking about God's power to deliver. Elijah's first thought was that Jezebel was more powerful than he. Eventually, he realized what he had done and did submit to God's Word.

So say what God has said, then make sure you submit to the sound words you are saying. You may be saying and believing the right things, but if you don't submit yourself to what you believe, you'll have a fit of carnality every day of your life.

Resist (Don't Assist) the Devil

Finally, resist the devil. Notice the order in James 4:7, "Submit yourselves therefore to God. Resist the devil, and he will flee from you." First, submit to God, then resist the devil.

For years I didn't know how to resist the devil. I blamed my temper on my Cajun heritage. Finally the Lord said, *Jesse, it's just you assisting the devil!*

As long as we are assisting the devil instead of resisting him, he's going to be running toward us and not away from us. We'll actually just be helping him with our fits of carnality.

Peter was known for fits like this. When the priests and soldiers came to arrest Jesus, Peter pulled out a knife and cut a guy's ear off. Just ripped it off, thinking he was helping.

Jesus picked the guy's ear up and put it back on his head, saying, "What's the matter with you, Peter?"

Peter was probably thinking: *I was just trying to help You out.*

You can be sitting in a meeting where there is a mighty move of God and be having a fit of carnality because you have not submitted yourself to God, and have not resisted the devil. Maybe your body is rebelling because the service is going so long. Or you may be embarrassed because under the anointing your wife seems out of control. You're assisting the devil, and you can grieve the Holy Ghost right in the middle of a powerful service. Someone may not get saved or healed because you had a fit of carnality.

Many of us are like Peter—we need time to grow. And the way we grow is by submitting ourselves to God. Then we can begin to resist the devil instead of assisting him. Soon we'll find Satan beginning to flee from us instead of coming toward us, and our fits of carnality will happen less and less.

Watch the Devil Run!

Don't misunderstand me. I'm not saying this life is easy. Everyone has aggravations. But an aggravation does not have to grow into a full-blown, no-holds-barred fit of carnality.

Hold fast to the form of sound words which you've heard of God. Live as a child of God, led by the Spirit of God, and submitted to Him. "For as many as are led by the Spirit of God, they are the sons of God" (Romans 8:14). You can walk in the spirit—all the time. The promise of that walk is life and peace (see Romans 8:6).

As you allow yourself to be led by the Spirit, He will give you opportunity to take authority over that aggravation so that it doesn't become a fit of carnality. Soon you'll be resisting the devil instead of assisting him.

Satan always works through a fit of carnality. If you will jump this hurdle and take away his ability to work up a fit of carnality in you, you will have closed the door to almost anything he could ever do to you. And whenever you're around, all he'll have left to do is to turn his tail and run!

Winning the Battle of the Flesh

Chapter 6

*Kenneth
Copeland*

"For though we walk in the flesh, we do not war after the flesh: (For the weapons of our warfare are not carnal, but mighty through God to the pulling down of strong holds;) Casting down imaginations, and every high thing that exalteth itself against the knowledge of God, and bringing into captivity every thought to the obedience of Christ."
— 2 CORINTHIANS 10:3-5

Do you know what it's like to be in a losing battle with your own body? I do...and I can tell you, it's miserable.

There have been times in my life as a believer when I wanted with all my heart to behave one way, and my body seemed absolutely intent on doing exactly the opposite. Times when I desperately wanted to lose excess weight, yet kept right on stuffing myself with every kind of unhealthy food I could get my hands on. Times, years ago, when I so longed to quit smoking that I threw my cigarettes out the car window...then turned the car around to go back and get them when I realized I didn't have the money for another pack.

You know what I'm talking about. You've been there too. Every Christian has in one way or another. We call it the battle of the flesh.

The crucial element in having victory is making a quality decision, one from which there is no retreat and about which there is no argument. It is the one thing God will not do for you. He has set before us life and death, but the actual choosing, the quality decision, is up to you.

But once you've made that quality decision, how do you stand when your flesh moans and groans and kicks and fusses? When you feel torn in two? When you're tempted to condemn yourself?

You take authority over your flesh—and you win.

Some people would say, "Oh yes, Brother Copeland. We have to fight our flesh constantly. It has an evil nature, the nature of the old man, you know, and it opposes the nature of God in us."

Please excuse me for being blunt, but I have to tell you, that's the most schizophrenic thing I've ever heard in my life. When we're born again, we're not half God and half devil. Jesus paid the price for our whole being on the cross—spirit, soul and body.

It bothers me when I hear a believer talk about his old, wicked, sinful, terrible flesh. We shouldn't talk like that! Jesus allowed stripes to be laid on His back so that our flesh could be healed. Ephesians 5:29 says, "No man ever yet hated his own flesh; but nourisheth and cherisheth it...." You're doing something that is unscriptural and unnatural in the sight of God when you begin to hate your own body.

"But I thought we were supposed to crucify our flesh!"

If you're born again, you've already done that. Galatians 5:24 says, "And they that are Christ's have crucified the flesh with the affections and lusts."

"Then why am I still having such a struggle?"

Quite simply, it's because you haven't developed your ability to walk in the spirit. For as Galatians 5:16 says, if you "walk in the Spirit...ye shall not fulfil the lust of the flesh." It does not say, "Hate your flesh enough, and someday maybe it will settle down."

Flesh Does What It's Told

To fully understand what I'm saying, there are some things you need to understand about your physical body. No. 1 is the fact that it has no nature of its own. It's just flesh, blood and bone that does what it has been trained to do.

Simply put, your flesh does what it's told to do. For example, if you decide to stand up, your body will stand up, right? But has your body ever just jumped up and run all around on its own without consulting you? Of course not! It's not made to do that.

Now once you train your body and teach it to do certain things and act in certain ways, it will expand and develop in those abilities. It will actually begin to do those things without conscious thought on your part. If it weren't that way, you'd still be struggling trying to button your shirt for 20 minutes like you did when you were 4 years old. You'd never be able to expand in any direction if your body couldn't accept training.

The problem most believers have with their flesh is that it's still living the way they trained it to live before they were born again. It's trying to go that same, old sinful way it has practiced for so many years. It doesn't yet know the believer has been saved.

What's more, it's being successful in going that way because instead of taking charge of their flesh and putting it under the direction of their spirit, those believers have let their flesh run the show.

Let me tell you, that's backward. Your flesh has no business lording it over your spirit. It does not have the equipment, the ability, the calling or the nature to rule this human system. It is merely a tool. It is a natural vehicle that enables the spirit man to live and have authority in this natural, physical world.

The body is not equipped to be in charge. Neither is the mind. When leadership pressure is put on the mind, eventually it will snap.

That's why it is so vital to understand that you are a spirit, you have a soul and you live in a body. Your spirit man, once it's been born again and re-created by the Spirit of God, is equipped to rule that system. A reborn spirit man has the capacity to take the mental computer God gave him and the body God put him in and bring them both into obedience to Christ Jesus. The spirit man is equipped for ascendancy over the human system. When he's in charge, taught and trained by the Holy Spirit and infused with power from on high, he simply cannot be beaten!

But far too many believers are living backward. They're allowing their bodies, which are highly skilled and trained in the ways of the world, to determine their choices in life. They know they shouldn't—and they struggle against it by trying to impose external rules and regulations on themselves. But that doesn't work. You can't train the flesh from the outside in; you have to do it from the inside out.

These believers are like the Galatians who reverted to living by Jewish law. Let's read what Paul wrote to them in Galatians 5:16-18, 22-23:

> This I say then, Walk in the Spirit, and ye shall not fulfil the lust of the flesh. For the flesh lusteth against the Spirit, and the Spirit against the flesh: and these are contrary the one to the other: so that ye cannot do the things that ye would. But if ye be led of the Spirit, ye are not under the law.... But the fruit of the Spirit is love, joy, peace, longsuffering, gentleness, goodness, faith, meekness, temperance: against such there is no law.

According to that scripture, if you're led by your spirit, there won't be any need to impose law on your flesh because your spirit man has been reborn. He's not going to break the law of God—it's written on his heart. (See Hebrews 8:10.) He has the Spirit of God living in there with him, teaching him.

I'll tell you something else that's exciting. If you'll develop your spirit man and put him in charge of your body instead of vice versa, eventually you'll be able to train that body to work with your spirit instead of against it. (That is great news to me. I get tired of fighting my flesh!)

Hebrews 5:13-14 says, "For every one that useth milk is unskilful in the word of righteousness: for he is a babe. But strong meat belongeth to them that are of full age, even those who by reason of use have their senses exercised to discern both good and evil."

Practice, Practice, Practice!

Let's look at those verses again. How do they say to bring your senses in line? First, by becoming skillful in the word of righteousness; and second, by reason of use, or by practice.

You have to practice walking in the things of the spirit. Practice walking by faith. Practice walking in love. Practice, practice, practice!

At first, your flesh will rebel against it. It's not been trained that way and it will be contrary for a while. Some people don't realize that; therefore they get discouraged when they stumble around and fall the first few times they try to walk by the spirit in some area.

They're like a little boy I heard about who used to bat cross-handed. He couldn't get a full swing at the ball because he had his grip reversed. One day his dad said, "Son, don't bat like that. Put your hands the right way so you can swing all the way around."

"I can't hit anything that way!" the boy protested.

"Yes, you can. Come on, I'll show you." The dad helped the boy get his hands right, then backed off and pitched a ball to him. When the boy swung and missed, he threw the bat down in disgust and said, "See there, I told you I couldn't hit anything like that!"

That's the way some Christians are. They decide to walk in love, mess up once and then say, "See there, I knew I couldn't do it!"

Don't be that way. Keep practicing. Pick out some old boy who's nearly impossible to love and start practicing on him. If you strike out the first time at bat, don't worry about it. There's more than three strikes in this game. You just keep swinging until you hit.

Somebody once asked me, "Don't you ever have any failures?" No, I don't, because I don't play nine-inning games. We play until I win. I have a lot of opportunities to fail if I receive failure. My shortcomings are many. I've fallen on my face many times. But I don't count that as failure. I just count that as practice. But when I win, praise God, that's for real!

"But Brother Copeland, that's not playing fair." You show me in the Word of God where it says we have to play fair with the devil. I don't play fair with him. I go in with a stacked deck. I go in with the Name of Jesus that's above every name. There's nothing fair about that. But that's OK because the devil is already whipped. We don't have to play fair with him anymore, we just go in and exercise the victory.

No Condemnation Allowed

There's one serious mistake we've made right here that has tripped us up in the past and kept us from playing until we win and it's this: We've let the devil put us under condemnation.

Romans 8:1 says, "There is therefore now no condemnation to them which are in Christ Jesus, who walk not after the flesh, but after the Spirit." The condemnation of the carnal mind will weaken the spirit man. Yet we use condemnation on ourselves and each other all the time.

Say, for example, a young man makes Jesus the Lord of his life. He's just gotten up from the altar. He has long hair, dirty feet and a pack of cigarettes he'll probably smoke as soon as he leaves the church. Don't you start condemning him for those things. That man is walking in the spirit in all the light he has.

Now, as he hears the Word of God on deliverance, one of these days, he'll reach in his pocket and pitch those cigarettes away. He won't need those anymore.

That's what happened to me. I fought cigarettes with everything I had. I threw away more of them than I smoked. I knew I ought not to be smoking those things. Yet I went from smoking a pack and a half a day to three packs a day after I got saved.

Some people would say that was proof I wasn't saved, but they'd be wrong. I was born again. I knew it!

Two and a half months later, I received the Baptism in the Holy Spirit and spoke with other tongues. Still, I was fighting those cigarettes with both hands and feet. Why? My spirit was trying to get me to believe God and quit, but my body was fighting to keep doing what it had been trained to do.

I was torn between the two. Every time I would light a cigarette, it would just tear me up inside. Yet I was walking in all the light I had. I didn't know how to break the power of that thing.

I finally went to a meeting in Houston, Texas, and heard godly men preach under the Anointing of God that Jesus was coming back. You know, the Word says when a man puts his hope in the return of Jesus, it will purify him, and that's what it did for me. I walked away from that meeting without any desire for tobacco. Years have come and gone since then, and I haven't had any desire for it at all.

My flesh had to get in line once this spirit man (the real me) was fed the food of the Word of God. It had to yield.

What you need to do is develop your own spirit and become skillful in the Word of righteousness in this area. Learn to confess, "There is no condemnation to those who are in Christ Jesus—and that's me. Therefore, there is no condemnation to me, praise God. I'm walking after the dictates of my spirit, not after the dictates of my flesh."

Then turn your ear off to anybody who tries to condemn you.

If you think I'm giving you license to sin, you're wrong. (I've found people don't need it. They sin without a license all the time.) I'm taking for granted you've come to know that sin doesn't work and that you're looking for a way to stop sinning.

With that said, what you need to realize is that you don't need somebody feeding you condemnation because of your flesh. You need somebody feeding you the righteousness of the Word of God so you can take authority over that flesh.

There may be some things in your life that are a little slow coming around. You will have to resist the devil in those areas. But you can stand against him. You can take the Word of God and put him out.

In the meantime, do not allow yourself to be subjected to harassment or condemnation whether it be physical or spiritual. It's dangerous.

Some years ago, there was a nurse who walked into a hospital room where some friends and I were praying for a man. You could tell when she came in that she would have given anything to join in on our prayer. Finally, one of the men turned to her and asked if she knew the Lord Jesus Christ. "Well, I used to know Him," she answered as tears started running down her cheeks. "But I'm beyond salvation now."

"What do you mean you're beyond salvation?" asked my friend. "What in the world did you do?"

Do you know what it was? She cut her hair! Now that may sound ridiculous to you, but to her it was very real. People in her denomination had so condemned her for cutting her hair that she believed with all her heart she was going to hell.

You can see how that kind of condemnation weakens a person's spirit. Satan uses it to get them to a point where they think, *Well, I'm going to hell anyway. I might as well just sin some more.* Of course, that's a lie. The deeper they get into sin, the more condemned they get and the devil just keeps tightening down the noose until it kills them.

Don't let yourself be subjected to that kind of condemnation. Don't believe it. Don't let yourself or anyone else say things like, "I'm so unworthy. I'm so bad. I'm so worthless." That's against the Word of God. If Jesus walked through the door and stood right here for the next 20 years, preaching every minute of every day, He would never call you unworthy. I can prove it to you in Hebrews 2:11. It says, "He is not ashamed to call them [us] brethren."

If Jesus isn't ashamed of you, then you don't have any business being ashamed of yourself!

So stop it and start believing what the Bible says. Believe that you're God's workmanship created in Christ Jesus. Start confessing that. Instead of talking about what a messed-up rascal you are, start agreeing with the Word and calling yourself the righteousness of God in Christ Jesus (2 Corinthians 5:21). Practice seeing yourself that way. Practice seeing yourself operating in the victory. After all, Jesus has already won it for you. So receive that victory by faith.

One time a fellow came up to me and said, "Brother Copeland, I'll tell you what my problem is. It's my flesh."

I said, "Well, overcome it."

"But, you don't understand!"

"No, but Jesus does," I answered. "And He said He's already overcome the world. So go get in the Word, pray, believe God and walk on off from that problem. The power is within you to do it."

Suddenly it hit him what I was saying. He stopped being hung up on the problem and started focusing on the answer.

That's what you need to do. Quit seeing yourself defeated by your flesh and start seeing yourself like the Word says you are—raised up together with Jesus and seated with Him in heavenly places! (See Ephesians 2:6.) Get your perspective on things from that heavenly position with Him.

Meditate in the Word and give your spirit man something to grow on. As 1 Peter 2:2 says, "Desire the sincere milk of the word, that ye may grow thereby." Then move on to the "strong meat [of the Word which] belongeth to them that are of full age, even those who by reason of use have their senses exercised to discern both good and evil" (Hebrews 5:14).

Bring your spirit man into ascendancy over your mind and your body. You'll still have to fight the fight of faith to keep them in line. But if you're walking in the spirit, you'll win every time. With a healthy Word-controlled, obedient body, you'll be glad you did.

You'll Never Have to Wonder Again

"...He was wounded for our transgressions, he was bruised for our iniquities: the chastisement of our peace was upon him; and with his stripes we are healed."

Gloria Copeland

— ISAIAH 53:5

Have you ever heard a group of people discussing someone else's tragic illness? Inevitably, one of them will shake their head and say, "Doesn't God work in mysterious ways?"

Then another from that same group will start praying, "God, if it's Your will, please heal so-and-so," as if they're not at all certain whether it's God's will or not.

If you've heard that kind of thing very much, you may well be wondering what to believe about the issue of sickness and disease. So let me help set things straight today: Sickness and disease are not the will of God. They never have been and they never will be. They're contrary to His will. How do I know? Because I've checked out the places where God's will is perfectly demonstrated and I found that sickness and disease weren't there.

Take heaven, for example. God's will is carried out there perfectly. Is there sickness in heaven? Of course not!

"But Gloria," you say, "maybe God's will for earth and God's will for heaven are different."

Jesus obviously didn't think so. He taught His disciples to pray for God's will to be done "in earth, as it is in heaven" (Matthew 6:10).

If you need more evidence that sickness isn't part of God's will, take a look at the Garden of Eden before the Fall of Man. God created that garden according to His own will. Everything He put there was good—just like in heaven. There was no death, no sorrow, no sickness and disease, no lack of any kind. Health, happiness and prosperity were there in abundance. Why?

239

Because that's what God wanted for man. It was His will then, and it still is now.

The Bible says God never changes (James 1:17). He couldn't change because He was right the first time. He has never changed His will, never changed His direction, never changed His plan for man.

The reason there's sickness and disease on the earth now is not because God's will changed. It's because man (who had been given dominion over the earth) stepped outside of that will through disobedience. Ever since the day that Adam and Eve yielded themselves to Satan in the Garden, God's will has not been done on the earth as a whole.

You may be wondering, *If that's the case, won't I have to put up with sickness and disease as long as I live on the earth?*

No, you won't!

Jesus came to earth and gave Himself as a sacrifice for sin in order to buy back for you everything that Adam lost. He came to destroy all the works of the devil—sickness and disease included! Isaiah 53:5 says, "He was wounded for our transgressions, he was bruised for our iniquities: the chastisement of our peace was upon him; and with his stripes we are healed."

Once you receive Jesus as Lord of your life, you're made right with God again. All the rights and privileges God originally intended you to have (the right to things like fellowship with God, health and prosperity) are restored.

"If that's true, then why are so many believers still sick?"

Because many have never exercised those rights!

You see, even though Jesus has already defeated the devil and taken away his authority in the earth, He's instructed us to enforce that defeat. The devil has no legal right to kill or steal from the children of God, but he's an outlaw! So he'll do it anyway as long as we'll let him get away with it.

We've got to enforce his defeat by speaking the Word of God in faith. As James 4:7 says, we've got to resist the devil and he will flee from us.

If you don't know how to do that, you'd better find out because as long as you remain passive, Satan will put sickness and disease on you every chance he gets. Ignorance is not bliss when it comes to spiritual things.

I've heard people say, "We did all we knew to do and that person died anyway." In the first place that is rarely ever true. Most of the time people do all that is comfortable to do and that is entirely different. Other times Christians might do all they know, but the problem is that they just don't know enough.

That's the reason God commands us to be diligent in His Word. We need to find out how God operates and how He wants us to operate. The more time we spend in His Word learning about that, the more victorious we're going to be.

This is serious business. Hosea 4:6 says, "My [God's] people are destroyed for lack of knowledge"! That's why so many die before their days are fulfilled. Not because it's God's will—but for lack of knowledge. They don't know the Word of God.

Jesus knew the Word of God and the will of God perfectly. He understood that sickness was a work of the devil. So He demonstrated God's will by setting people free from sickness and disease at every opportunity.

Colossians 1:15 says that Jesus is "the exact likeness of the unseen God" *(The Amplified Bible)*. That means you can see what God does by watching what Jesus does. And do you know what? Jesus healed everyone who came to Him in faith.

He never refused to heal anyone. He never said, "I'm sorry. I guess you'll have to keep that sickness because God has sent it to you for a purpose."

No! The Bible says:

Jesus went forth...moved with compassion...and he healed their sick.... and great multitudes came unto him, having with them those that were lame, blind, dumb, maimed, and many others, and cast them down at Jesus' feet; and he healed them: Insomuch that the multitude wondered, when they saw the dumb to speak, the maimed to be whole, the lame to walk, and the blind to see: and they glorified the God of Israel (Matthew 14:14, 15:30-31).

Religious tradition says that God gets glory when we bear up nobly under the agony of sickness and disease. But that's not what the Bible says. It says God gets glory when the blind see and the lame walk and the maimed are made whole!

And speaking of religious tradition, have you noticed that religious people always talk about the good old days when God did mighty miracles? They also talk about the great things He's going to do in the future. But when you start talking about now, they get upset. When you say Jesus heals today, they don't want to hear that.

Jesus ran into that situation. In His hometown of Nazareth, people were religious. They believed the Word of God—as long as it pertained to yesterday or tomorrow. But when Jesus told them, *"Today* is this scripture fulfilled in your ears," they got mad. And, the Bible says that as a result, Jesus was able to do no mighty works among them.

You can see that same principle at work in the world today. You can go preach the Word of God to religious folks—you can open the Bible and read it right to them—and they'll get all huffy and tell you that what you just read has passed away. They'll insist that God doesn't do those kinds of things anymore. What's more, they'll be proven right every time because their attitude will keep God from working even one miracle among them, just like it did at Nazareth.

But in Africa, where people haven't been taught such religious traditions, when somebody stands up and announces, "I come to you as a messenger from the Most High God," people believe what he has to say. When they hear that Jesus, Lord of lords and King of kings and Son of the Most High God, shed His blood for them, when they hear He's sent His messenger to tell them that He'll deliver them from sin and sickness and death today, they get excited.

They don't sit there and think, *Well now, that's not what my denomination teaches.*

They don't argue with the Word of God. They just believe it and people begin to get healed. People start throwing away their crutches and flinging off their bandages. They don't argue with the man of God. They believe him. That's why people get such dramatic results in countries like Africa. Simple faith is the result because the people just believe what they hear without reservation.

When we learn to hear the Word of God like that, the same thing will happen where we live. God is no respecter of persons. If He'll do that in Africa, He'll do it in Oklahoma City or Chicago or San Francisco. God is the same. It's how we receive the Word that makes the difference.

I want to give you a chance right now to receive God's Word like that. The Bible says, "By His stripes you were healed." Your healing has been bought and paid for by Jesus Christ. It belongs to you.

You may say, "Well, I sure don't feel healed." Listen. This is the Word of the Most High God. You act on it. Demand that sickness and disease leave you in the Name of Jesus. Resist the devil with all you've got, and he can't stay in your mind or on your body.

If you believe this good news I'm telling you, I want you to do something right now. I want you to stand up. Right there, with this book still in your hand, stand on your feet.

Now I want you to say aloud:

"This gospel that I've heard is the power of God toward me. I confess Jesus Christ is Lord over my life—spirit, soul and body. I receive the power of God to make me sound, whole, delivered, saved and healed right now.

"Sickness, disease and pain, I resist you in the Name of Jesus. I enforce the Word of God on you. I won't tolerate you in my life. *Leave my presence.* Jesus has already borne my sickness, my weakness and pain, and I am free.

"Sickness shall no longer lord it over me. Sin shall no longer lord it over me. Fear shall no longer lord it over me. I have been redeemed. I proclaim my freedom in Jesus' Name."

Now, don't ever look back. God's will is exactly the same now as it was in the Garden of Eden and in the life of Jesus. God's will is for you to be free. Rejoice. Believe the message. You'll never have to wonder again.

God's Medicine!

Chapter 8

"Death and life are in the power of the tongue:
and they that love it shall eat the fruit thereof."
— PROVERBS 18:21

Charles Capps

Medical science tells us there are many incurable diseases, such as some forms of cancer, arthritis, heart disease and AIDS, just to name a few. Even though there are no known medical cures for these diseases, God's Word is a supernatural cure and offers supernatural hope to all who are afflicted.

There is probably no other subject as important to healing and health than the principle of calling things that are not. This one principle could be the key to your being a partaker of God's provisions concerning your healing.

Calling things that are not is the principle by which Abraham became fully persuaded that God would do what He had promised. Paul said that Abraham believed God, "who quickeneth the dead, and calleth those things which be not as though they were" (Romans 4:17).

Here Paul is referring to Genesis 17. God called Abram the father of nations *before* he had the promised child, and He taught Abram to do the same.

God changed Abram's name to *Abraham,* which meant "father of nations, or multitude." This was the means He used to convince Abraham to call for what he did not yet have in reality. God had established it by promise, but Abram had to call it into reality by mixing faith with God's Word.

Every time he said, "I am Abraham," he was calling things that were not yet manifest. Abraham did not deny that he was old. He didn't go around saying, "I'm not old," because he was old. But he said, "I am Abraham," (Father of Nations). This was God's method of helping him change his image, and it caused him to be fully persuaded.

Just as Abraham, you also must call those things which are not yet seen in the natural, if you are to live in the reality of God's promise. For God uses unseen spiritual forces to overcome natural things. First Corinthians 1:27-28 says, "God hath chosen...things which are not, to bring to nought things that are."

Your part is to speak what is true according to God's Word.

David said, "I believed, therefore have I spoken..." (Psalm 116:10). Quoting David, Paul wrote, "We having the same spirit of faith, according as it is written, I believed, and therefore have I spoken; we also believe, and therefore speak" (2 Corinthians 4:13).

When it comes to divine healing, this is a vital principle. For God's Word is life, health and medicine to all your flesh.

Psalm 107:20 tells us that God "sent his word, and healed them, and delivered them from their destructions." (Notice that God did not send His Word to heal, but He sent His *Word and healed.*)

The truth is that by Jesus' stripes *"ye* were *healed"* (1 Peter 2:24). Your healing is a complete work as far as God's Word is concerned. Yet we must be fully persuaded of it and call it into manifestation.

Healing Is in Your Mouth

One way to administer God's medicine to your body is to keep God's Word in your mouth. For Paul said, "The Word is nigh you even in your mouth and then in your heart." But, instead of calling things that are not, most people make the mistake of calling things the way they are.

I read an article many years ago about a lady who had a fever continually for several months. Doctors couldn't find anything wrong physically.

They questioned her thoroughly and discovered that when she got upset about anything, she would always say, "That just burns me up." She used that phrase several times a day. The doctors were not sure if it had anything to do with her condition or not, but they asked her not to use the phrase anymore.

Within weeks, her body temperature was normal.

Now let me ask you, how many times have you said, "Every time I eat that, it makes me sick.... My back is just killing me.... Those kids make me so nervous.... I'm trying to take the flu..."?

Your own words are giving instructions to your body. Eventually your immune system will respond to your instructions and you will have what you have been saying.

God's method is to call for positive things, even though they are not yet a reality in your body. Call them until they are manifested. Exercise your God-given authority over your body.

Apply Spiritual Medicine

To exercise your authority over your body, God's Word must be allowed to become part of you. This process is called receiving the engrafted Word.

Just as you would take medicine into your physical body to aid healing by physical means, so you must receive God's Word concerning healing into your spirit for supernatural healing. Just as medical science aids healing through physical means by administering medicine into the physical body, God's medicine provides divine healing by administering the promises of His Word through the human spirit. God's Word will heal your body, but it does it through spiritual means.

Although it is a spiritual cure, God's Word is like any other medicine—in that it must be applied on a regular basis. You must apply God's Word to your individual circumstance or situation by the confession of your mouth. No one else can do it for you. James admonished us to "receive with meekness the engrafted word, which is able to save your souls" (James 1:21).

God's Word becomes engrafted into your heart as you speak it. It is first in your mouth, then in the heart...this is God's order.

"The righteousness which is of faith...saith.... The word is nigh thee, even in thy mouth, and in thy heart" (Romans 10:6-8). Nothing builds up your faith more than declaring with your own voice what God has said about you in His Word.

When you declare God's promises concerning your healing, you are establishing God's truth even before it is reality in your body. This is not denying that sickness exists. It is denying sickness the right to exist in your body. It is taking your rightful position as one who has been redeemed from the curse of the law and delivered from the authority of darkness (Galatians 3:13; Colossians 1:13).

Some people who have misunderstood this principle try to deny what exists. But there is no power in denying what exists. The power is in calling for healing and health, and you do that by mixing your faith with God's Word.

If you are sick, you don't deny that you are sick. On the other hand, you don't want to always be confessing your sickness. Denying sickness will not make you well, yet confessing sickness establishes you in your present circumstance and gives you a mind-set of fear.

Make a decision to mix your faith with God's Word and call for God's promises to be manifest in your body. The mixing of your faith with God's Word will cause you to be fully persuaded. When you become fully persuaded, healing is the result.

Do you want your flesh to reflect the life of God's Word? Let the Word become so infused into your spirit that it becomes a part of you. Not only will His Word become your thought and affirmation...but it will be you. When God's Word concerning healing takes root in your flesh, it becomes greater than pain, greater than disease, and God's Word through your words is made flesh!

Seeing Yourself Whole

When the Word of God is allowed to be engrafted into you, it creates in you an image of what is already reality in the spirit realm. When you speak that Word from your heart, then faith gives substance to the promises of God. Those images become stronger every time you speak your faith.

A healing image is created in you by God's Word and your continual affirmation and agreement with what God has said. That image is perfected by the Word of God until you begin to see yourself well. The Word engrafted into you is infusing its life into you (John 6:63; Romans 8:11).

This was demonstrated by the woman with the issue of blood, who followed Jesus saying, "If I may touch but his clothes, I shall be whole" (Mark 5:28). The verb tense is made more clear in *The Amplified Bible,* which says, "For she *kept saying,* If I only touch His garments, I shall be restored to health."

This woman hoped to be healed as she pressed through the crowd. She continued to speak until she saw herself well. Her hope was that she would be healed, although she didn't feel or look healed. But she began filling her hope with faith-filled words: "I shall be restored to health...I shall be restored to health...I shall be...I shall be...."

I'm sure her head demanded, *When? You don't look any better.* So she answered human reasoning by filling her hope with a faith image: *When I touch His garments.*

Those words penetrated her spirit and she began to see herself well. Images of despair and defeat gave way to faith-filled words. When she touched Jesus' garments, her touch of faith made a demand on the covenant of God and on the healing anointing that was upon Jesus. As faith gave substance to her hope, healing was manifested in her body.

Hope is a goal setter, but it lacks substance until it is filled with faith. Faith gave substance to her hope, laid claim to what was hers according to the promises of His covenant, and brought manifestation of her healing. "Daughter, thy faith hath made thee whole," Jesus told her (verse 34). "Whosoever shall say...he shall have..." (Mark 11:23). These are Bible principles of believing and calling for things that are not yet manifest.

The Language of Health

The words you speak are vital to your health and well-being. I believe there are some diseases that will never be cured unless people learn to speak the language of health that the body understands. That language of health is the engrafting of God's Word into you by giving voice to His Word with your own mouth.

Your words become either a curse or a blessing to you. I am convinced from my study of the Word of God that your own words can change your immune system for better or worse. (See James 3:2-7.)

Proverbs 18:21 tells us that "death and life are in the power of the tongue: and they that love it shall eat the fruit thereof."

In a recent study, men and women 65 and older were asked to rate their health as excellent, good, fair or poor.

The study showed that those who rated their health as poor were four to five times more likely to die within four years as those who rated themselves as excellent. This was true even when examinations showed the respondents to be in comparable health.

People who have an image of themselves being in poor health will talk about poor health. Even though they may be in good health, they seem to live out the reality of the image they have of themselves even unto death.

On the other hand, I believe that people who continually affirm the Word in faith will build into their immune systems a supernatural anointing that is capable of eliminating sickness and disease in a natural manner.

By being taught properly and by practicing your faith, you can grow to the point where it will be a common thing for you to receive healing through the Word of God. Yet, this doesn't happen overnight. Use some common sense and don't do foolish things through spiritual pride and call it faith.

It takes time to develop faith to operate in these principles, so don't let anyone put you under condemnation for going to doctors or having an operation. You must operate on your level of faith, but don't stay on that level forever. Continue in God's Word until you develop faith in the healing power of God's Word.

Confess the promises of God's Word concerning your health and healing daily. Confess the Word audibly over your body two or three times a day. Confess it with authority. Confessing God's Word is a way you can fellowship with the Lord and increase your faith at the same time.

Take God's Word on a regular basis, just as you would take any other medicine. Practice God's medicine; it is life to you and health to your flesh.

Four Steps to Lasting Results

"For whatsoever is born of God overcometh the world: and this is the victory that overcometh the world, even our faith. Who is he that overcometh the world, but he that believeth that Jesus is the Son of God?"

— 1 JOHN 5:4-5

Marty Copeland

I've got good news! Jesus wants you to be free from every kind of bondage—whether it be overeating, cigarette smoking, alcohol abuse or fear that you'll gain back the weight you've lost. But before you start a regular exercise plan and change your habits, be sure to put these four steps to work for you so your results will last.

1. Make Jesus Your Lord (1 John 5:1-4)

Making Jesus Lord over everything in your life—from your spirit to your physical body—will be the best decision you've ever made. It's also a very necessary decision in order to involve God's Anointing in your freedom. Isaiah 10:27 says God's Anointing is His burden-removing, yoke-destroying power...and it's just what you need to stop the power of sin and death once and for all.

2. Put Your Hope and Faith in God (2 Corinthians 10:4-5)

Too many times we put our hope in carnal weapons—diets, pills, certain kinds of exercise—and then, by faith, we believe that those things are going to win our warfare. But when you put your hope and faith in carnal things, there's no substance... you're deceived into fighting a spiritual warfare in the arena of the flesh. So put your hope and faith in God. It's the only sure way to lasting victory.

3. Realize the Past Doesn't Matter (2 Corinthians 5:17)

Once you were born again, all things became new. You were reborn with right-standing before God, and you received all the ability it takes to walk in victory all the days of your life. It doesn't matter how many times you've failed, put your hope in a weight-loss product or anything else...because now you can do all things through the Anointed One and His Anointing.

4. *Walk in the Spirit* (Galatians 5:16)

When you walk in the spirit, you won't fulfill the lust of the flesh. Instead, you'll begin to develop the fruit of the spirit as you fill yourself with God's Word and discover who you are in Christ. And it's the fruit of the spirit—patience, faithfulness and self-control—that gives you the power to overcome.

So get your hope off diets, "fast fixes" and carnal weapons today...and put your hope in God. Because when you put your hope and faith in Him, you'll release the power of His yoke-destroying anointing to produce burden-removing results that will last!

Entering God's Rest— What a Way to Live!

Chapter 10

"Come unto me, all ye that labour and are heavy laden, and I will give you rest."
— MATTHEW 11:28

Kenneth Copeland

These days a great many Christians—good, God-loving folks—are extremely weary. They shouldn't be. But they are.

I'm not criticizing them, because there have been times in the past when I felt like the most tired of the bunch. I was once so tired, I asked God to let me go on to heaven so I could get some rest.

Of course, He didn't pay any attention to that request. What He did instead, was show me how to be free from that fatigue. He revealed to me through His Word that I didn't have to put off resting until I got to heaven. I could—and should—be resting here and now.

That's right. Hebrews 4:3 says, "We which have believed do enter into rest." It doesn't say we will enter rest someday. It says we do enter it today.

Granted, the whole idea of resting is strange to most of the Body of Christ. Religion has so robbed us of the rest of God that most of us haven't even known that rest was available...much less how to enter into it.

But, the fact is, God's rest is ours if we'll do what it takes to enter it. So if you've been tired—tired of struggling and striving and worrying—and you'd like to kick back and enjoy your life in God for a change, pay attention here. You're about to learn how to do it.

A Day in the Life of Jesus

Someone might say, "Well now, Brother Copeland, you wouldn't be so quick to tell me I could rest if you knew my schedule. The demands of my life and ministry are overwhelming. The

253

devil is hounding me from every side and my circumstances are really rough. There's no way anyone could rest in the middle of all this."

Jesus could. We know He could because when we read the New Testament, we see times when He faced those same situations. Matthew 8 gives us a glimpse of one of those times. Let's read it and see what we can learn:

> And when Jesus was come into Peter's house, he saw his wife's mother laid, and sick of a fever. And he touched her hand, and the fever left her: and she arose, and ministered unto them. When the even was come, they brought unto him many that were possessed with devils: and he cast out the spirits with his word, and healed all that were sick: that it might be fulfilled which was spoken by Esaias the prophet, saying, Himself took our infirmities, and bare our sicknesses. Now when Jesus saw great multitudes about him, he gave commandment to depart unto the other side.... And when he was entered into a ship, his disciples followed him. And, behold, there arose a great tempest in the sea, insomuch that the ship was covered with the waves: but he was asleep. And his disciples came to him, and awoke him, saying, Lord, save us: we perish. And he saith unto them, Why are ye fearful, O ye of little faith? Then he arose, and rebuked the winds and the sea; and there was a great calm. But the men marvelled, saying, What manner of man is this, that even the winds and the sea obey him! (verses 14-18, 23-27).

Actually, to see the complete picture of this particular day in Jesus' life, you need to start in Matthew 5 because that day didn't start with the healing of Peter's mother-in-law. It started with Jesus going up onto the mountain and preaching one of the most extensive messages recorded in the New Testament. I'm sure that meeting took up much of the day.

When He was finished, Jesus came down and headed for Peter's house, no doubt so He could rest and eat supper. But He was delayed because on the way, He was approached by a man with leprosy and by a Roman centurion whose sick servant needed healing. Jesus ministered to both those situations, then headed on to the house.

When He got there, He found Peter's mother-in-law was sick. So He ministered to her. She got out of bed healed, and prepared their evening meal. But Jesus' ministry that day still wasn't finished.

When evening came, multitudes came to the door. Many of them were sick. Others were demon possessed. Don't you know that was a welcome sight after such a full day?

But Jesus didn't fall on His face and cry and kick the dirt. He didn't throw a fit and say, "Oh God, I'm so exhausted. I hope I have enough anointing left to heal all these people. I've already been preaching and healing all day long. These people just expect too much of Me!"

No, He didn't say any of those things. He just went outside and did the work His Father had given Him to do. He healed the sick and cast out devils.

When He finished, He didn't get to climb into a soft, warm bed, either. He got into a boat and a storm hit. Circumstances were so bad, His disciples were sure they would all die. But what was He doing? He was sleeping.

There in that boat, with the wind howling around Him and the waves slapping over the side, soaking Him with water, He was at rest. Think about that. He wasn't in a cabin cruiser. He was out there exposed to the elements, but they didn't bother Him one bit.

Believe and Obey

How did Jesus enjoy that kind of rest in the midst of those kinds of situations? He did it by faith.

255

Jesus was full of faith and had entered into the rest of His Father. That was why He could lie down in the back of the boat and go to sleep. The disciples could have enjoyed that same kind of rest if they'd used that same kind of faith.

"Oh, Brother Copeland, surely you don't think the disciples could have done what Jesus did!"

Why not? They had been given a faith command by the Son of the living God. He had told them to go to the other side of that lake. So they had the power and authority to do it. That must be true. Otherwise, Jesus didn't have any right to get on to them for being afraid.

The only obstacle that stood between the disciples and the rest of God was their "little faith." Jesus had big faith, so He had big rest. They had little faith, so they had little rest.

Remember that: Big faith—big rest. Little faith—little rest.

It was big faith that enabled Jesus to teach and minister to the multitudes from morning till night—and do it in the rest of God. It was faith that kept Him from being overwhelmed with the needs of the people.

It was Jesus' faith in His heavenly Father that kept Him at rest—regardless of the circumstances. Jesus, even though He is the sinless, spotless Son of God, didn't carry out His ministry trusting in His own divine abilities. On the contrary, the Bible says He laid aside the privileges of deity before He came to the earth. So He ministered not as God, but as a man in covenant with God.

Jesus wasn't trusting in Himself. In fact, He said, "I do nothing of Myself. It's the Father in Me that does the works."

Jesus' faith was in the Word of God and in the Anointing of God within and upon Him. He knew that anointing would supply the power to bring God's Word to pass. So He had nothing to worry about!

He didn't have to heal anyone. All He had to do was what God said to do, and go where He said to go...and God Himself would take care of the rest. God is the One who does the healing. God is the One who stops the waves. All Jesus had to do was believe and obey.

Notice, I said He obeyed. Sometimes we take for granted Jesus' unquestioning obedience to God. We assume it was easier for Him to obey than it is for us. But think about it for a moment.

Jesus was physically tired that evening. I'm sure He would have enjoyed spending the night at Peter's dry, comfortable house. It would have been reasonable for Him to say, "I'm having a good meeting here. The crowds are good. People are getting healed and delivered. I believe I'll just stay here and keep this meeting going for a few days."

But Jesus didn't do what was comfortable. He didn't do what was reasonable. He did what the Spirit of God told Him to do. So He left a good meeting and a good bed, crossed the lake in bad weather in the middle of the night, and went to face two demon-possessed people and a whole city of pig-loving unbelievers (see Matthew 8:28-34).

Jesus knew that no matter what natural evidence there might be to the contrary, as long as He obeyed God in faith, He didn't have to concern Himself with the outcome of any situation. He knew God had it well in hand, and He could enjoy complete rest.

What Do You Have to Worry About?

The same thing is true for us as believers. If we'll just believe the Word of God and obey Him, we can have the sweetest, most restful life imaginable, and kick the stuffing out of the devil while we're at it!

I realize that's hard for some Christians to swallow. They've been so brainwashed with religious tradition over the years that real spiritual truth goes down hard. They can't imagine how they could ever live like Jesus did. After all, He was Jesus! They're unworthy worms! They're just old sinners saved by grace.

That's what religion has told them. But that's not what the Bible tells us. It says we're united with Jesus. We are one Body with Him. As Hebrews 2:11 says, "Both he that sanctifieth and they who are sanctified are all of one: for which cause he is not ashamed to call them brethren."

You can live in Jesus' own rest because, if you've made Him Lord of your life, you're one with Him. The New Testament says again and again, you are in Him. That means you are everything to God that Jesus is. You have His Name. You're washed in His blood. You're in His house.

God loves you every bit as much as He loves Jesus (John 17:23). It seems almost unthinkable, but it's true. And if God loves us just like He loves Jesus, if He's given us His Word, and His Anointing, what could we possibly have to worry about?

Nothing, man! Absolutely nothing!

Since we're one with Jesus, we ought to be acting just like Jesus acts. We ought to be living just like He lives. Do you think He's running around heaven, wringing His hands with worry? Do you think He's looking at circumstances down here on earth saying, "Oh, no. It's looking really bad on earth. I'm not sure God will be able to pull off His plan now. I'm not sure His plan is going to turn out the way He said."

Hardly!

The Bible says God sits in the heavens and laughs at His enemies. He's not worried, He's laughing—and Jesus is right beside Him. Hebrews 10:12-13 shows us exactly what He is doing: "But this man [Jesus], after he had offered one sacrifice for sins for ever, sat down on the right hand of God; from henceforth expecting till his enemies be made his footstool."

Jesus is sitting down, expecting! He is at rest, expecting everything to turn out exactly as God has said.

That's exactly what we need to be doing. God has "raised us up together, and made us sit together in heavenly places in Christ Jesus" (Ephesians 2:6). So we don't have any more business wringing our hands than Jesus Himself does! We should be at rest, expecting the devil and all his works to be put under our feet!

Labor to Enter the Rest

I realize that sounds easier said than done. But it can be done if we will just do it! Hebrews 4:9-11 tells us how: "There remaineth therefore a rest to the people of God. For he that is entered into his rest, he also hath ceased from his own works, as God did from his [on the seventh day of creation]. Let us labour therefore to enter into that rest, lest any man fall after the same example of unbelief."

We have to labor to enter the rest. We have to stop struggling and striving to handle things in our own human wisdom and strength. We have to stop trying to wrestle our circumstances to the ground. Instead, we must labor spiritually and do what it takes to walk in faith.

We must read and meditate on the Word, and fellowship with the Lord over it—then cast down every thought contrary to His Word. We must stay in the Word and on our knees until faith rises in our hearts. We must keep at it until we can look the devil right in the face and laugh with joy because we know the battle has already been won! When we do that, we'll enter into God's rest.

You may be thinking, *Surely he's not serious! My bank account is completely empty and I have a stack of unpaid bills a foot high!... I'm dying and the doctor says there's nothing medicine can do for me!... My children are on drugs!... How could I ever laugh with joy in this condition?*

By looking to Jesus. He's the author and the finisher of our faith. He's our High Priest. He's the One with whom we're united. Hebrews 2:17-18 says, "Wherefore in all things it behoved him to be made like unto his brethren [once more, Jesus and us together], that he might be a merciful and faithful high priest in things pertaining to God, to make reconciliation for the sins of the people. For in that he himself hath suffered being tempted, he is able to succour them that are tempted."

You may think you're facing the most tremendous problems anyone ever faced. You may think you're under such severe pressure it would be impossible for you to rest in the midst of it. You may think there's no one who can understand, no one who can help you through it.

But Jesus can.

He knows what real pressure is. He has been there, my friend. You and I can't even imagine the kind of pressure Jesus faced. Consider it for a moment. If we sin, we repent and get cleansed of it. If Jesus had sinned, the whole world would have gone to hell. That's pressure!

He dealt with that pressure in the Garden of Gethsemane. He labored there in prayer and in fellowship with God until He entered God's rest. He stayed there until He could say, "Thy will be done." Then He got up and walked out of there for the joy that was set before Him. He went straight to the Cross, through hell, was resurrected and sat down at God's right hand!

"Oh, but that was Jesus!"

That's right. That was Jesus. Your blood Brother. The One who has declared you sinless, free and just like Him in the presence of Almighty God. The One who has given you His Spirit. The One who has given you His Name. The One who has given you His Word. The One who has given you His Anointing.

So enter His rest! Roll the care of that problem over on Him and expect the victory.

I know it can be done because I've done it. I had to do it years ago when our television bills got away from us, and we found ourselves several million dollars behind. For a good, long time, I took the care of that deficit myself. I worried over it. I tried to figure out how to fix it. I thought about selling the ministry property to pay it.

Then something interesting happened. I received our year-end report and found out we'd had the most productive year in ministry we'd ever had. We only had one major problem—and that was in the area I'd been trying to handle myself.

The Lord said to me, *See there, the area you hung onto is the one that's messed up.*

Immediately, Gloria and I saw what we had to do. We had to take authority over that situation and completely roll the care of it over on the Lord. We had to set our minds and hearts on God's Word and completely get into His rest.

I did it too...for about 30 seconds. Then I started thinking about it again. I was in such a habit of thinking about that deficit, it would slip back into my mind before I even realized it.

So every time it did, I said out loud, "No, that's not my thought. I refuse to think it. Get out of my mind. I bring my thoughts under obedience to the anointing of Jesus. I've rolled the care of this thing over on God and I'm not going to touch it." I did that time after time, day after day. I labored to enter God's rest.

The first week I had to speak out loud to those thoughts of care every few minutes—sometimes every few seconds. By the end of the second week, it was a few times a day.

By the end of the third week, I couldn't have cared less about that deficit. My thoughts had been brought into captivity in obedience to Christ. It wasn't my problem anymore. It was God's and I knew He could handle it.

Sure enough, He did. In six months the deficit was completely paid. What's more, for the first time in the history of this ministry, we were able to start paying our television bills in one payment each month instead of paying them a little at a time throughout the month. And we've been paying that way ever since.

Hallelujah, what a wonderful, powerful, victorious way to live!

Do you want to live that way? You can!

Receive Jesus' Anointing in Hebrews 3:1, as your High Priest. Keep your confession right. Keep your faith right. Go boldly before the throne of grace and receive mercy and grace to help in your time of need.

Then rest with Jesus. Sit down with Him, prop your feet up on the devil's head and expect the victory.

God Himself has already guaranteed—it's yours!

A Carefree Life?

"Humble yourselves therefore under the mighty hand of God, that he may exalt you in due time: Casting all your care upon him; for he careth for you."

— 1 Peter 5:6-7

Kenneth Copeland

Sitting in your living room. A fire roaring in the fireplace. Bills piled to the ceiling. Children running through the house. More laundry to do. Plans to make. Details to handle....

Can you really have a peaceful life with all those pressures bearing down on you?

Yes, you can—and you don't have to leave the country to do it. No matter how intense or how trivial the problems are that you're facing right now, you can live the most peaceful, carefree life you've ever lived—and you can start today.

How?

Look at 1 Peter 5:6-7 and I'll show you. It says, "Humble yourselves therefore under the mighty hand of God, that he may exalt you in due time: Casting all your care upon him; for he careth for you."

As a believer, you're probably familiar with that scripture. But have you ever taken it seriously enough to put it into action? There's a good chance you haven't because you haven't understood just how dangerous those cares you're carrying around actually are.

You probably haven't realized that they are a deadly part of the devil's strategy against you.

That's right. Worry is one of the chief weapons of his warfare. If he can get you to worry about them, he can use the financial and family pressures and scheduling problems that are just a "normal" part of everyday life to weigh you down, drain your spiritual strength, and drag you into more trouble than you care to think about.

You see, worry produces a deadly force—the force of fear. It is what Satan uses to govern his kingdom. He uses it to steal, kill and destroy. It's a killer force.

That's why all through the Bible the Holy Spirit commands, *"Fear not!"* He's not just giving friendly advice. He's giving us an order from our Commander in Chief, an order that will keep us from falling prey to the enemy's attack.

Medical science tells us that approximately 80 percent of the people hospitalized in the United States are there with ailments caused by worry and tension. Yet a great many believers worry without even thinking about it.

They'll worry about finding the time to get their hair cut. They'll worry about getting the right present for Grandma's birthday. They'll stew over this and that and then go to church and not even realize they've been sinning all week long!

"Sinning, Brother Copeland?"

Yes! For the born-again, Spirit-filled believer who owns a Bible—worrying is a sin.

I've had people say to me, "Brother Copeland, pray for me that I'll be able to bear these burdens." Well, I won't do it. Jesus said if you're burdened and heavy laden, to come to Him and He'd give you rest. He didn't say, "Pray and I'll give you the strength to bear your burdens." He said, "I'll give you *rest!"*

Let's get something straight right now. A mind that is burdened down with worry is not a godly mind. You may be born again and baptized in the Holy Spirit, but if your mind is controlled by worry it is not controlled by the Holy Spirit of God.

I don't care how major or minor your problem is, Philippians 4:6 says to be anxious about *nothing,* but in everything pray and give thanks and make your requests known to God. It doesn't say, "Worry about it for four or five days." It says, "Pray and give thanks."

That means if you're going to obey God, you must make a decision to quit worrying. You must realize that it's part of Satan's strategy.

"But what should I do with my cares," you say, "if I'm not going to worry about them anymore?"

You use the force of faith and do just what Jesus did when the devil came at Him.

Jesus said, "The prince of this world cometh, and hath nothing in me" (John 14:30). The devil never could get any of his junk into Jesus. He threw at Him everything he could throw, but Jesus wouldn't let it in.

He'd just say, "No, I don't live by that. I live by the Word, thank you." He wouldn't receive anything the devil said. He just trusted God and said, "It is written...."

When the devil attacked Jesus with worry, He didn't give in to it. He fought back with His double-edged sword. He clobbered the devil with the Spirit-power of the Word.

You see, the only way you can truly cast your care on God is by believing what He's already said about that care. The only way you can be free when it comes to finances is by believing that God has met all your needs according to His riches in glory by Christ Jesus (Philippians 4:19). The only way you can cast the care of sickness over on God is by believing that by His stripes you were healed (1 Peter 2:24).

That's why, when the devil wants to destroy you, he'll send a demon spirit to exalt himself against the Word of God.

If you're sick, he'll begin to tell you, "You're not healed. You know healing is not for today. Even if it were, it wouldn't work for you. It might for someone else, but not you."

When he starts to tell you that kind of thing, don't buy into it! Don't start worrying around about it and thinking, *Oh my, I'm afraid I'm not going to get healed. I sure don't feel healed. Why, I'm probably just going to get worse and worse....*

Don't do that! Do as Paul said in 2 Corinthians 10:5: "Casting down imaginations, and every high thing that exalteth itself against the knowledge of God, and bringing into captivity every thought...." Hit the devil with the Word, and cast the care of the situation over on God.

If you're thinking, *Yes, that sounds like a good thing to do, but I'm not Jesus! I'm just little old me,* remember that Jesus said He wasn't the One responsible for His success. He was using the Word of God. He said, "The Father that dwelleth in me, he doeth the works" (John 14:10).

Remember that. It's the Word that does the work, not the one holding onto it. It'll work for anyone who will put it to work. It will work for you just like it worked for Jesus. Just put it out there, and then get in behind it and hide. Let the Word fight its own fight.

When I first learned how to do that, I was down in South Texas preaching at a meeting that no one was coming to. I'm telling you, people were staying away from that meeting by the thousands. And after a service or two with just the pastor and me and one or two others there, I was starting to sweat it. But the Lord said, *Cast that care on Me,* so I did.

I started walking around grinning and whistling. I told the devil, "I'm not going to frown or have one worried thought. I came here to preach and that's what I'm going to do. It's God's business whether anyone shows up or not. I could care less!"

I went around so happy I felt downright foolish. The devil said, "What's the matter with you? Don't you even have sense enough to worry over something like this?" News got back to me that some of the people were saying, "I guess he's too dumb to worry. I think it's because he's never been to seminary. He can't tell a landslide from a flop."

But I told the Lord, "I have my care rolled over on You, and if nobody shows up but that one dear old woman, she's going to be the most preached-up old woman in the state of Texas because I'm going to preach just the same as if there was a crowd."

I didn't realize then what was happening, but that carefreeness put me in a noncompromising position with the devil. He couldn't get to me anymore. He couldn't pressure me and get me to compromise because I didn't care! I'd given all my care to God!

Once, when I was preaching in Louisiana, it was the last night of the meeting and the budget hadn't been met. We were $900 short. During those early days, $900 might as well have been $9 million.

The devil was jumping on me so bad I couldn't afford to let my mind run loose five seconds. So I went outside and started walking up and down the motel patio, praising the Lord out loud. I'd found that my tongue controlled my mind.

By the way, if you haven't discovered that, let me demonstrate it really quickly. Start counting silently from one to 10. Now, while you're still counting, say your name out loud. See what I mean? Your head had to stop counting and see what your mouth had to say, didn't it? Use that the next time your mind starts to worry about something. Make it stop by speaking the promises of God out loud.

Anyway, I was walking back and forth out there praying out loud, confessing the Word and praising God. Whenever I'd stop, the devil would say, "You ain't going to get it."

Then I'd say, "As far as I'm concerned I already have it. I prayed and cast that care over on God, and He pays His bills!"

I just kept it up and kept it up, holding the devil over in the arena of faith, rather than letting him pull me over in that arena of worry.

Suddenly a man pulled up into the motel driveway. He honked his horn and stuck his head out the window. "Brother Copeland, I'm so glad I caught you. I had to get by here to see you because I won't get to the meeting until late tonight and I didn't want to miss the offering."

He held out a check and said, "I wanted to make sure you got this." Then he turned around and drove off. The check was for $500. That night we went over the budget.

You see, God will handle it for you if you cast those cares on Him. Not only that, but He also says He'll exalt you. Exalt you above what? Above the devil and all his crowd. Above every problem he tries to use against you.

That's God's plan for your victory. It doesn't make Him any difference if it's December or the Fourth of July. It doesn't matter if the dog needs a bath, *again,* and everyone on your son's soccer team is coming to your house for dinner. The Bible says, "...delight thyself in the Lord; and I will cause thee to ride upon the high places of the earth" (Isaiah 58:14).

God is an exalter. He wants to lift you above that anxiety and care the devil uses to pull you down. You can understand now why the psalmist says, "He maketh my feet like hinds' feet..." (Psalm 18:33). A deer's feet touch the ground every once in a while, but most of the time, they're in the air!

Are you ready to be free of care? If you are, just lift your hands where you're sitting and make this confession of faith: "I'm a believer. I'm not a doubter. The Word works in me; and at this moment, I humble myself under the mighty hand of God. I cast the care of _____ (name it out loud) over on Him. From this moment forward, I refuse to worry. Instead, I will pray. I will use my faith, and He'll exalt me over the problem and over the devil. For I belong to Jesus. He's made me to sit with Him in heavenly places. I've put on the whole armor of God. From this very moment, with Jesus as my helper, I'm carefree. He has my cares. He'll work them out. He'll do it. He'll finish the work."

Shout, "Thank God I don't have a care!"

Now, go ahead and have a truly peaceful life, you carefree thing you!

One Word From God
Can Change
Your Destiny

Hope: The Blueprint of Faith

Chapter 1

"Where there is no vision, the people perish."
— PROVERBS 29:18

Kenneth
Copeland

If I asked you to explain to me what hope is, what would you say? What example would you give me from your own life?

Would you think back to a time when you hoped for something...just to have those hopes dissolve into disappointment?

Most people would. That's because, in their minds, hope and disappointment keep very close company. Such close company, in fact, that even the word itself, "hope," has a ring of uncertainty. "Maybe it will happen—maybe it won't," they say. "All we can do is hope."

But there's something very wrong about that perspective. It flatly contradicts the Word of God. He says "hope maketh not ashamed," or as another translation puts it, "hope does not disappoint us" (Romans 5:5).

"Brother Copeland, how in the world can you say hope won't leave us ashamed?" you may ask. "There have been many times when I've hoped and prayed with all my heart and nothing happened. So how can you stand there and tell me hope won't disappoint me?"

I'm not the one who's telling you! I didn't write Romans 5. It was written by the Apostle Paul under the inspiration of the Holy Ghost. So it was God, not I, who said hope won't disappoint you. And if He said it, it has to be true.

That's why there's no use in you or anybody else whining to me about how it failed you and left you ashamed. I know it didn't. HOPE didn't. If you ended up disappointed, you must have been using something other than hope because God says real, Bible hope won't leave you that way.

"Well, I guess I must not know what real hope is, then!" you say.

That's true. There's a good chance you don't. So maybe we'd better go to the Word of God and find out.

Hebrews 11:1 says, "Faith is the substance of things hoped for...."

The first thing we can learn about hope from that scripture is that faith won't do us any good without it. Hope serves as the blueprint for faith. Without it, faith has nothing to do. Hope is the plan that faith carries out. It's the inner image—the picture that the Holy Spirit paints on the inside of you, a picture that's based on the Word of God. Its opposite is despair, which is an image of disaster based on the lies of the devil. Despair says there is no hope.

Did you catch what I said a moment ago about hope being based on the Word of God? That's most important. You may wish that you were two inches taller or that you had a million dollars in the bank. You may even be optimistic enough to think those wishes might come true. But you will not have the hope-that-does-not-disappoint until you go to the Word and find out what God has promised you about those things, and then base your hope on His Word instead of your wishes.

You see, the Bible contains the only workable blueprint for your life (or any other human life for that matter). It's the manufacturer's operating manual. If you ignore the instructions in it, your life simply won't work. It's like putting water in the gas tank of your car. You can do it, but it won't get you anywhere. Your car's operator's handbook will tell you to put water in the radiator and gas in the fuel tank and then it will work. The Word is the manual of life.

Now let's go back to Hebrews 11:1. We've already learned from that scripture that hope must be present for faith to produce. But the reverse is also true. Hope can't produce anything without faith! Faith is the substance.

I remember years ago when I first started studying the subject of faith, I discovered that many people were trying to get by on hope alone, and it wasn't working. They'd say, "We're just hoping and praying," and I'd know right then they wouldn't get anything, because without faith their hope had no substance.

Hope is only the blueprint. You can't take a blueprint all by itself and make a house out of it. You won't be able to live in the thing because it's paper. But if you'll take some substance—lumber and steel and stone—you can follow the blueprint and build a place fit to live in. Faith and hope. Blueprint and building materials. You must have them both.

Remember though, as I said before, the only truly workable blueprint comes from the Word of God. All other blueprints will let you down.

That's why you often hear people say, "Don't get your hopes up." They've had experience with natural hope (hope based on circumstances and human knowledge instead of on the Word of God), and they know that kind of hope will leave you disappointed more often than not.

In Colossians 1:23, Paul warns us not to be moved away from the "hope of the gospel." That's because any other hope besides "gospel hope" can be spiritually dangerous.

Say, for example, you were dealing with a physical disease and your doctor told you that you only had a small chance of recovering. He'd say that because, based on the natural information he'd have, that might be all he could medically expect—and he wouldn't want to offer you a false hope that might leave you disappointed.

But the Bible says when we operate in the hope of the gospel, we'll not be ashamed. So, instead of clinging to that flimsy thread of limited hope which man has offered you, you'd be much safer going to the Word of God that says, "By his stripes ye were healed"! Because those words aren't based on fragmented human information. They're based on the knowledge of God Himself.

Instead of holding on to natural hope, if you built up supernatural hope by meditating on that truth and looking at it night and day, you'd soon have some inner images of strength you could wrap your faith around. You'd even be able to use that supernatural hope to combat the natural evidence around you. Then, instead of having a small hope for recovery, you could have a sure hope for recovery!

Look at Romans 4:18 and you can see what happened when, in the midst of a naturally hopeless situation, Abraham chose to build his life on that kind of supernatural hope. He had received a promise from God that he would become the father of many nations. The problem was, he was already old. So when he turned around and looked at his 90-year-old wife and he looked in the mirror and saw a 100-year-old man, he had no natural hope.

Natural knowledge told him there was no way he could ever have a child. Don't you know that negative knowledge bombarded his thinking? So what did he do? He took the promise of God and the hope of that promise and combated the negative hope coming against him which said, "No way, you can't do it. It's hopeless."

The Bible actually says, "He hoped against hope." In other words, he used supernatural hope to overcome natural hope. He locked his mind onto what God said and drove out everything else.

Verse 19 says, "Being not weak in faith, he considered not his own body now dead...neither yet the deadness of Sarah's womb."

Now, how did he do that? How can you consider not your own body when you're 100 years old and thinking about having a baby? It would be tough, but Abraham was able to do it because "he staggered not...through unbelief; but was strong in faith, giving glory to God; and being fully persuaded that, what [God] had promised, he was able also to perform" (verses 20-21). God's promise was at the center of his hope, his faith and his persuasion.

Abraham was fully persuaded. You can be fully persuaded, too. But you can't get that way by sitting around watching television or by spending all your time messing around with the world. You get fully persuaded by purposely meditating on the promise of God until it gets inside you so deeply that no one can get it out.

Another thing that caused Abraham to be fully persuaded was the fact that God changed his name. God stopped calling him Abram and started calling him Abraham, which means "father of a multitude."

If you'll pay attention to this principle, you'll find you can use it in your own life. For example, I learned a long time ago to stop calling myself "poor boy." It didn't matter that on the outside I looked broke. I decided—based on the Word of God—if anyone hollered, "Poor boy!" I wouldn't answer, ever again.

Now, if they were to start hollering for someone who has all his needs met according to God's riches in Christ Jesus, I'd come running. But I decided I wouldn't go by what things looked like anymore. I wouldn't go by what I felt. I had based my life on something bigger than feelings. I had gotten the hope of the gospel inside me.

Abraham called himself "father of a multitude." That was his new name. He wouldn't let anyone call him anything else. People probably thought he'd flipped out. But Abraham knew what he knew. He was the father of a multitude. He'd seen the blueprint.

Let me give you another example. If I said to you, "Come over here and see my dream house. Man, is it something!" You might say to me, "Where is it?"

I'd answer, "Right here on this piece of paper!"

Then you might tell me, "You don't have any house."

"I certainly do," I'd say. "I just got back from the architect, and you ought to see it. Sit down and I'll show you my house."

Now, that house is real. It started as an image in my mind. Then I described it to the architect and he translated it into symbols and lines. If it hadn't been a picture in my mind and on paper, if I hadn't called it my house, then it would never have been built.

Hope works just like that. People of faith look into the Word of God and they begin to see things. They see things like, "By his stripes ye were healed."

I remember the first time I ever saw that particular part of God's blueprint. My mind just wouldn't accept it. If it hadn't been right there in the Bible, I never would have believed it because it was obvious to me I wasn't healed. But the Bible said, "Ye were healed." And if "ye were," then I knew I must be.

Once I received that, I started meditating on it. I started building it up on the inside of me. Eventually I was able to see myself healed.

Soon, every time some symptom suggested to me that I wasn't healed, I'd begin to resist it and reject it. You couldn't tell me healing didn't belong to me any more than you could tell me that blueprint wasn't my house. I knew it did. I had a picture of it on the inside of me.

Now I realize there's been some controversy in Christian circles about the right and wrong of visualization. But I can put that argument to rest by assuring you, you are always visualizing something—whether you want to or not. Our minds have been divinely programmed to do that. You have an imagination.

Now, we can either use that programming the way God designed it to be used, and live, or we can use it pervertedly, the way Satan has trained us to use it, and die. But we're going to be using it, one way or the other.

Look at the way we talk. Words are simply inner-image transferring devices. When I say, "Dog," I transfer an image from the inside of me to you. You don't sit there thinking, "D-O-G." You see an inner image of a dog. If I say, "Big, black, barking dog," I can modify that image. So when we speak, we're actually exchanging pictures.

As you speak out those inner images, if they are based on the Word of God, faith comes alongside to give them substance. Hope is the blueprint. Faith is the substance. It's a powerful process. How you use it will literally determine your destiny.

There is, however, one thing you need to know: Destiny is not built overnight. It's not what you thought once or twice that got you where you are today. It's what you've thought over and over again. Those inner images are created by repetition, and repetition takes time.

I remember how long it took me to start seeing myself with my needs met according to God's riches in glory by Christ Jesus. The outside of me kept saying I was broke. It said, "You will live in this shack all your life, boy. There's no way you can ever get out of here."

But I started meditating on the Word of God. I practiced thinking about myself God's way. It wasn't easy at first. It felt awkward and unnatural. But that's how you feel when you do something new.

That's how I felt the first time I tried to fly an airplane. During those first few hours, that thing was a monster. When I tried to land it, I hit the nose gear on the ground first and bounced the thing like it was a basketball. Then the next time I landed it, I kept the nose too high and fell several feet, slamming into the ground. I couldn't find the ground. But now, after more than 11,000 hours and 52 years of flying, I don't feel awkward anymore.

That's exactly how you learn to operate in the things of God. You practice. You get into the Word and you meditate on it until the Word begins to change your inner image of yourself and you begin to see yourself with your needs met instead of without. You begin to see yourself in Christ Jesus. You think about it. You talk about it. You start believing in God's promises and acting on them.

"But what if I fail?"

So what if you do! Don't call it a failure. Just get up and go after it again. Learn some more, and learn some more. Work at it. Determine to develop inside you the hope of the gospel.

Just remember, this isn't something that happens in a day or two. It takes time. Before I came to Jesus in 1962, I was one of the most efficient sinners you ever saw. I could sin without even thinking about it. When I got into the things of God and started trying to turn that around, it wasn't easy to do. It didn't take much of anything for Satan to knock me off course.

But over the last 42 years you might say I've had a lot of Holy Ghost flying lessons. I've done a lot of spiritual bouncing and slamming, but I've learned a lot, too. Some of the things Satan used to knock me off balance with years ago won't even get to first base with me now. So be diligent. Stick in there. It will pay off if you don't give up.

The Bible solemnly says, "Where there is no vision, the people perish" (Proverbs 29:18). That's how important it is for you to get a grip on God's blueprint for your life.

It's not an option. It's an absolute necessity, because like it or not, your hope, your vision, that inner image inside of you, is determining your destiny—for better, for worse...forever.

Discovering the Power in Supernatural Expectancy

"Now faith is the substance of things hoped for, the evidence of things not seen."
— HEBREWS 11:1

Kenneth Copeland

Have you ever been in the midst of a faith stand when suddenly it seemed like your faith just quit working?

Maybe you were believing God for healing or financial deliverance or the salvation of your family. Spiritually, everything was in place. You found the scriptures that promised you what you needed. You were firing off confessions of faith like a machine gun.

But as time went by, your spiritual battery began to weaken. The power you had when you first took your stand began to wane, and you developed a gnawing suspicion that nothing would happen.

In desperation, you tried to shove those doubts away by confessing louder and longer. You frantically tried to force your faith to work. But to no avail.

You wound up still sick, still broke, still surrounded by unsaved relatives...and wondering what went wrong.

In the end, you probably just chalked it up as a faith failure.

But I'm about to tell you something that will change your life if you'll pay attention to it. It certainly changed mine. It's this: *What you experienced was not the failure of your faith...it was a breakdown of your hope.*

Faith...or Desperation?

Most believers don't pay much attention to hope. They don't think of it as very important. They certainly don't consider it to be as important as faith. But the fact is, faith won't function without hope.

That's because "Faith is the substance of things hoped for" (Hebrews 11:1). Sometimes I say it this way, "Hope is the blueprint of faith." When hope is lost, faith loses its aim. It no longer has a mission to accomplish. It just scatters uselessly in every direction.

I remember one time in particular some years ago, when that happened to me. At God's instruction, I had given my airplane to another preacher and then ordered another to replace it. During the weeks while the new plane was being manufactured, I began to believe God for the full amount I needed to pay for it.

I hooked up my faith to the promises of God and I was going along fine for awhile. But just a few days before the plane was scheduled to be delivered to me, I realized I was $20,000 short.

As the delivery date grew closer, I became more and more alarmed. I started making faith confessions as fast as I could. I'd say, "Thank God, I have that $20,000. In Jesus' Name, I-have-it-I-have-it-I-have-it-I-have-it."

But the problem was, I was no longer confessing in faith, I was confessing out of desperation.

I knew something had to change, so I gathered up my Bible and my tapes, got in my boat, and went out to the middle of the lake to spend some time with the Lord. But when I got out there, I was still saying, "Thank God, I have that $20,000. In Jesus' Name, I-have-it-I-have-it-I-have-it-I-have-it."

Suddenly, the Lord spoke up on the inside of me: *Kenneth, be quiet!* He said, *I'm tired of hearing that. Just hush and let Me show you what I can do.*

When He said that, something happened inside me. My hope came alive again. Suddenly I was expectant instead of desperate. I started eagerly anticipating what God was about to do, instead of fearing what would happen if He didn't come through in this situation.

Sure enough, the $20,000 I needed for that airplane came in and the pilot who delivered it to me ended up getting saved and filled with the Holy Spirit in the process. But none of that would have happened if I hadn't pulled aside, locked myself away with the Word for several hours, and let the Spirit of God rebuild and rekindle the hope inside me.

Supernatural Expectancy

Before you can understand how important hope is, you have to realize that real, Bible hope is not "wishing." That's worldly hope. People in the world say, "I sure wish I would get a raise at work," when what they mean is, "I want a raise. I don't think I will get it...but it would be nice if I did."

The kind of hope the Word of God talks about is much stronger than that because it's not based on wishing or wanting. It is based on your covenant with God and the anointing God has provided to carry out that covenant in your life.

In fact, Ephesians 2:12 says before you knew Jesus, you were "without Christ [or without the anointing], being aliens from the commonwealth of Israel, and strangers from the covenants of promise, having no hope, and without God in the world."

"But Brother Copeland," you say, "I'm a believer. I know God's promises. Doesn't that mean I have all the hope I need?"

Not necessarily. You see, hope comes when you take those promises, keep them before your eyes and in your ears until they begin to build an image inside you. Hope comes when you begin to see yourself *with* what God has promised you—instead of seeing yourself *without* it.

When you have hope, you have a supernatural expectancy that what God has promised will come to pass in your life.

The Apostle Paul talks about that kind of supernatural expectancy in Philippians 1:19-20 where he says, "I know that this shall turn to my salvation through your prayer, and the supply of the Spirit of Jesus Christ, according to my earnest expectation and my hope, that in nothing I shall be ashamed."

In that scripture, Paul uses two different words from the Greek language, each of which can be translated *hope*. One of them means "the happy anticipation of good." The other can be defined as "eager longing, strained expectancy, watching with an outstretched head, and abstraction from anything else that might engage the attention."

When divine hope comes alive in you, you're so locked in on the Word of God, you can't be distracted from it. I know what that's like. There have been times in my life when I was so focused on something God had called me to do, and I was so tuned in to what the Word said about it, I couldn't think about anything else.

People would try to have a conversation with me and I'd always end up talking about my hope. It would come up so big inside me that at those times, I was bigger on the inside than I was on the outside.

When your hope gets that strong, it doesn't matter what kind of unbelief the devil tries to throw your way, it just bounces off you. You're so one-track minded, you can't be drawn off course.

Back when Gloria and I first found out about faith, I was like that all the time. If someone walked up to me and said something that sounded like unbelief, I would just explode all over them! (I'm still like that, actually, I've just learned to be a little more gentle about it.)

One night I was in a bookstore in a church where I was preaching when such an explosion took place. I had stepped up to the cash register to buy my book and when I reached in my pocket to get my money, I sniffed.

I just sniffed! I don't know why I did it. I guess I just felt like sniffing. When I did, the lady running the bookstore said to me, "Is it a cold or hay fever?"

Almost before I knew what I was doing, I had opened my mouth and started spurting the Word as fast as I could talk. *"The Word of the Living God says in Galatians 3:13, I'm redeemed from the curse of the law. Deuteronomy 28:61 says all sickness and disease is under the curse, and I am redeemed from the curse of hay fever. I don't have colds, in Jesus' Name! I've been washed in the blood of Jesus! And by Jesus' stripes I am healed! He bore my sicknesses and carried my diseases...."*

I nearly pinned that lady to the wall with the Word of God. Finally, she exclaimed, "Forgive me, Brother Copeland. I knew I was in trouble when I said that! But I finally understand what you've been preaching about. I've had migraine headaches all my life. I have one right now, but if you'll lay your hand on me, I'll be healed."

I did—and she was!

What happened to her? That explosion of the Word went into her heart and suddenly she could see herself healed. Her hope came to a crisp sharpness. She saw an inner image of who she is in Christ Jesus and that no migraine could stay in her body. The minute she did, the force of faith went to work and brought that image to pass!

That's what the Bible means when it says "faith is the substance of things hoped for"!

Stick Your Neck Out

How do you develop that kind of hope? You stay in the Word until your neck stretches out. I particularly like that part of the definition of hope because I know what it means to have your neck stretched.

When I was a little boy, my grandfather was my hero. He was a full-blooded Cherokee Indian and I wanted to act like him, look like him, curse like him, chew tobacco like him and spit like him—much to my mother's chagrin. When my mother would tell me that he and my grandmother were coming to see us, I would get so excited I could hardly wait.

Every minute or two, I'd run to the window to see if they had arrived. Every noise sent me running for the door. I tell you, my neck was stretched out in anticipation. My Pawpaw was coming and I expected him any moment.

That may sound like a silly example, but the Lord once told me if people would just expect Him to move as much as a child expects his grandparents to arrive, He could move on their situation and change things drastically by the power of His Spirit.

That's what happened in Acts 3 to the crippled man at the gate Beautiful. He had been sitting by that gate begging, his head down and his eyes to the ground. But when Peter and John walked by and said, "Look on us!" that man lifted his head and began to expect.

Hope rose up in him because he was "expecting to receive something of them" (verse 5).

Of course, he received a lot more than he was expecting—he expected alms, but he got legs! That's because his expectancy hooked into their expectancy—and, believe me, their expectancy was running high!

It hadn't been more than a few days since Jesus had risen from the dead, defeated the devil and all of hell with him. It hadn't been but a few days since Jesus had looked the disciples straight in the eyes and said, "Now, you go into all the world and use My Name to cast out devils. You lay hands on the sick and they'll recover" (see Mark 16:15-18).

I can just imagine Peter saying, "Hey, John, you know that crippled beggar down there by the temple? Come on, let's go use the Name on him!"

They could see themselves doing what Jesus said they could do. Their hope was "white hot." So they went charging down to the temple and said to that cripple, "In the Name of Jesus Christ of Nazareth rise up and walk."

When they said it, they grabbed him. He had to walk, brother! They yanked him completely off the ground (Acts 3:1-8).

What made them do such a thing? Expectancy!

They didn't tiptoe up to that gate, look around to make sure no one was watching and then whisper, "Dear Lord, if it be Thy will, heal this poor crippled man."

The only people who pray "if it be Thy will" are those who don't have any hope or expectancy. If you've been praying that way, stop it! Go to the Word and find out what God's will is. The Word of God is His will. It is His will for you to be well. It is His will for you to be prosperous. It is His will for you to lay hands on the sick and it is His will for them to recover.

So stay in the Word until you're so confident and expectant that your neck is stuck out in anticipation. Meditate on the Word until your hope gets crisp and that image inside you gets strong and clear.

Stay in there until you're so full of expectancy that when someone walks up to you and says, "Good morning," you jump on them like a chicken on a bug saying, "Yes! Bless God! It is a good morning. Do you have anything wrong with you? I'll lay hands on you right now and you'll get healed!"

Once hope gets that strong, it becomes courage...and hope plus courage equals the spirit of faith in action!

The Spirit of Faith

The Apostle Paul refers to the spirit of faith in 2 Corinthians 4:13 saying, "We having the same spirit of faith, according as it is written, I believed, and therefore have I spoken; we also believe, and therefore speak."

The spirit of faith speaks! It calls things that be not as though they were. It makes faith confessions—not because it's "supposed to" or out of desperation, but because it's so full of eager anticipation and confident expectation it can't keep its mouth shut!

The spirit of faith says, "I don't care what God has to do, He'll turn the world upside down if He has to, but He will change this situation for me."

Every time I talk about the spirit of faith, I think about my high school football team. For years, the teams from that school had been losing teams. But something happened to the bunch on my team. A spirit of winning got into them.

When we were sophomores, we were on the B squad. We were the nothings. But somehow we got the idea that we could win. Every year the B squad would have to scrimmage the varsity team, and usually the varsity just beat the daylights out of the sophomores.

But the year our B squad played them, that changed. We didn't just beat them, we had them down by several touchdowns, just daring them to get the ball, when the coach called off the game. He was so mad at the varsity team, he didn't even let us finish.

What happened to that little B squad? We reached the point where we expected to win. We had an inner image of ourselves as winners, and it eventually took the best team in the state to beat us.

The same thing happened to Gloria and me in 1967 when we went into the ministry. We began to have an inner image of preaching the Word of God to thousands upon thousands of people. It was 10 years before we could gather up more than a handful of them at a time for one service, but we didn't let that stop us.

We saw the thousands in our heart and in our mind and we just kept our necks stuck out—in more ways than one—expecting God to bring the people. Sure enough, He did.

Of course, there were some hard times. Times when people stayed away from our meetings by the millions. Times when I preached to 17 people with the same intensity that I would preach to 6,000.

That's what hope does. It keeps you intensely focused on God's promise. It keeps you seeing that promise on the inside, even when you can't see it on the outside. It keeps you operating by the spirit of faith.

When you have hope, the devil can't beat you down. He can't tear you down. He can't stop your faith from working. Everyone around you can just stop in their tracks, but you'll keep right on going.

When the devil knocks you down, you just get up with a deeper resolve to hit him harder the next time...and harder the next time...and harder the next time.

You get to the point where you expect God to move with such vigor that all the distractions in the world can't turn your head. All the failures of the past drift into nothingness. You can't even remember them anymore because you're so absorbed with the expectation of what God is about to do.

When that happens, you no longer sit around wondering what went wrong. You blast off into the glory of God, laying hold of His promises and watching your dreams come true. You live the kind of life that those who give up hope will never know.

Good News!

"God was in Christ, reconciling the world unto himself, not imputing their trespasses unto them; and hath committed unto us the word of reconciliation."

     — 2 CORINTHIANS 5:19

Happy Caldwell

"Go ye therefore and teach all nations that God is mad at them."

That's not what Jesus said in the Great Commission. But all too often, that is the message traditional religion has preached.

People (believers and unbelievers alike) have been told how unworthy they are. They've been told what sorry creatures they are. They've been told they don't act right or talk right or pray right.

Sound familiar? If so, I have some good news for you today: God is not mad at you. In fact, He's not mad at anybody!

The Bible says He [God] "was in Christ, reconciling the world unto himself, not imputing their trespasses unto them" (2 Corinthians 5:19). Every person ever born on this earth has already been guaranteed by God the right to stand before Him without any sense of guilt or shame. Every person, no matter how covered in sin he may be, qualifies to receive God's righteousness. Not everyone takes advantage of it, but everyone has the opportunity.

Statements like that shock religious people. Do you know why? Because, as Romans 10:3 says, "They being ignorant of God's righteousness, and going about to establish their own righteousness, have not submitted themselves unto the righteousness of God."

That's what religion always does. It tries to establish its own righteousness, its own rules, its own right-standing with God. Religion says, if you act right, talk right, dress right and look right, then God will give you favor.

But God isn't religious. He says, *I don't want you to establish your own righteousness. I want to give you Mine. But before you can receive it, you have to quit trying to establish your own.*

You can't earn the righteousness of God. There's nothing you can do to deserve it. It's God's gift. All you can do is receive it.

When I accepted Jesus Christ as my Lord, God declared me righteous. I didn't look very righteous. I called on liquor stores back then. Alcohol was my business. I sold it and I drank it. But the day I submitted to Jesus, my life changed.

I went back to work the next Monday morning in those same liquor stores. I didn't know a thing about the Bible. I only knew I was different. Soon, I began to tell people that I had two kinds of spirits, alcoholic spirits and the Holy Spirit. "Which one do you want to hear about first?" I'd ask.

I found that many of them were interested in Jesus. They weren't interested in religion, but they were interested in knowing that God was no longer *"imputing their trespasses"* to them. They were interested in knowing that He had settled the account of the whole world's sins. That was good news!

The sad thing is many believers—people who have already been made righteous in Jesus—don't fully grasp that news. They don't realize God isn't mad at them. They don't realize they can go boldly before the throne of God without shame—dressed in the righteousness of Jesus Christ.

That's because they've been taught to focus more on how they've messed up than on what Jesus has done for them. They're more sin-conscious than they are righteousness-conscious.

One of the first steps to becoming righteousness-conscious is to learn the difference between having your sins forgiven, and having your sins remitted. Remitted is a word that should never be used in connection with a believer because a man's sin is remitted only once.

When sin is remitted, at the moment of salvation, the Word tells us we become "a new creature: old things are passed away; behold, all things are become new" (2 Corinthians 5:17).

You see, the problem we had before we were saved was not all those little individual sins we committed. They were only the symptoms. The problem was the condition of our heart. The problem was our sin nature. No matter how hard we tried to be good and act right, that nature kept us imprisoned in sin.

But when we made Jesus the Lord of our lives, our sin nature died and a righteous nature was born in us. Sin no longer had dominion over us. Righteousness set us free!

That kind of freedom wasn't available to people in Old Testament days. Back then, before the blood of Jesus had been shed, there was a "reckoned righteousness" with God, gained through the blood of sacrificed bulls and goats. Those sacrifices covered the individual sins, but they didn't change the hearts of people. People kept on committing the same sins every year because their nature was still the nature of sin.

"For it is not possible that the blood of bulls and of goats should take away sins" (Hebrews 10:4). But what the blood of bulls and goats could not do, Jesus' blood did. "...This man, after he had offered one sacrifice for sins for ever, sat down on the right hand of God.... For by one offering he hath perfected for ever them that are sanctified" (verses 12, 14).

How long will Jesus' sacrifice for sin last? Forever. You are forever righteous through the blood of Jesus.

I know you still miss it and sin sometimes. But even when you do, it's not the same because your heart is different. God doesn't see you the same way He did before you were born again.

Think of it this way. If you're a parent, you may know your child has done something wrong, but as far as you're concerned, he's still your child and he's wonderful. He may need to be corrected, but there's nothing wrong with him. You know he wants to please you. He just needs more training so he can learn to do things right.

Do your children fall out of good standing with you just because they mess up? Certainly not. It's the same way in the family of God. Once you've been born again, your nature is changed. You don't want to sin even when you do.

And when you do sin, you have Someone on your side. "...If any man sin, we have an advocate with the Father, Jesus Christ the righteous" (1 John 2:1). "If we confess our sins, [God] is faithful and just to forgive us our sins, and to cleanse us from all unrighteousness" (1 John 1:9).

While remission changes your nature, forgiveness erases your mistakes. And that's the final word on sin. God has taken care of the sin problem forever. When Jesus became sin and put sin away, the sin problem became a closed issue with God.

You can still sin if you choose. God won't stop you. The Holy Spirit will deal with you if you'll listen...but if you won't, you can do what you will. But you don't *have* to sin. You don't have a sin nature anymore. You have a righteous nature.

God "hath delivered us from the power of darkness, and hath translated us into the kingdom of his dear Son" (Colossians 1:13). You've been translated out of one kingdom and into another one.

People are so worried about the devil. They're fighting the devil and bombarding the gates of hell all over the place. But I like what one author wrote: "If you really understand your righteousness in Christ and your authority as a believer, you will pay no attention to the devil. You'll just go on and do your job."

Jesus said, "I beheld Satan as lightning fall from heaven. Behold, I give unto you power to tread on serpents and scorpions, and over all the power of the enemy: and nothing shall by any means hurt you" (Luke 10:18-19).

Satan has no authority over you unless you give it to him. Jesus has stripped him of all authority and placed it in your hands. As He said in the Great Commission, "All power is given unto me in heaven and in earth. Go ye therefore..." (Matthew 28:18-19).

That's good news, Church! Let's tell it!

The Forgotten Power of Hope

"...God is able to make all grace abound toward you; that ye, always having all sufficiency in all things, may abound to every good work."
— 2 CORINTHIANS 9:8

Kenneth
Copeland

I want you to look with me at a word most people think they understand. It's a word you've heard thousands of times, in church and out. A word you've used yourself over and over again—probably without having the foggiest notion what it really means.

I'm talking about the word *hope*.

"Oh, Brother Copeland, I know what the word *hope* means!"

No, you don't. Not unless you've studied it in the Word of God. Because in today's language the word *hope* has lost its meaning. It doesn't even resemble the hope spoken about in the Bible.

For example, these days you might hear someone say, "I sure do hope Joe is coming for dinner." What does that mean? It means, "I don't know if Joe is coming for dinner, but I sure wish he would." In that context, the word hope is the same as the word wish. It carries with it an element of doubt.

But real Bible hope isn't like that at all. In fact, it's just the opposite. If you look up the Greek definition of the word *hope,* you'll find it means "to be intensely expectant, to be confidently looking forward to something you fully expect to happen."

You can see this kind of hope in action in Philippians 1:19-20. There, the Apostle Paul says, "I know that this shall turn to my salvation through your prayer, and the supply of the Spirit of Jesus Christ, according to my earnest expectation and my hope...." For emphasis, Paul used the two Greek words there that mean earnest expectation. In other words, he was saying to them, "This thing is so inevitable I'm just burning up with expectancy!"

Most believers don't know anything about that kind of burning-up-with-expectancy hope. They just know about the wishing kind of hope. You ask them, "Will you get your healing?"

"Oh, I hope so...," they answer. Then they just go on and on expecting to be sick—and of course they are—and never understand why.

Wishing won't accomplish anything in the kingdom of God. But hoping will, especially when you couple it with faith and love! First Corinthians 13:13 says, "And now abideth faith, hope, charity [or love], these three...." That puts hope in some very powerful company! It is one of the three most powerful elements in the universe. It is one of the three eternal and living substances that run the entire kingdom of God.

I preach a lot about faith. I'm constantly teaching believers that they can't get anything done in the kingdom of God without faith. But do you want to know something? Faith can't get anything done without hope—intense expectation!

Hebrews 11:1 says, "Now faith is the substance of things hoped for...." In natural terms you might say faith is the building material and hope is the blueprint. You have to have hope before faith can begin building anything in your life.

Now when I say you need to have hope, I'm not saying you just need to start thinking optimistically. Positive thinking is fine and it certainly is better than negative thinking. But just thinking optimistically will never cause you to burn up with confident expectancy like the Apostle Paul did. Positive thinking will never give you Bible hope.

Real Bible hope has to be based on God's Word. Otherwise, it has no foundation under it.

For instance, someone who has liver cancer might say to me, "I fully expect to be healed of this liver condition." I might say to them, "What makes you believe that when the doctor just declared your condition incurable?"

Now, that person can respond in one of two ways. He can tell me he believes he'll be healed just because he wants it to be true. If he does, he has no foundation beneath him. He's just wishing. That's the world's kind of hope, but it definitely isn't the Bible kind.

If he has Bible hope, he'll say, "I will be delivered from this liver condition because God's Word says every sickness and every disease is under the curse of the law, and Galatians 3:13 says Jesus has redeemed us from the curse of the law, being made a curse for us. In other words, Jesus has already redeemed me from the curse of this liver condition. That's why I fully expect to be delivered from it."

When you have that kind of clear, Word-based image inside you, you have real Bible hope—and it's an absolute must for anyone who wants to live by faith. Without that kind of hope, your faith has nothing to grab onto and you'll let the devil talk you out of your healing (or whatever else you need to receive from God). He'll look you right in the face and say, "Well now, I don't see any healing taking place in your body. It looks to me like you're as sick as you've ever been. Obviously, this healing business just isn't working for you."

The devil will feed those kinds of words into your mind and try to get you to think about them. If you do, you'll be in trouble. But if you'll dwell on the Word of God until the hope of the gospel rises up on the inside of you...if you'll meditate on God's promises until you begin to have an inner image of yourself healed and strong...if you'll speak those promises day after day...you'll be able to look at the devil and say, "Oh, shut up! I know what I know and I know God's Word is working for me. That Word says I'm healed and that's what I'm looking at and nothing else."

I don't mind telling you, it's rarely easy to do that. (If it were easy, everybody would be doing it!) Sometimes you have to get rough on yourself to make yourself stand on the Word of God when you're in great physical pain. Your emotions will want to take over. They'll push you to start crying and feeling sorry for yourself.

But don't do it. Instead, take charge of those emotions by the Spirit of God within you. Don't ever let your emotions cause you to back away from hope. If you do, you'll kill it.

Yes, I said you'll kill it. You see, hope is a living thing. Paul says hope "abides." To abide means to live. Only living things abide, so hope is a living thing and you have to guard it and nourish it with the Word of God. You have to feed it with the Word so it can grow.

If you'll do that, hope will paint a picture on the inside of you, a picture of God's promise fulfilled in your life. It will give you an inner image of yourself healed and prosperous, with your loved ones saved, your marriage restored or whatever else you've been hoping for. Hope will paint that picture so clearly inside you and make it so real, you'll begin to be blind to what you see on the outside.

Let me give you an example: You've prayed for your son or daughter to be set free from a drug habit. You can get such a clear picture of what that child will be like after he has been delivered that he starts looking great to you now—even though he still may be giving you trouble!

You'll actually get to the point where you won't see what a louse he or she is being right now because you've seen him in Jesus with the eyes of your spirit. People will say, "I don't know what she sees in that child." They won't understand that you're looking at him through eyes filled with hope.

If you'll continue to look at him that way and not let the devil shake you, if you'll refuse to jump up in that child's face and tell him what a sorry old thing he is, one of these days that child of yours will look on the outside just like you see him on the inside. He'll be delivered!

No doubt about it, that kind of hope is strong spiritual stuff! Where do you go to get it?

You go to the same place you go to get faith—the Word of God. You bathe your brain in that Word every day. You think about it all the time, wherever you are and whatever you are doing.

You keep your faith tapes going. You keep someone preaching to you all the time. Because as you keep feeding your spirit on God's Word, hope will begin to rise up. God's pictures will start to develop in your spirit. You'll begin to see them on the inside of you. In fact, they'll get bigger inside you than the circumstances around you.

Then, when the devil comes and tries to show you an image of some beaten-up, run-down person wearing your name, you'll just send him packing. You'll shake your head and say, "No sir, that's not a picture of me. *This* is a picture of me," and you'll start talking the Word of God!

As you meditate on those inner pictures hope has painted with God's Word, you'll begin to believe you are what the Word of God says you are. You'll begin to realize you're not what the world says you are. You're not what your parents or your friends say you are. You're not even what you think you are. You are what GOD says you are! You're the righteousness of God in Christ Jesus (2 Corinthians 5:21)!

When the devil comes at you with his junk, you'll reach in, get out that picture hope has given you, and put it in front of your eyes. You'll say, "Devil, I'm not looking at you. That sick, poverty-stricken, failure-bound person you're describing isn't me. This is me. I'm the fellow with the healed body. I'm the fellow with all my needs met according to God's riches in glory. I'm the fellow who is more than a conqueror in Jesus!"

Power pictures. That's what hope produces. Inner pictures faith can build on. But you need to understand, these are not instant photos. The development of hope takes time.

For instance, when I discovered healing, I didn't have any trouble with that. I could easily see that if God made a body, He could certainly fix it. That seemed obvious. But I had a difficult time seeing how God could ever fix my financial problems. I couldn't see the prosperity picture clearly at all.

But the more I studied the Word and meditated on it, the more my thinking changed. Hope began to develop. I grabbed hold of 2 Corinthians 9:8 that says, "God is able to make all grace abound toward you; that ye, always having all sufficiency in all things, may abound to every good work."

An inner image of all my needs being met with plenty left over for every good work began to grow by God's Word. I began to see it on the inside. I got a revelation of it.

After that it wasn't a matter of how God would meet my financial needs. It was a matter of fact that He'd already met them. All I needed to do was get in line with Him.

After a while, that revelation was so real in my consciousness that I began to think like a man without debt. I began to talk like a man without debt.

It wasn't long until Gloria and I were totally, completely debt free. We didn't owe anybody anything and God was the One who had done it. We hadn't asked anybody for a dollar.

I've never written an appeal letter in this ministry and I never will because I don't have to. My needs aren't met by your giving. My needs are met by my giving because I'm standing on the Word that says, "Give and it shall be given unto you again." That's why my needs are met. God is my source, so I don't have to put any pressure on you. Now, God may use your giving to meet my need, but that's not where my earnest expectation is built. My hope is built on the forever Word of God's promises.

I learned how to think that way by studying Jesus. He never looked to people to meet His need. It's a good thing, too. One time when He was preaching, everyone in His congregation walked out. They just got up and left. The only people who stayed were the members of His own staff.

Did He get upset about it? No, He just went right on to the next place and held another meeting. That time He had a landslide. But the landslide didn't affect Him any more than the walkout because those people weren't His source. God was His source. He was there to help them. He didn't call them there to help Him. They did help Him, but not because He pressured them to.

Do you get the picture? I did. Many years ago, it came alive inside me. I took hold of it and it changed my financial life forever.

I got a picture of prosperity from God's Word, and faith made that picture a reality. That's how the process always works. First you have to have the hope, then faith goes into action. Hope is the inner image that your faith becomes the substance of. Hope is the blueprint. Faith is the material.

Faith can't build on wishes. How many times have you heard someone say, "I sure do wish God would do something for me"? The rest of the statement hangs unspoken in the air, "...but He probably won't."

That's not faith. That's unbelief. But it works the same way faith works—only backward. Fear is actually faith in the negative dimension. It's faith in failure, danger or harm. When someone is meditating on negative thoughts or, "worrying," as we call it, he or she is developing inner pictures. Not pictures of hope, but pictures of despair.

Just as fear is the flip side of faith, despair is the flip side of hope. It's an inner image of failure, sickness, poverty or whatever else the devil wants to inject into you. Despair is actually hope in the negative and fear, like faith, brings it to pass.

Do you see how powerful this process is? This is the process that controls the course of your life. These inner images, whether they be of hope or despair, become the blueprint for your faith or fear, and ultimately control your destiny.

Once you understand that, you hold the key to your future. You hold the key to becoming everything God wants you to be. It doesn't matter where you are right now. You may be sick. You may be broke. You may be defeated. It doesn't matter!

What you must do is dig into the Word and begin building your hope. Start developing God's pictures within you. As long as you have an image of your own defeat on the inside of you,

you're destined to be defeated on the outside as well. But change that inner image with the Word of God and no demon in hell will be able to hold you down.

Jesus came to change the inner man. "If ye continue in my word," He told us, "then are ye my disciples indeed; and ye shall know the truth, and the truth shall make you free" (John 8:31-32).

Get that truth working inside you. Put it in there until hope begins to paint new pictures in your heart. Then hang on to those pictures relentlessly. Don't ever let them go. Eventually—inevitably—faith will make those pictures as real on the outside as they are on the inside.

"For as he [a man] thinketh in his heart, so is he" (Proverbs 23:7). It's the pictures inside you that determine your destiny. Get yourself some power pictures. God's Word is full of them. The question is, are you?

The Anointing Factor

"Wherefore remember, that ye being in time past Gentiles in the flesh...were without Christ [the Anointed One], being aliens from the commonwealth of Israel, and strangers from the covenants of promise, having no hope, and without God in the world: But now in Jesus [the Anointed One] ye who sometimes were far off are made nigh by the blood of Christ [the Anointed One]."
— EPHESIANS 2:11-13

Kenneth Copeland

In May of 1993, hopelessness hit the headlines. It grabbed the attention of the nation as it drove angry, violent crowds into a destructive rage on the streets of east Los Angeles.

Businesses were burned and stores looted. Innocent bystanders were injured and even killed as people who felt trapped by circumstances, condemned to poverty and powerless over their own futures, erupted in frustration.

As the startling scenes reached into living rooms across this country by television, people began to ask, "What can we do? These people are hopeless! How can we change this situation?"

Some answered by calling for more government programs. Others cried out for financial aid. Still others called for more educational and employment opportunities.

But I can show you by the Word of God that none of those things by themselves would have solved the situation. They wouldn't have gone to the source of the problem. In Ephesians 2:11-12, the Lord reveals what that source is. Describing the condition all of us were in before we were born again, He says: "Wherefore remember, that ye being in time past Gentiles in the flesh...were without Christ, being aliens from the commonwealth of Israel, and strangers from the covenants of promise, having no hope, and without God in the world."

According to the Word of God, hopelessness isn't caused by lack of money. It isn't caused by lack of education. It isn't caused by negative circumstances. Hopelessness comes from being without God in the world. It comes from being a stranger to His covenant.

Anybody anywhere can have hope if they know Jesus and the covenant promises of God. Your background, race, or financial status doesn't matter. You can live in the worst ghetto in the world and still have hope in God because He isn't limited by man's resources. He isn't limited by man's prejudices. God is an equal opportunity employer!

Some people have said to me, "You ought not preach that prosperity message in poverty-stricken areas. You'll get those people's hopes up, and they don't have the same opportunity to prosper that you do."

Yes they do!

I've seen God prosper people in places where there was absolutely nothing. No food. No jobs. No welfare program. Nothing! There is one country in Africa where the government wanted a tribe to die out so they just stopped the flow of food and began to starve them to death. But that plan failed because some Holy Ghost-filled African Christians refused to give up hope. They knew their covenant, so they prayed, "Give us this day our daily bread." Do you know what happened? The people got fed and the government went under!

More Than Wishful Thinking

Understand this, though. When I say hope, I'm not talking about the weak, wishful-thinking kind of attitude most people call hope. Real, Bible hope isn't a wish. Hebrews 11:1 says, "Faith is the substance of things hoped for...." There's no room for faith in wishing! For example, take the statement, "I sure do wish God would bless me financially." There's no place in that statement for faith. It just won't plug in anywhere.

The Apostle Paul said in Philippians 1:20, "According to my earnest expectation and my hope, that in nothing I shall be ashamed...." If you'll look up the two Greek words translated earnest expectation and hope, you'll find they're two different words that both mean the same thing. So hope is earnest expectation.

There's plenty of room for faith in earnest expectation. Say, for instance, "I earnestly expect to receive financial blessings. I earnestly expect to be free from poverty." Faith can plug right into that statement. It just follows naturally. Faith becomes the substance of that statement.

Someone might ask, "How can you so intensely expect to prosper when the unemployment rate is up and the economy is down?" You can answer, "What I'm earnestly expecting isn't dependent on the world's economy. It's based on what God has promised in His covenant. Because He said it, I earnestly expect it!"

Can you hear the faith in those words? Certainly! Real, Bible hope just opens the door so faith can walk right in!

Why don't we see more of that kind of hope in the Body of Christ? Because it is born out of the promises of God's covenant. And most Christians are using their believing faculties to believe some sort of religious system that men have designed instead of believing the Word of God. Despite the fact that they're born again with the seed of hope inside them, baptized in the Holy Spirit and walking around with a Bible tucked under their arm, they've become strangers to the covenants of promise.

You can tell those folks that 2 Corinthians 8:9 says Jesus became poor so we might be rich and they'll answer, "Oh, yes, amen. I know it says that, brother. But I just don't know whether to take the Bible literally or not."

The reason they don't know whether or not to take the Bible literally is because they're not spending any time in the Word as a covenant. That's what the word *testament* means. Did you know that? The New Testament is the new covenant! It's not some kind of religious book. It is God's will and testament written down. It is a covenant of promise. It is God's blood-sworn oath.

I want you to imagine for a moment that you made a blood covenant with someone. You both cut your wrists, bound your hands together, mixed your blood and swore an oath to each other in your own blood. That would be serious, wouldn't it?

You know it would! But you have a covenant even more serious than that with Almighty God. It's a covenant ratified not by the tainted blood of a sinful man, but by the sinless blood of Jesus.

I've meditated on that fact until it's real to me. So when I pick up the New Testament, I'm not just reading a history book. I'm reading a copy of God's will and testament and in my mind, I have Jesus by the hand and His blood is flowing down my wrist. Once you get a revelation like that, hope is no problem!

Figure In the Anointing

With those things in mind, let's go back to Ephesians 2 and dig a little deeper into what God is telling us about hope: "For we are (God's) workmanship, created in Christ Jesus unto good works, which God hath before ordained that we should walk in them" (verse 10).

Before we read any further, I want you to stop for a moment and notice the phrase "created in Christ Jesus." To truly understand that phrase, you need to realize that the word *Christ* is a Greek word. Why the English translators failed to translate it, I don't know. But that failure has cost us a great revelation.

You see, the word *Christ* isn't Jesus' last name. It's not a title. It's a word with a very significant meaning. *Christ* actually means *anointed*. To *anoint* is literally "to pour on, smear all over, or rub into." So the Anointing of God is to have God poured on, smeared all over, and rubbed into.

Some time ago, the Spirit of God further clarified that definition for me. He said, *The Anointing of God is God on flesh doing those things only God can do.*

Practically speaking, what does that Anointing of God on flesh do for us? According to Isaiah 10:27, it destroys the yoke of bondage.

Some people say the anointing breaks the yoke. But the word used in Isaiah isn't *break*, it is *destroy*. It literally means to obliterate so completely that there is no evidence the yoke ever even existed.

Now, let's go back and read Ephesians 2, translating the word Christ: "Wherefore remember, that ye being in time past

Gentiles in the flesh...were without [the Anointed One], being aliens from the commonwealth of Israel, and strangers from the covenants of promise, having no hope, and without God in the world: But now in [the Anointed] Jesus ye who sometimes were far off are made nigh by the blood of [the Anointed One]" (verses 11-13).

According to those scriptures, before you were born again, you were without the Anointed One. Well, if you were without the Anointed One, you were also without the anointing, right? But now, you are in the Anointing of Jesus. That anointing is available to you in every situation to destroy (obliterate completely!) every yoke of bondage.

That's why you can have hope in the most hopeless situations. It doesn't matter who you are or what color your skin is. It doesn't matter if you never made it past the sixth grade. You can break out of that hopeless situation if you'll factor in the anointing.

The anointing factor is what the world always forgets. They say, "We'll build this wall so big nobody will ever get through it. We'll build it big enough to block out the gospel and keep the people under our thumb." But they fail to figure in the anointing factor. It will destroy that wall. If you don't believe it, ask the believers in Berlin!

I strongly suggest you begin factoring in the anointing in your life from this moment forward. If someone says, "Well, brother, you can't expect to succeed. You can't expect to prosper. You can't expect to get healed," ask yourself, "Is there a yoke holding me back?" If the answer is yes, then rejoice because the anointing will destroy it!

"But Brother Copeland, I can't ever expect to get a good job because I can't read."

Is that your yoke? Then, believe God and He'll destroy it.

I know a fellow who hadn't gone to school at all. God taught him how to read the Bible, but for a long time he couldn't read anything else. One day, he walked into the principal's office in the local high school and said, "I want to earn my diploma."

The principal looked across his desk at this 40-year-old man and said, "OK, we can probably work something out. How much schooling have you had?"

"None," the man answered.

Shaking his head, the principal told him there just wasn't any way to overcome that kind of obstacle. But the man was persistent. "Now wait a minute," he said. "The Lord Jesus Christ has let me know that if I do my part and you do your part, He'll do His part. Yes, sir. There is a way."

Sure enough, in less than a year he had his high school diploma.

Don't Be a Stranger

Nothing is too big a problem when you figure in the anointing! So take hold of that anointing by beginning to expect. Start expecting something good to happen to you. Lay hold of the hope that's set before you in the promises of God.

Don't be a stranger to those promises. Dig into them, find out what God has said about your situation. Then start saying, "I expect it because God promised it!"

Think about that promise and meditate on it. Let it build an image inside you until you can see yourself well...until you can see yourself with your bills paid...until you can see yourself blessed and prosperous in every way.

If you'll do that, you'll eventually get bigger on the inside than you are on the outside. Your hope will grow so strong that the devil himself won't be able to beat it out of you.

Most believers never experience that kind of confident hope because they allow their emotions to pull them off course. They don't feel healed or they don't feel blessed, so they let the promises slip.

You can avoid that pitfall by anchoring your soul. Anchor it by becoming a follower of people like Abraham "who through faith and patience inherit the promises." (See Hebrews 6:11-20.)

The Bible says Abraham hoped against hope (Romans 4:18). He used the hope of the promise of God to fight against the natural "hope" (or hopelessness) that told him it would be impossible for Sarah and him to have a child.

Romans 4:21 says he was "fully persuaded that, what (God) had promised, he was able also to perform." Now, Abraham wasn't always fully persuaded. There was a time after God had promised to give him a child when he asked, "How can I know these things will happen?"

God answered him by cutting a covenant with him. Abraham killed the covenant sacrifice animals, split them down the center, laid the halves opposite each other and God walked in the blood of those animals. I believe with all my heart Abraham saw God's footprint in that blood.

From then on, Abraham's soul was anchored. His mind couldn't argue with him. His emotions couldn't argue with him. His old, dead body couldn't argue with him. His barren wife couldn't argue with him. That covenant put an end to all arguments. From then on, Abraham was fully persuaded. Fully expectant.

Anchor Your Soul

God has made a covenant with you just as surely as He made it with Abraham. But instead of making it in the blood and body of animals, He made it with the broken body and shed blood of His own Son—Jesus the Anointed One. That's what should be on your mind when you take communion. Hebrews 6:17-19 says:

> Wherein God, willing more abundantly to show unto the heirs of promise the immutability of his counsel, confirmed it by an oath: That by two immutable (unchangeable) things (the body and the blood of Jesus), in which it was impossible for God to lie, we might have a strong consolation, who have fled for refuge to lay hold upon the hope set before us: Which hope we have as an anchor of the soul, both sure and stedfast....

Friend, we have hope because we're in blood covenant with Almighty God! Through Jesus we have access to Him. We "are no more strangers and foreigners, but fellowcitizens with the saints, and of the household of God" (Ephesians 2:18-19)!

When we're confronted by impossible situations in this world, we have a covenant right to factor in Jesus! Factor in the power of His Word! Factor in His Anointing!

Some say, "That sounds too easy." No, it's not easy! When the devil begins to pull the noose of hopelessness around your neck with poverty or sickness or some other terrible situation, you have to fight and fight hard. Not by burning buildings and robbing stores—but by grabbing hold of the hope in the Word and using it to demolish every thought that would rise up against it.

"Casting down imaginations, and every high thing that exalteth itself against the knowledge of God, and bringing into captivity every thought to the obedience of Christ" (2 Corinthians 10:5).

The battleground where hope is won or lost is not on the streets, it's in the mind. It's in the imagination where expectancy begins to take form. So take your stand on that battleground. Begin now to expect the anointing to destroy the yokes in your life. Begin now to expect God to keep His covenant promises to you.

Fight for that expectancy in the Name of Jesus. Take your hope, fill it with faith and storm the gates of hell. They will not prevail against you!

Renewing Your Mind

"But we all, with open face beholding as in a glass the glory of the Lord, are changed into the same image from glory to glory, even as by the Spirit of the Lord."
     — 2 CORINTHIANS 3:18

Gloria Copeland

Christianity is not just another religion. It is the life of God abiding within and flowing out of the believer. Other religions leave you the same person you were before. But the wonderful thing about the Christian life is that it will completely transform you.

When you are born again, your spirit is instantly transformed into the image of God. The spirit is the part of you that takes on the nature of God. According to the Word, once that happens you should immediately start the process of changing your soul. The Bible calls it "renewing the mind."

Your soul is your mind, will and emotions. Spiritual growth is determined by how much your soul is changed by the Word of God. The more you know the Word, the more you conform to the image of Jesus. When you are born again, nothing is wrong with your spirit—the life of God is in there—but you are hindered from living a spiritual life by a soul (mind) that thinks like the world instead of like God.

After becoming a Christian, the Bible instructs you to "put on the new man, which after God is created in righteousness and true holiness" (Ephesians 4:24). This means that your soul and body are to take on the same image that is in your spirit. This happens through the process of changing your mind, your will and your emotions to understand and walk in the ways of God. We are to conform to the image of God's Son (Romans 8:29). You and I ought to act just like Jesus. The only thing that stands in the way is our soul. Without a renewed mind, we could not dare to walk and act like Jesus.

That's why Romans 12:2 tells us "be ye transformed by the renewing of your mind." The word *transformed* is translated from the Greek word from which we get the term *metamorphosis*. This Greek word is used in the Scripture in two other places.

One such account is when Jesus was transfigured on the Mount. The other is in 2 Corinthians 3:18: "But we all, with open face beholding as in a glass the glory of the Lord, are changed into the same image from glory to glory, even as by the Spirit of the Lord." Changed is the same word in the Greek as *transformed* and *transfigured*. Our souls are changed when we spend time beholding the Lord in the Word and in prayer. It is a natural process like metamorphosis.

Renewing our minds causes our outer being to be transformed in much the same way as a caterpillar is changed into a butterfly. As we behold Him, our outer man changes to match the inner man which is created in righteousness and true holiness.

The world would have you think that God is a liar. Yet God tells you that Satan is the liar, and in between these two adversaries is your soul. Here is where the spiritual battle is fought. Therefore, your soul must be anchored. Anchored to what? To the Word. To eternal things. If it is moored to this world, you will never walk in victory or in the power of God. If your soul is not fixed on eternal things, it will not hold steady in the time of crisis.

When you become a Christian, you are sustained from the inside. Your spirit is steady in adversity. You are upheld and maintained by your spirit man and not by your intellect or reasoning. "For the word of God is quick, and powerful, and sharper than any twoedged sword, piercing even to the dividing asunder of soul and spirit, and of the joints and marrow, and is a discerner of the thoughts and intents of the heart" (Hebrews 4:12).

God's Word divides (distinguishes between) the soul and the spirit. Nothing else can cause you to recognize whether you are being led by your soul and natural thinking or whether you are following your spirit which is led by the Holy Spirit.

Every problem, weakness or difficulty you have could be solved immediately if you could know the mind of God. But it takes effort, dedication and faithfulness to renew your mind. Mind renewal is not like the new birth. It is a process and doesn't come overnight. Though your spirit is renewed and transformed, your soul must be saved. Saved from what? From the world's influence and thinking.

James 1:21 is quite clear concerning this: "Wherefore lay apart all filthiness and superfluity of naughtiness, and receive with meekness the engrafted word, which is able to save your souls." You can't just read the Word. It must be implanted in your soul (your mind) and be received with meekness.

Meekness is often misunderstood. It is a thing of power, not weakness. It is an attitude in which we accept God's dealing with us as good. Therefore, we do not resist His correction or guidance. Meekness is giving your will to God and letting Him change it. So, your soul is saved as you yield your will to God's will.

The Scripture says that God energizes and creates in us the power and the desire to will and to work for His good pleasure (Philippians 2:13). He works from the inside out, not from the outside in. He takes the image of the Word that is in our spirits and grafts it into our souls as we behold Him. Only then can we outwardly express the image of Jesus that we inwardly possess.

But this takes conscious effort. If you are just going to give God a couple of hours a week, your mind will not be renewed. The Word won't be implanted in you. You might know it with your head, but it's the engrafted Word in your soul that changes you. It's the Word of God that controls your thinking and transforms your life.

So, take the time to get away from the world and study God's Word. Meditate on it, and let it change you from the inside out. "Draw nigh to God, and He will draw nigh to you"

(James 4:8). Make a conscious effort to allow the Word of God to be engrafted into you. Only then will you begin to understand His Word and His will. Only then will you be on your way to renewing your mind.

More Than You Can Dream

"...hope maketh not ashamed; because the love of God is shed abroad in our hearts by the Holy Ghost which is given unto us."
— ROMANS 5:5

Kenneth Copeland

These days, when I say the Word of God can heal your body, pay off your debts and bring you victory in every area of your life, not everyone believes me. Most wouldn't admit it outright, but it's true nonetheless.

They don't intentionally doubt the Word, of course. They're just so overwhelmed by the problems in their own lives, they're not sure anything (natural or supernatural) can help.

When they see Gloria and me so blessed and prosperous, they think, *Sure, it's easy for you to live by faith. You have a great life. But what can God do with a life as messed up as mine?*

If you ever struggle with that question, let me tell you. God can do for you exceeding, abundantly above all that you can ask or think. After more than 42 years of ministry, I can say that, not only because it's the Word of God, but also because it's a living reality for me.

You see, I wasn't always blessed. When I first learned about faith, I was a failure looking for somewhere to happen. I wasn't just scraping the bottom of the barrel, I was underneath with the barrel on top of me! Then one day I was reading Deuteronomy 28 and I saw all the blessings God's people are supposed to have in their lives.

I got mad. *Where are all these blessings that are supposed to belong to me?* I thought. As far as I could see, I didn't have even one of them. Yet the Bible clearly said:

> ...all these blessings shall come on thee, and overtake thee, if thou shalt hearken unto the voice of the Lord thy God. Blessed shalt thou be in the city, and blessed shalt thou be in the field. (I wasn't blessed anyplace!)

Blessed shall be the fruit of thy body.... (My children kept getting sick so they weren't very blessed, either.) Blessed shalt thou be when thou comest in, and blessed shalt thou be when thou goest out. (I wasn't.)

The Lord shall cause thine enemies that rise up against thee to be smitten before thy face: they shall come out against thee one way, and flee before thee seven ways.

The Lord shall command the blessing upon thee in thy storehouses, and in all that thou settest thine hand unto; and he shall bless thee in the land which the Lord thy God giveth thee (Deuteronomy 28:2-4, 6-8).

I didn't have any land. I didn't have any storehouse. In fact, I'd heard that God wouldn't bless you with a storehouse at all because He didn't want you to have anything.

And the Lord shall make thee plenteous in goods, in the fruit of thy body, and in the fruit of thy cattle, and in the fruit of thy ground, in the land which the Lord sware unto thy fathers to give thee. The Lord shall open unto thee his good treasure, the heaven to give the rain unto thy land in his season, and to bless all the work of thine hand: and thou shalt lend unto many nations, and thou shalt not borrow (verses 11-12).

I don't mind telling you, that looked good to me. All I'd ever known how to do was borrow, and I had depended on borrowed money all my adult life.

From Galatians to the Garage

Religion might have tried to explain the absence of those blessings in my life by telling me God made those promises to the Israelite nation, not to me. But I had already found out from Galatians 3:29 that everything God promised Abraham belongs to the gentiles now through Christ Jesus. For "if ye be

Christ's, then are ye Abraham's seed, and heirs according to the promise."

No, there was no doubt in my mind that these blessings were legally mine. The only question I had was, "How can I get my hands on them?"

As I dug into the Word, I found the answer. To enjoy the blessings of Abraham, I was going to have to walk in the same kind of faith he did.

Now, as in Abraham's day, faith opens the door to God's promises. To me, that was good news.

Not everyone sees it that way, however. Some people want the blessings without having to walk by faith. But like it or not, that's just not the way things work.

"Well," you say, "I wish they did!"

No, you really don't. God didn't set up the system of faith and prayer in order to make things difficult for you. He did it because Satan and his crew are always trying to steal our blessings. God's system is designed to keep them from pilfering our inheritance.

That's not hard to understand. After all, we protect things of value, even in the natural world. Think about how your bank works, for example. You have money deposited there. You know it belongs to you. But if you want to receive it, there are some things you have to do.

Why is that? It's certainly not to keep you from getting your own money—it's to keep other people from getting it. The procedures are for your benefit.

Of course, if you want to, you can ignore the procedures. You can go into the bank and squall and cry, beg, plead and jump up and down, but if you don't follow the established procedures, you won't get your money.

In that same way, God's promises belong to you. They're locked up in the spiritual treasure house of Almighty God. To access them, you'll have to take the time to learn the procedures. You'll have to study God's Word and discover His ways.

My willingness and even eagerness to do that was about all I had going for me back there in those early days, but it was enough. I was so desperate to learn faith that I locked myself in my garage with some tapes of Kenneth E. Hagin's messages about our inheritance in Christ Jesus.

For a week, I didn't talk to anyone else; I didn't listen to anyone else. I just went out there with the garbage, my Bible and my tape recorder. I told Gloria, "Don't call me more than once for a meal. If I don't show up in five minutes, go ahead and eat without me. I'll come in and sleep when I'm ready and then I'm coming right back out here. If anybody calls me, I'm not available."

I stayed out there with those tapes hour after hour. I couldn't get enough of the Word of God.

I'm the same way today. I can't get enough of it. I don't care what else is going on in the world, I'm going to stick with the Word. It brought me out of debt. It healed me. It healed my children. It has taken me through everything that has ever come my way, and I'm not about to turn loose of it now.

Build a Dream

Let me make it clear though, I didn't get a new set of circumstances overnight. When I walked out of the garage at the end of that week, my debts were just as big and my problems just as real as when I began. But something inside me had begun to change.

Hope had been born in me.

When I say "hope," I don't mean the weak "I wish" kind of hope the world gives. I mean the Bible kind of confident expectancy that comes when you get an inner image of something that hasn't happened yet. That kind of hope, Romans 5:5 says, never disappoints you.

Most people aren't familiar with godly hope. They are, however, quite experienced in "worry," which is a negative form of it. Worry begins with a thought in someone's mind. As it progresses, that thought becomes a mental picture.

Once the picture is formed, every time the person thinks of that thing, he can see it happening. As he concentrates on that picture, mulling it over again and again, it gets stronger and clearer.

What he's actually doing is meditating on something that hasn't come to pass yet. Eventually, he'll begin to talk like it has already happened because of the inner image he has built inside his consciousness. If he talks it long enough, that image will show up as a reality in his world.

Hope works that same way. The difference is, hope's pictures are not based on natural circumstances and devil-inspired fears, but on the Word of God.

If you're going to follow the faith of Abraham, you need to practice developing that kind of hope.

"But, Brother Copeland, I told you before, my situation is hopeless!"

It's probably not any more hopeless than mine was—and it certainly is not any more hopeless than Abraham's was. When God told him he was going to have a son, he was already 100 years old. Obviously there was no natural hope for that to happen. To make matters worse, his wife, Sarah, was in her 90s and had been barren all her life.

Yet the Bible says Abraham hoped against hope (Romans 4:18). He built a picture in his mind because of God's promise to him, a picture that was contrary to the pictures of childlessness that his circumstances had given him.

Abraham drew hope from what God had said to him and hung on to it. He drew it into his spirit and imagined having a son. He built it into his consciousness until he drove out every other idea.

It doesn't matter how far down you are today—financially, physically or any other way—you can do the same thing. You can begin to build dreams out of God's Word. A good foundation for them is Deuteronomy 28. It's God's Word and I can tell you from experience, it is good dream-building material.

God intended for man to be a dreamer. He built into us the capacity to do it. But He didn't intend for us to be limited by natural thoughts and circumstances. He meant for us to dream beyond them.

That's what Abraham did. He locked into God's dream—and it was bigger than anything he could have thought up on his own.

It will be that way for you too. God's dream is bigger than your dream for yourself. It is, as I said before, exceeding, abundantly beyond all you can ask or think! (See Ephesians 3:20.)

What Are You Becoming?

Once you get that dream inside you, things will begin to change. No, all your problems won't disappear overnight any more than mine did. But you'll respond to them differently. When they rise up in front of you and threaten to defeat you, God's dream will stir in your heart.

You'll start saying, "Wait just a minute. I'm the head, not the tail. I'm blessed, not cursed. I don't have to put up with this mess. I happen to be a child of the King Himself. He sets my table in the presence of my enemies. No weapon formed against me can prosper!" (See Deuteronomy 28:13, Psalm 23:5 and Isaiah 54:17.)

Once you start dreaming from the Word of God, you'll start acting on those dreams and your faith will bring them to pass.

That's what Dr. David Yonggi Cho did in Korea. He was a dying man, riddled with tuberculosis, when he came into the kingdom of God and started studying God's Word. He didn't have any religious people around him to tell him not to dream. He just took his Bible and started building dreams in his heart—things he wanted to do for God, for his nation, for his people.

He dreamed of building the biggest church in the world. He dreamed of sending missionaries all over the world. Today, that dream is a reality.

Dr. Cho pastors a church in Seoul, Korea, with over 700,000 members. Although the nation had no money when the church started, his church is able to send out millions of dollars a year to the foreign mission field.

Just think, all that started with one man dreaming by the Word of God. Like Abraham, he hoped against hope. He wrapped his faith around the supernatural picture painted by the Word of God, instead of the impossibilities painted by the world.

Look at Romans 4:18 again. It says Abraham "believed in hope, (notice the next phrase) that he might become...."

What are you becoming? Abraham was 100 years old and still planning what he would become. He still had his eye of faith focused on something he couldn't attain on his own. Something that couldn't come to pass without the supernatural power of God. He set out to become the father of many nations at 100 years old.

You know, when you get right down to it, it doesn't really matter much what you've been in the past. It doesn't matter whether you've left a colossal mess behind you or 25 years of ministry—what matters is what you're becoming today.

The Apostle Paul put it this way: "...this one thing I do, forgetting those things which are behind, and reaching forth unto those things which are before, I press toward the mark for the prize of the high calling of God in Christ Jesus" (Philippians 3:13-14).

Better Than Good

If you're not sure what you're becoming, let me give you a hint. You're going to become whatever you think about and talk about all the time.

I can listen to you talk for 30 minutes and tell you exactly what you're going to become. It doesn't take a prophet to do that. It just takes someone who will listen to your words.

So, listen to yourself. If you don't like what you hear, change it. Become someone better by beginning to think God's Word, talk God's Word and act on God's Word.

Nobody on earth can determine what you're going to become but you. Yes, you! Don't blame it on the devil. He can't change it. Don't blame it on your parents, your background or your circumstances.

Forget those things which are behind...and do what Abraham did. The Bible says "he considered not his own body now dead, when he was about an hundred years old, neither yet the deadness of Sarah's womb..." (Romans 4:19). He just said to himself, "Old man, you don't count. Neither do you, Granny. What counts is God's Word, and I am exactly who God says I am."

Do you want to become who God says you are? Do you want to be healed? Do you want to become free financially? Do you want to become a powerful witness in your neighborhood?

What is your dream? You can have it if you'll learn to live by faith.

If you don't have a dream yet, get one. Fill your heart full of the Word of God. Let Him show you what's possible. Trade your negative, natural hope for the supernatural promises of Almighty God and learn to "hope against hope."

I can tell you, your life will really be good when you're living Matthew, Mark, Luke and John instead of the 6 o'clock news. No, it will be better than good—it will be miraculous.

So miraculous, in fact, that sometimes when you tell people the Word of God will heal them, prosper them and set them free, they'll look at your life and say, "Sure it's easy for you to live by faith. You have a great life. But what can God do with a life as messed up as mine?"

Then you'll just smile and say, "Friend, God can do more for you than you'll ever dream. I can tell you that from experience. You see, I wasn't always this blessed...."

You Are a Candidate for a Miracle

Chapter 8

Jesse Duplantis

"Be thou strong and very courageous, that thou mayest observe to do according to all the law, which Moses my servant commanded thee: turn not from it to the right hand or to the left, that thou mayest prosper whithersoever thou goest. This book of the law shall not depart out of thy mouth; but thou shalt meditate therein day and night, that thou mayest observe to do according to all that is written therein: for then thou shalt make thy way prosperous, and then thou shalt have good success. Have not I commanded thee? Be strong and of a good courage; be not afraid, neither be thou dismayed: for the Lord thy God is with thee whithersoever thou goest."
— JOSHUA 1:7-9

If you're facing an impossible situation today, if you can't see a way out and you're so discouraged you're ready to quit, I have seven words for you that can change everything. Seven words that can—if you'll dare to believe them—turn total defeat into the most glorious opportunity for victory you've ever known: You are a candidate for a miracle.

That's right. If you're in Christ today (Notice I said "in Christ" not "in church." These days there are a lot of people in church who aren't in Christ.), you should be expecting God to do the impossible for you.

You should be running for a miracle today the same way a political candidate runs for office. But with one big difference. You don't have to be voted in to get your miracle. You just have to enter the race—because your miracle has already been won!

Every challenge you face today was overcome by Jesus 2,000 years ago when He went to the cross. He paid the price to heal every sickness or disease that may be in your body. Because of Jesus, there's an answer that's older than any problem you now have.

If you have cancer, you're a candidate for a miracle.

If you have diabetes, high blood pressure, heart trouble (or whatever!), you're a candidate for a miracle.

If you're financially broke, you are a candidate for a miracle.

If you're looking for someone to marry, you're a candidate for a miracle.

No matter what kind of need you may have today, you're a candidate for a miracle!

Problems, Get Out of My Face!

The first chapter of Joshua tells us about one particular man who was a candidate for a miracle. His associate, Moses, had just died and Joshua was facing the task of taking 5 million notoriously rebellious Israelites into the Promised Land.

God said to him, Now, Joshua, here's the situation. "Moses my servant is dead; now therefore arise, go over this Jordan, thou, and all this people, unto the land which I do give to them, even to the children of Israel" (verse 2).

Notice that God didn't tell Joshua about all the trouble he was going to meet when he got over there. He didn't tell him about the wall at Jericho. He didn't tell him there would be fierce giants to defeat.

He just said, "Arise and go, Joshua. You're a candidate for a miracle."

Then He said, *If you'll get up and go...*

Every place that the sole of your foot shall tread upon, that have I given unto you, as I said unto Moses. From the wilderness and this Lebanon even unto the great river, the river Euphrates, all the land of the Hittites, and unto the great sea toward the going down of the sun, shall be your coast. There shall not any man be able to stand before thee all the days of thy life: as I was with Moses, so I will be with thee: I will not fail thee, nor forsake thee (verses 3-5).

Look again at that last verse. Notice God didn't say that no one would stand against Joshua during this "Promised Land Campaign" he was about to begin. He said, "All the days of your life, Boy, nobody will be able to get in your face and knock you down" (my paraphrase, of course).

God told Joshua he'd be a candidate for a miracle all his life. That's good news, isn't it?

"Yeah, Brother Jesse, but that promise was for Joshua, not you and me."

God is no respecter of persons! God didn't love Joshua any more than He loves us. So if we'll do what God told him to do, no one will be able to stand before us either.

Forward...or Back?

What exactly did God instruct Joshua to do?

> ...be thou strong and very courageous, that thou mayest observe to do according to all the law, which Moses my servant commanded thee: turn not from it to the right hand or to the left, that thou mayest prosper whithersoever thou goest. This book of the law shall not depart out of thy mouth; but thou shalt meditate therein day and night, that thou mayest observe to do according to all that is written therein: for then thou shalt make thy way prosperous, and then thou shalt have good success. Have not I commanded thee? Be strong and of a good courage; be not afraid, neither be thou dismayed: for the Lord thy God is with thee whithersoever thou goest (verses 7-9).

Just like Joshua, if you meditate on the Word of God, if you believe it and obey it, you're a candidate for a miracle today. You may feel like you're in the desert, but you're standing on the boundary of the Promised Land.

The only question is: Will you go forward...or will you turn back?

The devil is going to try to convince you to turn back. He's going to work to distract you from the Word of God and scare you into settling for a nice life in the desert.

But listen to me. You may build 100 churches in the desert. You may draw water out of the Jordan, cultivate the dry land and think you've found heaven. But you'll be mistaken. Don't live in the desert in a church with a cultivated yard! You'll be outside of the will of God. He wants you in the Promised Land.

"But, Brother Jesse, it would take a miracle to get me past all these problems I have and into the Promised Land."

No problem! You're a candidate for a miracle!

Well, then, you may wonder, *why am I having such a hard time receiving one?* Because you remember too well that fallen state you were in before God saved you.

Most Christians have that problem. That's why they have difficulty believing God will work a miracle for them. They believe, for instance, that God will heal...but they're not sure He will heal them!

But it's time we change that kind of thinking. We need to quit dwelling on that old, fallen state and focus instead on the fact that God has made us His righteousness in Christ Jesus! We are in Him!

Sometimes I speak so boldly, it makes people mad. They say, "Who do you think you are?!" I ask them, "How much time do you have? It would take me a long time to tell you who I am because I'd have to tell you everything Jesus is. I'm in Him!"

Hey Everybody, Watch This!

Because of that attitude, when a big obstacle arises in my life, the first thing I say is, "Well, it's miracle time. It's time to grow. It's time to get in the Word of God."

I had to learn that early in my ministry because I faced some situations where a miracle was the only thing that was going to get me through.

I'll never forget one particular time, just after my brother-in-law, Jules, was saved. He was a very successful lawyer and through Cathy's and my witness, he had come to the knowledge of Jesus Christ. Of course, we'd told him about the healing power and promises of God and—as baby Christians usually do—he just believed without question and said, "Wow! That's great!"

I was getting ready to preach a meeting one night when my brother-in-law called me. He said a woman had come into his office who had been in an accident in the restaurant where she worked. She had been paralyzed as a result of it and wanted to sue the restaurant.

Jules said, "Well, lady, you have two choices. We can take the legal route and get you a lot of money...or you can go with me to my brother-in-law Jesse's meeting tonight and get healed. Which do you want?"

She said, "Well, I guess I'll go to the meeting."

So Jules called me and said, "Jesse, I'm bringing this paralyzed woman tonight and I've told her she'll get healed. That's right, isn't it?"

I assured him that was right and then after I hung up, I said, "God, what are we going to do?" You see, I had a problem because I had seen some people get healed and some not.

We're at the Promised Land, Jess, God answered. *Are we going to walk across or are we going to drag this paralyzed woman back to the desert and bury her?*

That night I preached as long as I could. (I was hoping she might get tired and go home.) Finally, I couldn't put it off any longer and I said, "All right, it's time for God to heal."

When Jules brought the woman up front, I determined to pray for her as quietly as possible so as not to attract any attention. But Jules had other ideas.

"Hey, everybody!" He called out. *"Watch! God's going to heal this woman.* OK, Jesse, now do it."

That woman was a candidate for a miracle—and so was I! I tried to make things easier by closing my eyes while I prayed for her but the Lord said, *Open your eyes.*

"No!" I answered.

Open your eyes, Jesse!

So I opened my eyes, told the woman God was going to heal her and then prayed with every fiber of my being. All of a sudden—wham!—both her hands went up in the air, she was knocked down by the power of the Holy Ghost, and was totally, miraculously healed!

You may think that's an unusual incident. And, to some it might be. But you and I serve an unusual God, and we should expect the unusual to be "the usual" in our lives.

Why? Because we are candidates for a miracle.

I want to burn that phrase into your mind. I want it to so mark your thinking that any time you have trouble from now on, instead of slipping automatically into despair, you'll follow the instructions God gave to Joshua. You'll get into the Word of God and not turn from it to the left or to the right. You'll go to bed reading it. You'll get up reading it. You'll meditate on it until you digest all the nutrients in it and it fills you with the power of God.

You'll say boldly, "No, I'm not giving up, praise God. I'm going on. I'm stepping into the Promised Land because I'm a candidate for a miracle!"

Turn Your Hurts Into Harvests

Chapter 9

"My God shall supply all your need according to his riches in glory by Christ Jesus."
— PHILIPPIANS 4:19

Kenneth Copeland

What do you do when someone mistreats you?

I didn't ask what you want to do. I didn't ask what your automatic fleshly reaction is. I already know that.

Your natural, knee-jerk response is the same as mine. You want to strike back. You want to do something or say something that will even the score. If you can't manage that, you might settle for a few hours (or days or years) of feeling sorry for yourself. You might try to ease your wounded feelings by telling someone how wrongly you've been treated.

On a purely natural, human level that's how we all want to react when someone does us wrong. But I want to tell you something today. If you're a born-again child of the living God, you have no business just reacting to things on a natural, human level.

God has called and equipped you to live on a higher level. He's given you the power to respond in a supernatural way when someone does you wrong. He's given you the power to respond in love.

"Oh, Brother Copeland, that's too hard. I don't want to do that!"

Yes, you do—and here's why. If you will train yourself to respond God's way, you can take mistreatment and transform it from the curse the devil intends it to be into a seed of tremendous blessing in your life.

When you learn to obey God in the face of persecution, you can literally get rich—in the areas of finances, favor and opportunity—off the very persecution the devil sent to keep you down.

Serious Business

Make no mistake, that is the devil's intention. He sends people across your path to offend you and mistreat you for the express purpose of stealing the Word of God—and the anointing that goes with it—out of your life. Mark 4:17 says, "Persecution ariseth for the word's sake...."

The devil knows how powerful you are when you are anointed. He knows because he once was anointed himself. The Bible says before evil was found in him, he was the "anointed cherub." So it is his one ambition to trick you into cutting yourself off from that anointing.

That's why he sends bigots to insult you and thieves to steal from you. That's why, whenever he can, he goads people around you into being insensitive and unappreciative. He wants you to get offended and cut off your supernatural power supply.

Most believers don't realize it, but that's what offenses do. You can see that in Matthew 11:4-6. There, the disciples of John the Baptist came to Jesus and asked if He was truly the Anointed One. Jesus answered and said to them: "Go and show John again those things which ye do hear and see: The blind receive their sight, and the lame walk, the lepers are cleansed, and the deaf hear, the dead are raised up, and the poor have the gospel preached to them. And blessed is he, whosoever shall not be offended in me."

We need to realize, my friend, that offenses are serious business. They are sent by the devil to rob us of the anointing and block the flow of the blessings of God. That fact alone should be enough to make us decide never, ever, to be offended again.

I know I've made that decision. I've determined that no matter how someone may insult my intelligence, my beliefs or even my race, I'm not willing to lose my anointing over it.

No matter how they treat me, or what they might call me, I will not take offense.

Now, I realize someone may be reading this and thinking, *Yeah, that's easy for you to say! Nobody says and does the things to you like they do to me!*

That may be true. Although I am an Indian, and have had ample opportunity for offense, where race is concerned, I know there are many people who have suffered much more mistreatment than I have. But I can say this: No matter what color you are, you are welcome in more churches than I am. I've had entire books written for the express purpose of criticizing me. How many books have they written about you?

I only bring those things to your attention because I want you to know that dealing with offenses isn't any easier for me than it is for anyone else. I've come up against some hard people and some hard situations in my life. So I know if God can see me through, He can do the same for you.

Rejoice!...No Kidding

Once we decide we will take a devil-sent opportunity for offense and turn it into a harvest of blessing, the first thing we need to know is what God wants us to do in that situation. If we're not supposed to strike back, if we're not supposed to get our feelings hurt and go off in a huff, what are we supposed to do?

First Peter 4 answers that question: "Beloved, think it not strange concerning the fiery trial which is to try you, as though some strange thing happened unto you: But rejoice, inasmuch as ye are partakers of Christ's sufferings; that, when his glory shall be revealed, ye may be glad also with exceeding joy. If ye be reproached for the name of Christ, happy are ye; for the spirit of glory and of God resteth upon you..." (verses 12-14).

God doesn't want us to cry and complain when someone does us wrong. He doesn't want us to sue them. He wants us to *rejoice!*

I can just hear your old flesh groan: "Man, you have to be kidding! I'm supposed to rejoice when someone does me wrong? What do I have to rejoice about?"

Plenty!

According to Jesus, persecution sets you up for blessing. It opens you up for great rewards! Jesus made that very clear in Luke 6. He said, "Blessed are ye, when men shall hate you, and when they shall separate you from their company, and shall reproach you, and cast out your name as evil, for the Son of man's sake. Rejoice ye in that day, and leap for joy: for, behold, your reward is great in heaven" (verses 22-23).

To get the full meaning of what Jesus was saying there, you have to realize what the word *blessed* means. It's not just a weak, religious sentiment. To be God-blessed means you're empowered by Almighty God Himself to prosper and succeed. It means you're empowered by the Holy Spirit to be exceedingly happy with life and joy in spite of any outside circumstances.

Think about that for a moment. When people mistreat you, they're actually giving you the opportunity to receive greater measures of power and success from the Spirit of God. They are opening the door for you to step up to a higher plane of heavenly reward!

Religion has taught us that we couldn't enjoy such heavenly rewards until after we die. But nothing could be further from the truth. God intends for us to make use of our heavenly rewards here on this earth where we need them!

You see, as believers, we each have a heavenly account that functions much like a natural bank account. The Apostle Paul refers to that account in his letter to his Philippian partners. He commended his partners for giving to him, not because he wanted gifts from them, but because he desired fruit that would abound to their account.

Paul's partners had made deposits in that heavenly account through their giving, so he was able to boldly say, "My God shall supply all your need according to his riches in glory by Christ Jesus" (Philippians 4:19).

Jesus also spoke of that heavenly account when He said, "Lay not up for yourselves treasures upon earth, where moth and rust doth corrupt, and where thieves break through and steal: But lay up for yourselves treasures in heaven, where neither moth nor rust doth corrupt, and where thieves do not break through nor steal: For where your treasure is, there will your heart be also" (Matthew 6:19-21).

If you've studied the Word under this ministry any length of time, I'm sure you already know how to lay up treasure in your heavenly account by giving financially into the work of God. You know about the spiritual law of seedtime and harvest. You know that when you give to God of your material resources, He multiplies it and gives it back to you a hundred-fold (Mark 10:30).

But let me ask you this: Did you know you can do the same thing with persecution? Did you know that you can plant it as a seed by obeying God, by leaping and rejoicing in it instead of taking offense?

Sure you can! And when you do, it will bring forth a harvest of blessing!

What's more, because persecution attacks your soul and the very Anointing of God on your life—which is far more precious than anything money could buy—the value of the harvest it brings is absolutely priceless. The seed of persecution when planted according to the Word will be worth far more to you than any financial seed you could ever plant!

Now, I'll admit, it's a tough seed to sow. You have to sow it out of commitment. It doesn't feel good to do it. But the harvest is worth the pain.

I know that not only from my own experience, but from watching the experience of others. For instance, one friend of mine has refused to take offense at the bigotry directed against him because of the color of his skin. He has so succeeded in blessing and loving the white people who have persecuted him that now some black people are mad at him. "He doesn't even know he's black anymore!" they'll say.

But my friend doesn't take offense at them either. He just prays for them and goes right on gathering up his harvest. It's quite a harvest, too! That man has favor everywhere he goes. He's invited to places few people get to go. He's blessed financially beyond most people's wildest dreams.

The man is getting rich off racism!

It's Worth More as a Seed

Someone might say, "Well, that sounds good! I wonder if it would work like that for me?"

It will if you'll put it to work. Look back at that passage in Luke 6:27 where Jesus explains this principle and says, "I say unto you which hear...." In other words, this will work for anyone who will listen. All you have to do is hear it and do it.

> Love your enemies, do good to them which hate you, bless them that curse you, and pray for them which despitefully use you. And unto him that smiteth thee on the one cheek offer also the other; and him that taketh away thy cloak forbid not to take thy coat also. Give to every man that asketh of thee; and of him that taketh away thy goods ask them not again.... But love ye your enemies, and do good, and lend, hoping for nothing again; and your reward shall be great, and ye shall be the children of the Highest: for he is kind unto the unthankful and to the evil. Be ye therefore merciful, as your Father also is merciful. Judge not, and ye shall not be judged: condemn not, and ye shall not be condemned: forgive, and ye shall be forgiven: Give, and it shall be given unto you; good measure, pressed down, and shaken together, and running over, shall men give into your bosom. For with the same measure

that ye mete withal it shall be measured to you again (verses 27-30, 35-38).

For the most part, we've misunderstood what Jesus was saying about turning the other cheek and giving to the guy who tries to steal from us. We thought He was saying we should just lie down and let people run over us. But that wasn't His point at all!

He was trying to teach us about this seedtime, harvest principle. He was trying to show us how to get blessed. He was saying, "Don't sue the person who stole your shirt and try to get your shirt back. Give it to him. Then give him your coat too. Those things will be worth more to you as seeds than they would be if you kept them. If you'll sow them instead of fighting to keep them, the power of God will go to work on your behalf. He'll multiply that seed and bless you with a hundred times as much!" If you fight, you do it on your own. If you give, all of heaven will get in the situation with you.

I'll never forget the first time God was able to get the truth of that principle through to me. It was years ago when Gloria and I were on our way to preach a meeting in San Francisco. I was walking through the airport with a little Minolta camera hanging over my shoulder. Back then, that was the ministry camera and Gloria was the ministry photographer. So that camera was important to us.

I had walked around that airport for a while when suddenly I realized my camera was gone. Someone had stolen it right off my shoulder! To put it very mildly, I was irritated.

I started looking around the airport for the thief. I thought, *If I find you, you turkey, I am going to whip you good!*

But right in the middle of my upset, the Spirit of God interrupted my thinking. *If you take that attitude,* He said, *you'll lose that camera!*

"What are you talking about, Lord?" I answered. "I've already lost it!"

No, it isn't gone yet.

I'd learned from Oral Roberts about the seed, plant, harvest principle, so I caught on to what the Lord was telling me in a flash. I said, "Lord, I see it!" Then I turned to Gloria and said, "Listen, let's agree on this. I'm giving that camera to whoever took it off my shoulder. I'm sowing it as a seed into that person's life and I'm praying that God will use it to get him saved. I'm believing that every time he touches that camera, the Anointing of God will come on him and draw him to Jesus. Even if the police catch the thief with the camera in his hand, I will say, 'Don't charge that man with any crime. I have given him that camera.'"

Of course, Gloria agreed and we boarded the plane to San Francisco. After we got settled in our seats, I started talking to the Lord about the seed I'd planted. I said, "Lord, I know that camera had value and we need a camera in this ministry. But I don't want another Minolta. It's a good camera, but it doesn't have enough range to do what I need. What I want is a Nikon F."

This was back in the early '70s when just the body of a Nikon F was worth anywhere from $700 to $900. The two lenses I needed were worth about the same amount, so to buy the whole outfit, I might have to pay up to $1800. But I wasn't worried. I had my seed in the ground and I started getting excited. I started expecting the harvest.

What a Deal!

Can you see what happened to me? I could have been sitting there seething over that stolen camera. I could have been sitting there getting offended, cutting myself off from the Anointing of God. But I wasn't! I had forgotten all about that thief. I was too busy being thrilled with the new camera God was giving me to worry about how the thief had done me wrong!

A few days later, Gloria and I were walking along the street in San Francisco when I spotted a Nikon F camera box sitting in the window of a small shop. I went in and asked the store clerk how much they wanted for it.

"We don't have a Nikon F," she answered.

"Yes, you do. It's right there in the window."

She reached over and got it, looked puzzled and carried it to a Japanese gentleman in the back of the store. "How much is this?" she asked him.

He threw up his hands and said something in Japanese that I didn't understand. So I just dug around in my pocket and found some traveler's checks. "Here," I said, "I have $250. Will you sell it to me for that?"

"OK!" said the Japanese man.

Of course I was excited about getting just the body of a Nikon F for that price. But before I had a chance to say anything about it, the store clerk dug around in a drawer, found a Nikon 50 mm lens and handed it to me along with the camera. Glory to God, my crop was coming up!

It wasn't finished yet, either. Just a few days later in another city, Gloria and I were walking along the street again and we stopped in a camera store. I looked up and noticed that way up high on the top of a display shelf there was a lens case for a Nikon 200 mm lens.

The same thing happened again. The store owner didn't know he had it, and didn't know what to charge for it. So he sold it to me for $100!

I don't mind telling you, by the time that deal was done, I was almost hoping someone would steal something from me. But then I realized, *Hey, I can give it—without someone having to steal it!* I liked that kind of harvest!

You'd like that kind of harvest too, wouldn't you?

Well, you can have it. Just start taking those opportunities for offense and planting them as seeds. Instead of crying over how badly you've been hurt, turn those hurts into harvests and start laughing at the devil. Take everything ugly he has ever thrown at you and sow it as a seed.

Begin now by praying:

"Father, in the Name of Jesus, right now I sow as seed in the kingdom of God every hurt, every bad feeling, every theft, and every evil thing any person has ever done or said to me, my family or my ministry. I release every person who has ever hurt me and I forgive them now. I lift each one of them up to You and I pray for those people. I pray, Father, that they'll come into a greater knowledge of You. I pray that their spirit be saved in the Day of the Lord.

"Now I declare before You, My God in heaven, that I expect a reward. I believe Your Word and by faith I set my sickle to my harvest. I believe I receive a hundredfold return for every wrong deed done to me, every unkind word spoken to me and every dime stolen from me. I expect to receive a blessing of equal benefit. I claim it. It's mine and I have it now in Jesus' mighty Name!"

Think Again! The Only Thing Powerful Enough to Keep You From Receiving Is Your Own Thinking

Chapter 10

Kenneth Copeland

"According as his divine power hath given unto us all things that pertain unto life and godliness, through the knowledge of him that hath called us to glory and virtue: Whereby are given unto us exceeding great and precious promises: that by these ye might be partakers of the divine nature...."
— 2 Peter 1:3-4

What would you say if I asked you to tell me the biggest problem you're facing right now?

Would you say your finances? Family problems? Sickness? Job frustrations? Your weight?

If you said any of those—in fact, if you listed any circumstance at all—I have some startling news for you.

You're mistaken.

That's right, you're mistaken! I can tell you without even knowing the details of your life that, if you're a born-again believer, money is not your problem. Sickness is not your problem. Your family, weight, job, background, lack of education...none of those things is your problem.

Your problem is the way you've been thinking about those things.

"Oh now, Brother Copeland, be realistic. These are hard times. The economy is bad. The government is a mess. Everything is going downhill. Those things aren't just figments of my imagination. They're real. What difference could it possibly make how I think about them?!"

I'll show you. Look at 2 Kings 6, beginning in verse 24. There, God gives us a dramatic illustration of what a difference your thought patterns can make—even in the worst of situations. He tells us of a time when the city of Samaria was in deep trouble. An enemy king had surrounded it with fortified troops and put it under total siege. No one could go into the city and no one could go out.

"And there was a great famine in Samaria: and, behold, they besieged it, until an ass's head was sold for fourscore pieces of silver, and the fourth part of a cab of dove's dung for five pieces of silver."

(That's worse than a recession folks! It's worse than any economic depression any of us have ever seen!)

"And as the king of Israel was passing by upon the wall, there cried a woman unto him, saying, Help, my lord, O king. And he said, If the Lord do not help thee, whence shall I help thee?"

This king was saying, "Look, lady, the government is just as broke as you are. What do you expect us to do?"

"And the king said unto her, What aileth thee? And she answered, This woman said unto me, Give thy son, that we may eat him today, and we will eat my son tomorrow. So we boiled my son, and did eat him: and I said unto her on the next day, Give thy son that we may eat him: and she hath hid her son. And it came to pass, when the king heard the words of the woman, that he rent his clothes."

This situation had gone way beyond serious. It was pathetic, and tragically hopeless. Listen to what the king said next: "He said, God do so and more also to me, if the head of Elisha the son of Shaphat shall stand on him this day.... Behold, this evil is of the Lord; what should I wait for the Lord any longer?"

All he knew to do was get mad at the preacher and blame the problem on God. Have you ever had thoughts like that? Well, sure you have! We all have!

But when the king sent someone to cut off Elisha's head, Elisha delivered a surprising message from the Lord. "Then Elisha said, Hear ye the word of the Lord; Thus saith the Lord, Tomorrow about this time shall a measure of fine flour be sold for a shekel, and two measures of barley for a shekel, in the gate of Samaria" (2 Kings 7:1).

Don't you know those words were a shock to those who heard them? Here they are in the midst of the most desperate situation they've ever seen. There's no sign of hope anywhere and the prophet of God says, "Hey, good news! This is all going to be over by tomorrow and we'll all be enjoying prosperity!"

God wasn't the one creating the disaster. He was the One with the solution to it. Yet, instead of rejoicing over this thrilling word of hope, "A lord on whose hand the king leaned answered the man of God, and said, Behold, if the Lord would make windows in heaven, might this thing be? And he [Elisha] said, Behold, thou shalt see it with thine eyes, but shalt not eat thereof" (verse 2).

This man, who actually served as the "vice president" of Samaria, didn't respond to God's Word in faith. He responded to it with skepticism. He thought, *Even if God got involved, this situation is too bad to be turned around now!* His thinking was so geared toward the negative that he couldn't even imagine a positive turn of events.

As all this was going on, there were four lepers sitting outside the city's gates. They'd been thinking negative, fear-filled thoughts just like everyone else. But then, something happened.

When Elisha spoke God's plan, the Holy Spirit moved on these men. Suddenly, their thinking changed. They didn't know it—but they began thinking the thoughts of God. "And they said one to another, Why sit we here until we die? If we say, We will enter into the city, then the famine is in the city, and we shall die there: and if we sit still here, we die also. Now therefore come, and let us fall unto the host of the Syrians: if they save us alive, we shall live; and if they kill us, we shall but die" (verses 3-4).

Do you see the change in their thought pattern? Up to that time, they had been famine thinkers and leprosy thinkers. But now they were saying, "Why are we just sitting here waiting to die? Let's do something!"

When their thinking changed, their actions changed. Instead of sitting around feeling sorry for themselves, they jumped up and headed toward the Syrian camp. Do you know what they discovered when they arrived? No one was there!

The camp was abandoned. It was filled with an abundance of food and clothing and supplies—but all the soldiers were gone.

These lepers had stumbled onto a spiritual law. It's this: When hard times come, they're never as hard as they look. That's so important, I'm going to say it again. Hard times are not as hard as they look—unless you're looking in the wrong place, through the wrong eyes, thinking the wrong thoughts, and imitating the wrong people.

You may say, "But Brother Copeland, the lepers' thinking patterns didn't change that situation. God changed the situation. He made the Syrian army hear the sound of warriors coming and it scared them away!"

Exactly. But that miracle of God would never have been a blessing to those lepers—or anyone else for that matter—if they hadn't changed their thinking.

As a born-again believer, you're in much the same situation. God has already moved on your behalf. He sent Jesus to the cross to bear your sickness, weakness and pain (Isaiah 53:4-5). He healed you by His stripes (1 Peter 2:24). He became poor so you could be rich (2 Corinthians 8:9). He covenanted with you to meet all your needs according to His riches in glory by Christ Jesus (Philippians 4:19).

He has given you "all things that pertain unto life and godliness" (2 Peter 1:3). The only thing powerful enough to keep you from receiving those things is your own thinking.

Wrong thoughts will paint the wrong pictures in your mind. They'll tell you things are worse than they are. They'll tell you that you can't do what it takes to succeed in life. But I'm here to tell you, you can succeed!

It doesn't matter how bad the economy is. People who understand money aren't afraid of hard times. In fact, it's the ungodly people who are money minded that actually wish for hard times. Such people made great fortunes back during the depression years. They bought up goods at about 10 cents on the dollar and ended up rich while others went broke.

But, of course, as believers, that's not our motive for prospering during hard times. We want to prosper in order to help others get back on top.

We want to say, "Hey friend, let me teach you how to prosper with me. Come on over here in the kingdom of God. Get over here in my house. No flood of recession or depression is going to tear it up. It's built on the Rock!" (See Matthew 7:24-26.)

If people are sick, we can say to them, "Don't let sickness and disease knock your feet out from under you, friend. Come on over here to my house. It's a healing house. By the power of God, we can show you how to be well!"

That's what the good news is really about. If we'd preach it that way instead of preaching it as some kind of religious club people need to join, they'd come running to us. If we'd preach the gospel to the poor and let them know they don't have to be poor anymore because of Jesus, they would beat down the church door just to get in there with us.

But we aren't preaching that way because we aren't thinking that way!

So, how do we change our way of thinking? God tells us in Isaiah 55:

> Seek ye the Lord while he may be found, call ye upon him while he is near: Let the wicked forsake his way, and the unrighteous man his thoughts: and let him return unto the Lord, and he will have mercy upon him; and to our God, for he will abundantly pardon. For my thoughts are not your thoughts, neither are your ways my ways, saith the Lord. For as the heavens are higher than the earth, so are my ways higher than your ways, and my thoughts than your thoughts. For as the rain cometh down, and the snow from heaven, and returneth not thither, but watereth the earth, and maketh it bring forth and bud, that it may give seed to the sower, and

bread to the eater: So shall my word be that goeth forth out of my mouth: it shall not return unto me void, but it shall accomplish that which I please, and it shall prosper in the thing whereto I sent it (verses 6-11).

If we want to live the kind of life God has in mind for us, we must trade our thoughts for His thoughts. We must lay down the perspectives we've gained through past experiences and instead pick up the wisdom of God.

Just look at what Proverbs 4 says about the importance of that wisdom: "Wisdom is the principal thing; therefore get wisdom: and with all thy getting get understanding. Exalt her, and she shall promote thee.... She shall give to thine head an ornament of grace: a crown of glory shall she deliver to thee" (verses 7-9).

Acquiring the wisdom of God is the number one top priority in our lives. Some people think prayer is top priority. But prayer without wisdom won't get you anywhere.

How many times have you prayed and failed to receive your answer? It wasn't because God missed it! The Word of God says you ask and receive not because you ask amiss (James 4:3). You need wisdom, you need God's thoughts about the situation before you can pray effectively.

Many times you may be crying out to God for healing when what you actually need is a miracle. You may be praying about a money shortage when what you have is a giving shortage. You may even be causing the problem yourself without knowing it.

You need God's wisdom!

How do you get it?

Jesus shows us in Luke 11:49. There, He says, "Therefore also said the wisdom of God, I will send them prophets and apostles, and some of them they shall slay and persecute."

Think about this for a moment. Jesus said, "Therefore...said the wisdom of God...." Then He began to quote Scripture. He called the written Word of God the wisdom of God.

God's Wisdom Is His Word

Do you want to know the thoughts of God? Do you want to know the wisdom of God? Well, go get your Bible, open it up, and read it!

If you're holding a Bible, you have God's wisdom right there in your hand.

About 20 years ago I was driving down the highway pleading with God. I had some questions I wanted to ask Him. I had some problems in my life I needed Him to address. "Oh, God," I said, "You spoke to Moses face to face. You spoke to Elijah. You spoke to Elisha. You spoke to Joshua. I want You to talk to me so badly I can hardly stand it."

Suddenly, right on the inside of me I heard His voice. *Why, Kenneth,* He said, *You have a record of everything I said to Moses. You have a record of everything I said to Joshua. You have everything I said to Elijah and Elisha. You have everything I said to Daniel and Jesus. It's lying right next to you on the seat of your car.*

I looked over and there was my Bible. I'll tell you, I shouted. "Praise God! Praise God! Praise God!"

I pulled over to the side of the road and shouted and wept with joy. I was driving an old car that had more than 98,000 miles on it (actually, it had 98,000 miles on it when I got it!) and it was leaking at every joint. At that moment, I realized that the new car I so desperately needed was laying right there on the seat by me.

The wisdom of God—all it would take for me to have that car—was right there. The wisdom of the ages was at my fingertips and I could read every word of it and stand on every word of it.

You can, too. But first, you have to be willing to forsake your old ways of thinking. "Let the wicked forsake his way, and the unrighteous man his thoughts" (Isaiah 55:7). Do you know what wicked means? It means twisted.

Twisted thoughts produce twisted results. Poor thinking produces poverty. Sick thinking produces sickness. You can't hold on to those kinds of thoughts and walk in the power of God.

"For my thoughts are not your thoughts, neither are your ways my ways, saith the Lord" (Isaiah 55:8). Let's face it. God is just plain smarter than we are. He's been around a lot longer—and what He thinks is a whole lot different than what we've been thinking.

So let the Word of God, the wisdom of God, begin to influence your thinking. Soak your mind in it. Don't just scan it lightly. Dig in it. Learn it. Take it seriously.

Then begin to pray in the spirit. Let the Spirit of God start a process of spiritual insight in your heart as you pray and worship in the spirit. After awhile, you'll begin to understand things in a new way. You'll begin to have a whole new interpretation of the problem.

You may suddenly have a realization, a deep conviction, an inner knowing. Someone may call you on the telephone and say, "I just got a word from the Lord this morning and I'm so excited about it...." And what they say is exactly what you need to hear.

However you get it, remember—wisdom is the principal thing. God's way of thinking will save your life, pull you out of debt and put you on the road to prosperity. It will introduce you to possibilities you have never seen before. They're out there now...just beyond your thinking.

So quit focusing on your seemingly hopeless situation, get your Bible out, and say—just like the leper—"Why sit we here till we die?"!

Then get moving. There's a word full of abundance just waiting for you.

Rejoice!

Chapter 11

"A merry heart doeth good like a medicine."
— PROVERBS 17:22

Kenneth Copeland

With the busy schedules, high expectations and financial pressures we all face, it's easy to let joy slip through your fingers. But don't do it. Instead, get a revelation of joy that will inspire you to hang on to it all year round.

If you've recently been in many services where the Holy Spirit is moving, you've heard the laughter. You've seen, and perhaps experienced, spontaneous outbreaks of joy that range from a few quiet chuckles to uproarious laughter that literally leaves believers rolling in the aisles.

It's glorious. There's no denying that. But what is it all about?

The answer to that question is even more thrilling than the laughter itself.

Jesus is building up His Church. He is strengthening us out of the rich treasury of His Glory. He is arming us with the spiritual might we will need to march out of every bondage and crush the devil under our feet—once and for all.

If you don't understand what all that has to do with laughter, read Nehemiah 8:10 and you'll find out. It tells us "the joy of the Lord is [our] strength."

Many believers don't realize how literally true that verse is. So they drag around in defeat, never knowing why. "I just can't figure it out," they'll say. "I believe the Bible. I believe Jesus has set me free from this sickness...I believe He has set me free from this sin...I believe He has set me free from this lifestyle of lack. But I still can't get the victory."

The problem is, those people are too spiritually weak to receive what Jesus has given them. They need a tonic that will put some muscle back in their believing. They need something to put a sparkle in their eye, a spring in their step, and give them the spiritual might they need to knock the devil in the head and take back what belongs to them.

That's exactly what the joy of the Lord will do.

To understand why, you must realize that joy is not happiness. Happiness is a fleeting, temporal condition that depends on the comfort of your flesh. Joy, on the other hand, is a vital spiritual force. It is not based on outward circumstances, but upon the condition of your heart.

Happiness is wimpy. It disappears every time there's trouble. But joy is tough. If you'll let it, it will keep flowing in the midst of the most miserable situation. It will enable you to stand as solid as a stump until the time of trouble is over.

I realize if you're sitting there right now in the midst of trouble, you probably feel like it will never be over. But, believe me, it will!

Psalm 30:5 says, "weeping may endure for a night, but joy cometh in the morning." If you're a person of faith, it doesn't matter how dark conditions may seem to be right now, you can rest assured, a brighter day is on the way. That's because the devil cannot sustain an attack. He doesn't have the power. So if you'll let the force of joy keep you strong, you will outlast him and he'll eventually have to give up and admit defeat!

The Apostle Paul confirms that fact in Galatians 5:22-23. There he lists joy as a fruit of the spirit and says, "against such there is no law." That means there is no force in existence that can rise up and overcome the fruit of the spirit.

Here's why. The devil is not a creator. He can't come up with anything original. All he can do is take what God has made and twist it into its opposite, or reciprocal, form. Since something that's been twisted and corrupted is always weaker than it was in its original state, the devil's forces must yield when God comes on the scene. Hate must yield to love. Fear must yield to faith. Joy whips weakness and discouragement every time!

More Than a Holy Ghost Giggle

Now let me show you how that information relates to the laughter and the outpouring of God's glory we've begun to experience.

The word *glory* as used throughout the Old Testament literally means "to be heavy laden with everything that is good," and it relates directly to the presence of God's Spirit. Some years ago, I learned from Billye Brim, who has studied Hebrew extensively, that the word *grief* is the exact opposite. It means to be heavy laden with everything that is bad.

Grief is the satanic reciprocal of glory. So, when the glory of God comes on you, grief doesn't stand a chance. It has to flee! When it does, the joy of the Lord that's in you just starts bubbling out. There's nothing to hold it back.

Of course, that's a lot of fun. We all enjoy it. But actually, the Lord is not just out to give us a good time and a Holy Ghost giggle. He has a greater purpose. He wants us to be full of joy because it's the force that will make us strong enough to carry out His plan in this final hour. It will give us the spiritual, mental and physical fortitude to rise up in the fullness of God's glory—fully healed, fully delivered, fully prosperous—so we can reap the final harvest and march out of here into the rapture.

Listen to me. The Church will not slip out of this earth in defeat and disgrace. We will not leave here like some whipped pup. No, God will take us out in glorious victory. He will do for us even more than He did for the Israelites when they left Egypt. Psalm 105 says:

> He brought them forth also with silver and gold: and there was not one feeble person among their tribes. Egypt was glad when they departed: for the fear of them fell upon them. He spread a cloud for a covering; and fire to give light in the night. The people asked, and he brought quails, and satisfied them with the bread of heaven. He opened the rock, and the waters gushed out; they ran in the dry places like a river. For he remembered his holy promise, and Abraham his servant. And

he brought forth his people with joy, and his chosen with gladness (verses 37-43).

Look at that last verse again. It says God "brought forth his people with joy." No wonder none of them was sick or feeble! Joy made them strong from the inside out.

"Brother Copeland, are you saying joy heals?"

Yes, I am. Proverbs 17:22 plainly says, "A merry heart doeth good like a medicine." Even modern research has proven that joy and healing are connected. There are documented reports of people who've been healed watching old Laurel and Hardy movies. They just released a small measure of joy and their bodies responded.

Get Another Load

The reason we haven't seen more of that kind of thing is that until recently, the Body of Christ has put very little emphasis on joy. There was even a time when we thought the more grief-stricken you were during church, the more spiritual you were.

There is nothing further from the truth. God is full of joy. Jesus is a man of joy. So if we're going to follow after Him, we'll have to be full of joy too!

Joy used to be my weakest area, spiritually. I spent so much time majoring on faith that I didn't pay much attention to it. But the Lord eventually taught me that you can't live by faith without joy.

That's because it takes strength to live by faith. We're surrounded by a world that is flowing toward death. The natural pull of it is always negative. When you leave things alone and don't work against that negative flow, they always get worse—not better. If you leave a garden unattended, it dies for lack of water or gets taken over by weeds. If you leave a house unattended to, the paint peels off and the boards begin to rot.

To move toward life you must constantly swim upstream. If you ever get too weak spiritually to do that, you'll find yourself being swept back toward sickness, lack or some other form of defeat. So you can never afford to run out of strength.

No wonder the Apostle Paul wrote, "Rejoice in the Lord always: and again I say, Rejoice" (Philippians 4:4)! To rejoice means to re-joy, to back up your spiritual truck and get another load of it.

Paul understood the link between joy and strength. That's why he prayed for the Colossians to be "strengthened with all might, according to [God's] glorious power, unto all patience and longsuffering with joyfulness" (Colossians 1:11). If you were to diagram that sentence and take out the intervening phrases, you would find it actually says we are strengthened with all might with joyfulness!

Paul reaffirmed that what was true in Nehemiah's day under the Old Covenant is still true today under the New Covenant. The joy of the Lord is our strength!

Learn to Do It Yourself

Read Colossians 1:11 again and you'll see it is that joy-inspired strength which enables us to be patient and long-suffering. (So, if you've been running short of patience lately, check your joy supply. That could be what you're lacking.)

Read Ephesians 6:10 and you'll see it takes that same strength to operate your spiritual armor. If you don't have the joy of the Lord, you'll eventually get too weak to wear it!

The fact is, joy and the strength it provides are far more vital than we ever imagined. Study Ephesians 3:16-19 and you'll see what I mean. There Paul prays:

That [God] would grant you, according to the riches of his glory, to be strengthened with might by his Spirit in the inner man; that [the Anointed One and His Anointing] may dwell in your hearts by faith; that ye, being rooted and grounded in love, may be able to comprehend with all saints what is the breadth, and length, and depth, and height; and to know the love of [the Anointed One and His Anointing], which passeth knowledge, that ye might be filled with all the fulness of God.

According to those verses, we can't abide in the anointing without joy. We can't comprehend the love of God without joy. We can't be filled with all the fullness of God without joy. We can't do any of those things without joy because we simply wouldn't be strong enough!

Can you see now why joy is such a major force in this end-time move of God? Even more importantly, can you see why joy must be a major force in your life if you're to be a part of that move?

"Oh yes, Brother Copeland, I do. So I'm planning to attend every Holy Ghost meeting within 100 miles of my house."

That's great. But, frankly, even if you do, it won't be enough. You see, as wonderful as it is to be in services where there is Holy Ghost laughter, you need joy all the time. And since you can't carry Kenneth E. Hagin or Rodney Howard-Browne around in your pocket, you'd better learn to release the joy of the Lord yourself!

Start With the Word

You may not feel like you have any joy to release right now. But I can assure you, you do. If you're a born-again child of God, you have His own joy residing in your spirit. You just need to prime the pump so it will start to flow. You need to purposely stir up the joy of the Lord.

How can you do that?

First, by meditating on the Word of God. You can understand why the Word is so important to your joy when you read some of the last things Jesus told His disciples before He went to the cross. He said:

If ye abide in me, and my words abide in you, ye shall ask what ye will, and it shall be done unto you.... If ye keep my commandments, ye shall abide in my love; even as I have kept my Father's commandments, and abide in his love. These things have I spoken unto you, that my joy might remain in you, and that your joy might be full.... Ask, and ye shall receive, that your joy may be full (John 15:7, 10-11, 16:24).

When you meditate on the Word of God and revelation begins to rise in your heart, joy comes! It comes because you begin to have a deeper and clearer knowledge of the Father. It comes because you realize you can go boldly before Him in prayer on the basis of the Word, and be confident your prayers will be answered.

If you've been sorrowing over a wayward child, for example, you can replace your sad thoughts with a revelation of God's promise in Isaiah 54:13, and joy will come into your heart. Suddenly, instead of crying over what the devil is doing to that child, you start shouting about what God will do. You laugh and say, "You might as well forget it, devil. Just pack it up and go home right now, because as far as I'm concerned, the victory is won. All my children shall be taught of the Lord. And great shall be the peace of my children!"

Then when the devil comes back at you and says, "Maybe so, but aren't you sorry over all the years that child has wasted?" you can shoot the Word right back at him. You can say, "No, I'm not sorry. I don't have to be sorry because Jesus bore my griefs and carried my sorrows (Isaiah 53:4). So I believe I'll just go ahead and have myself a grand time rejoicing in Him!"

Proverbs 15:23 says, "A man hath joy by the answer of his mouth." When you start answering the troubles and trials you're facing with the Word of God, it will release joy in you and run the devil off. He can't stand the joy of the Lord!

Jump Into the River

Another way to stir up joy is to fellowship with the Holy Spirit. Romans 14:17 says, "For the kingdom of God is not meat and drink; but righteousness, and peace, and joy in the Holy Ghost."

There's joy in the Holy Ghost—so hook up with Him! Pray and sing in other tongues. Jump into the river of the Spirit with praise and thanksgiving. You may start out thinking you don't have anything to thank God for—but you'll quickly find out that you do.

You can begin by thanking Him for the blood of Jesus that has washed away your sin. You can thank Him that you're on your way to heaven. If you can't think of any other reason to praise Him, just center up on those two things. Keep shouting, "Thank God, my sins are washed away!" until joy rises up within you.

"I can't do that. I just don't feel like it."

That doesn't matter! You don't have to feel any certain way to rejoice. Joy is bigger than your emotions. In Psalm 27, King David wrote, "And now shall mine head be lifted up above mine enemies round about me: therefore will I offer in [God's] tabernacle sacrifices of joy; I will sing, yea, I will sing praises unto the Lord" (verse 6).

Rejoicing is an act of the will. When you don't feel like rejoicing, set your will and rejoice anyway.

If you're having financial problems, don't stay up all night worrying about how you will pay your bills. If you're going to stay up, stay up and praise God. Sing. Dance. Give thanks. Shout the Word of God and laugh at the devil until joy comes. Then keep on rejoicing until you're so filled with the strength and might of God that nothing can stop you.

Keep on rejoicing until your body is well. Keep on rejoicing until every chain the devil has used to keep you in bondage snaps like a thread. Keep on rejoicing until people start coming to you—and they will!—saying, "Hey, I want some of that joy! Can you tell me how to get it?"

Think about it. Wouldn't it be wonderful if we started rejoicing and just kept on rejoicing every day from now on until this whole earth was filled with the Glory of God? I believe with all my heart that's what God is calling us to do.

Let's get on with it so we can rejoice our way right into the rapture.

Let's rejoice in the Lord, always. And again I say, rejoice!

Prayer for Salvation and Baptism
in the Holy Spirit

Heavenly Father, I come to You in the Name of Jesus. Your Word says, "Whosoever shall call on the name of the Lord shall be saved" (Acts 2:21). I am calling on You. I pray and ask Jesus to come into my heart and be Lord over my life according to Romans 10:9-10: "If thou shalt confess with thy mouth the Lord Jesus, and shalt believe in thine heart that God hath raised him from the dead, thou shalt be saved. For with the heart man believeth unto righteousness; and with the mouth confession is made unto salvation." I do that now. I confess that Jesus is Lord, and I believe in my heart that God raised Him from the dead.

I am now reborn! I am a Christian—a child of Almighty God! I am saved! You also said in Your Word, "If ye then, being evil, know how to give good gifts unto your children: HOW MUCH MORE shall your heavenly Father give the Holy Spirit to them that ask him?" (Luke 11:13). I'm also asking You to fill me with the Holy Spirit. Holy Spirit, rise up within me as I praise God. I fully expect to speak with other tongues as You give me the utterance (Acts 2:4). In Jesus' Name. Amen!

Begin to praise God for filling you with the Holy Spirit. Speak those words and syllables you receive—not in your own language, but the language given to you by the Holy Spirit. You have to use your own voice. God will not force you to speak. Don't be concerned with how it sounds. It is a heavenly language!

Continue with the blessing God has given you and pray in the spirit every day.

You are a born-again, Spirit-filled believer. You'll never be the same!

Find a good church that boldly preaches God's Word and obeys it. Become part of a church family who will love and care for you as you love and care for them.

We need to be connected to each other. It increases our strength in God. It's God's plan for us.

Make it a habit to watch the *Believer's Voice of Victory* television broadcast and become a doer of the Word, who is blessed in his doing (James 1:22-25).

Books Available From
Kenneth Copeland Ministries

by Kenneth Copeland

* A Ceremony of Marriage
  A Matter of Choice
  Blessed to Be a Blessing
  Covenant of Blood
  Faith and Patience—The Power Twins
* Freedom From Fear
  Giving and Receiving
  Honor—Walking in Honesty, Truth and Integrity
  How to Conquer Strife
  How to Discipline Your Flesh
  How to Receive Communion
  In Love There Is No Fear
  Know Your Enemy
  Living at the End of Time—A Time of
      Supernatural Increase
  Love Letters From Heaven
  Love Never Fails
* Mercy—The Divine Rescue of the Human Race
* Now Are We in Christ Jesus
  One Nation Under God (gift book with CD enclosed)
* Our Covenant With God
  Partnership—Sharing the Vision, Sharing the Grace
* Prayer—Your Foundation for Success
* Prosperity: The Choice Is Yours
  Rumors of War
* Sensitivity of Heart
* Six Steps to Excellence in Ministry
* Sorrow Not! Winning Over Grief and Sorrow
* The Decision Is Yours
* The Force of Faith

*Available in Spanish

by Gloria Copeland

* Love—The Secret to Your Success
   No Deposit—No Return
   Pleasing the Father
   Pressing In—It's Worth It All
   Shine On!
   The Grace That Makes Us Holy
   The Power to Live a New Life
   The Protection of Angels
   There Is No High Like the Most High
   The Secret Place of God's Protection (gift book with
        CD enclosed)
   The Unbeatable Spirit of Faith
   This Same Jesus
   To Know Him
   True Prosperity
   Walk With God
   Well Worth the Wait
   Words That Heal (gift book with CD enclosed)
   Your Promise of Protection—The Power
        of the 91st Psalm

Books Co-Authored by Kenneth and Gloria Copeland

   Family Promises
   Healing Promises
   Prosperity Promises
   Protection Promises

* From Faith to Faith—A Daily Guide to Victory
   From Faith to Faith—A Perpetual Calendar
   He Did It All for You
   Lifeline Series: Practical Tools for Everyday Needs
   • Healing & Wellness: Your 10-Day Spiritual Action Plan
   • Your 10-Day Spiritual Action Plan for Complete
     Financial Breakthrough
   One Word From God Can Change Your Life

*Available in Spanish

One Word From God Series:
- One Word From God Can Change Your Destiny
- One Word From God Can Change Your Family
- One Word From God Can Change Your Finances
- One Word From God Can Change Your Formula
  for Success
- One Word From God Can Change Your Health
- One Word From God Can Change Your Nation
- One Word From God Can Change Your Prayer Life
- One Word From God Can Change
  Your Relationships

Load Up—A Youth Devotional
Over the Edge—A Youth Devotional
Pursuit of His Presence—A Daily Devotional
Pursuit of His Presence—A Perpetual Calendar
Raising Children Without Fear

Other Books Published by KCP

Hello. My Name Is God. by Jeremy Pearsons
John G. Lake—His Life, His Sermons, His
  Boldness of Faith
Protecting Your Family in Dangerous Times
  by Kellie Copeland Swisher
The Holiest of All by Andrew Murray
The New Testament in Modern Speech
  by Richard Francis Weymouth
The Rabbi From Burbank by Isidor Zwirn and Bob Owen
Unchained! by Mac Gober

Products Designed for Today's Children and Youth

And Jesus Healed Them All (confession book and CD gift package)
Baby Praise Board Book
Baby Praise Christmas Board Book
Noah's Ark Coloring Book
The Best of Shout! Adventure Comics

The Shout! Giant Flip Coloring Book
The Shout! Joke Book
The Shout! Super-Activity Book
Wichita Slim's Campfire Stories

*Commander Kellie and the Superkids*_{SM} Books:

The SWORD Adventure Book
Commander Kellie and the Superkids_{SM}
   Solve-It-Yourself Mysteries
Commander Kellie and the Superkids_{SM} Adventure Series:
   Middle Grade Novels by Christopher P.N. Maselli:

   #1 The Mysterious Presence
   #2 The Quest for the Second Half
   #3 Escape From Jungle Island
   #4 In Pursuit of the Enemy
   #5 Caged Rivalry
   #6 Mystery of the Missing Junk
   #7 Out of Breath
   #8 The Year Mashela Stole Christmas
   #9 False Identity
   #10 The Runaway Mission
   #11 The Knight-Time Rescue of Commander Kellie

World Offices
Kenneth Copeland Ministries

For more information about KCM and our products,
please write to the office nearest you:

Kenneth Copeland Ministries
Fort Worth, TX 76192-0001

Kenneth Copeland
Locked Bag 2600
Mansfield Delivery Centre
QUEENSLAND 4122
AUSTRALIA

Kenneth Copeland
Private Bag X 909
FONTAINEBLEAU
2032
REPUBLIC OF
SOUTH AFRICA

Kenneth Copeland Ministries
Post Office Box 84
L'VIV 79000
UKRAINE

Kenneth Copeland
Post Office Box 15
BATH
BA1 3XN
U.K.

Kenneth Copeland
PO Box 3111 STN LCD 1
Langley BC V3A 4R3
CANADA

To receive a FREE subscription to
Believer's Voice of Victory, write to:

Kenneth Copeland Ministries
Fort Worth, TX 76192-0001
Or call:
800-600-7395
(7 a.m.-5 p.m. CT)
Or visit our Web site at:
www.kcm.org

If you are writing from outside the U.S., please contact the KCM office nearest you. Addresses for all Kenneth Copeland Ministries offices are listed on the previous pages.

We're Here for You!

Believer's Voice of Victory Television Broadcast

Join Kenneth and Gloria Copeland and the *Believer's Voice of Victory* broadcasts Monday through Friday and on Sunday each week, and learn how faith in God's Word can take your life from ordinary to extraordinary. This teaching from God's Word is designed to get you where you want to be—*on top!*

You can catch the *Believer's Voice of Victory* broadcast on your local, cable or satellite channels.* Also available 24 hours on webcast at BVOV.TV.

* Check your local listings for times and stations in your area.

Believer's Voice of Victory Magazine

Enjoy inspired teaching and encouragement from Kenneth and Gloria Copeland and guest ministers each month in the *Believer's Voice of Victory* magazine. Also included are real-life testimonies of God's miraculous power and divine intervention in the lives of people just like you!

It's more than just a magazine—it's a ministry.